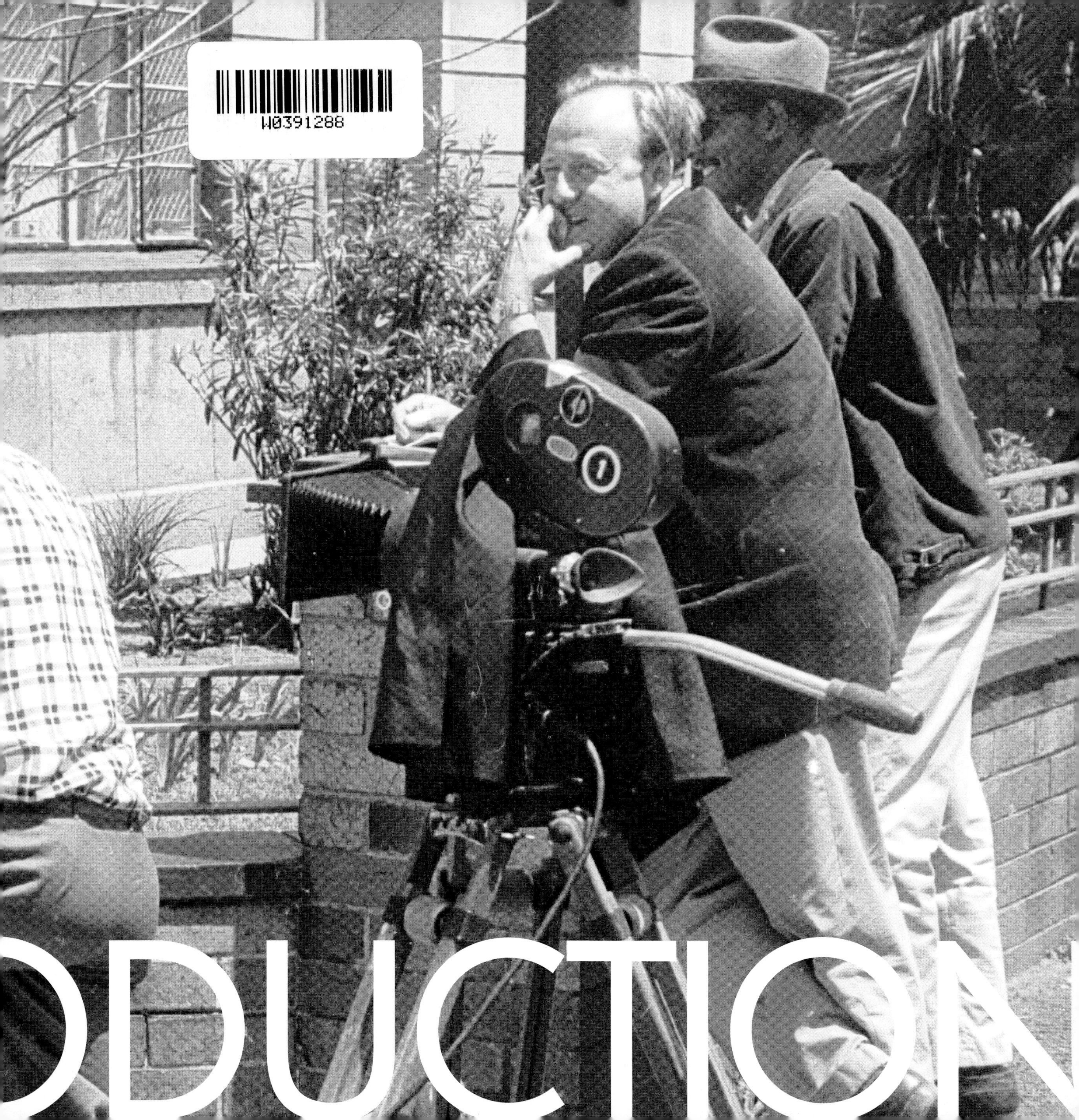
ODUCTION

LIONEL ROGOSIN,

22 January, 1924 - 8 December, 2000

Lionel Rogosin died on 8 December, 2000, and was buried in the Forever Hollywood cemetery on Santa Monica Boulevard in Los Angeles. He would have appreciated the irony: maverick film-maker Rogosin was never part of Hollywood, never wanted to be, and was anathema to just about everything that Hollywood stands for. A pioneer of what later came to be called docudrama, he was suspicious of glamour and sentimentality. Among his subjects were alcoholic deadbeats in New York City, exploited woodcutters in Mississippi, the Holocaust and the Arab-Israeli conflict. In South Africa, he will be best remembered for his classic portrait of the life of a migrant worker under apartheid, *Come Back, Africa.*

Rogosin had been educated to be a chemist, but after serving in the Second World War he decided that he wanted to be a film-maker instead. He made his name with *On the Bowery*, a film about down-and-outs in New York. Set on New York's skid row, the film established Rogosin's trademark — a concern with society's ills, performed by amateur actors who were not so much playing a part as going through their daily routine, in their natural surroundings. A sequence of actions that appeared to be observed, rather than artificially created, as haphazard as life itself. Heavily influenced by De Sica and by Flaherty, Rogosin's style could be called neo-realist. *On the Bowery* was critically acclaimed, but its distribution was severely limited. Nevertheless, Rogosin had won an international name, and proved himself a film-maker to be taken seriously.

For his next subject, he chose racism in South Africa: "I heard about South Africa and the rise of apartheid, and it sounded very ominous to me. And I was very concerned about the reawakening of fascism. Because we had defeated fascism in World War II, but I didn't feel it was defeated. I felt it would re-emerge and continue in different forms." (Interview by Riesenfeld and Davis, 1989).

This concern seems to have begun as early as 1954, but it was in May, 1957 that Lionel Rogosin and his wife Elinor finally arrived in Cape Town, South Africa. This was towards the end of the first decade of apartheid — that massive and lamentable reorganisation of society that would become the central fact of life in South Africa for most of the second half of the twentieth century. I think of this first decade as "the best of times, the worst of times". It was a period of mass removals of Africans from their homes, clearing "black spots" for whites to occupy. It was a time of increasing repression of opponents of the ruling National Party, of censorship, of the introduction of laws forbidding interracial sex, of draconian restrictions on movement and job opportunities for non-whites, of severe limitations on education, of the growing power of the Special Branch. At the same time, paradoxically, it seems to have been a period of great optimism for Africans. The recent war had opened up new vistas, there was an increasing awareness of the world, a growing militancy for rights for Africans, and, emanating from the world forum of the United Nations, the sense that colonialism and the colonial ethos were in retreat, racism everywhere in decline.

To many in the townships, the Afrikaner Nationalists could appear not so much vicious as delusional, their dream of a complete separation of the races in South Africa a mad fantasy. It is true that when the Rogosins arrived in Africa, 156 leaders of the African National Congress and its allies, including Nelson Mandela, were on trial for high treason, and that this trial would continue the whole time the Rogosins were in the country. But it is also true that the trial itself was clearly a travesty, which the accused often treated like a college common-room.

It is noticeable that none of the characters in *Come Back, Africa* use the word "apartheid". It came into prominence outside South Africa in the sixties, after the full force of its meaning was imposed upon the world with the Sharpeville Massacre of 21 March, 1960. Apartheid was by definition a racist agenda, and it was implemented at a time when most of the world was moving away from colonialism and when the horror of the Holocaust, the nadir of racism, was fresh in everyone's minds.

That being said, the cause of human rights in South Africa was not high on the agenda of Rogosin's country, the United States. Indeed, African campaigners for equal rights were lumped together with black activists as "communist agitators". South Africa, safe in white hands, was in the Cold War considered a vital bulwark against communism. It should not be forgotten that the United States in which Rogosin was formed still was, and would continue to be for some time, an openly racist society. This racism found expression in many ways, and not the least of these was demeaning portrayals of Africans in cinema. Africa was the white man's

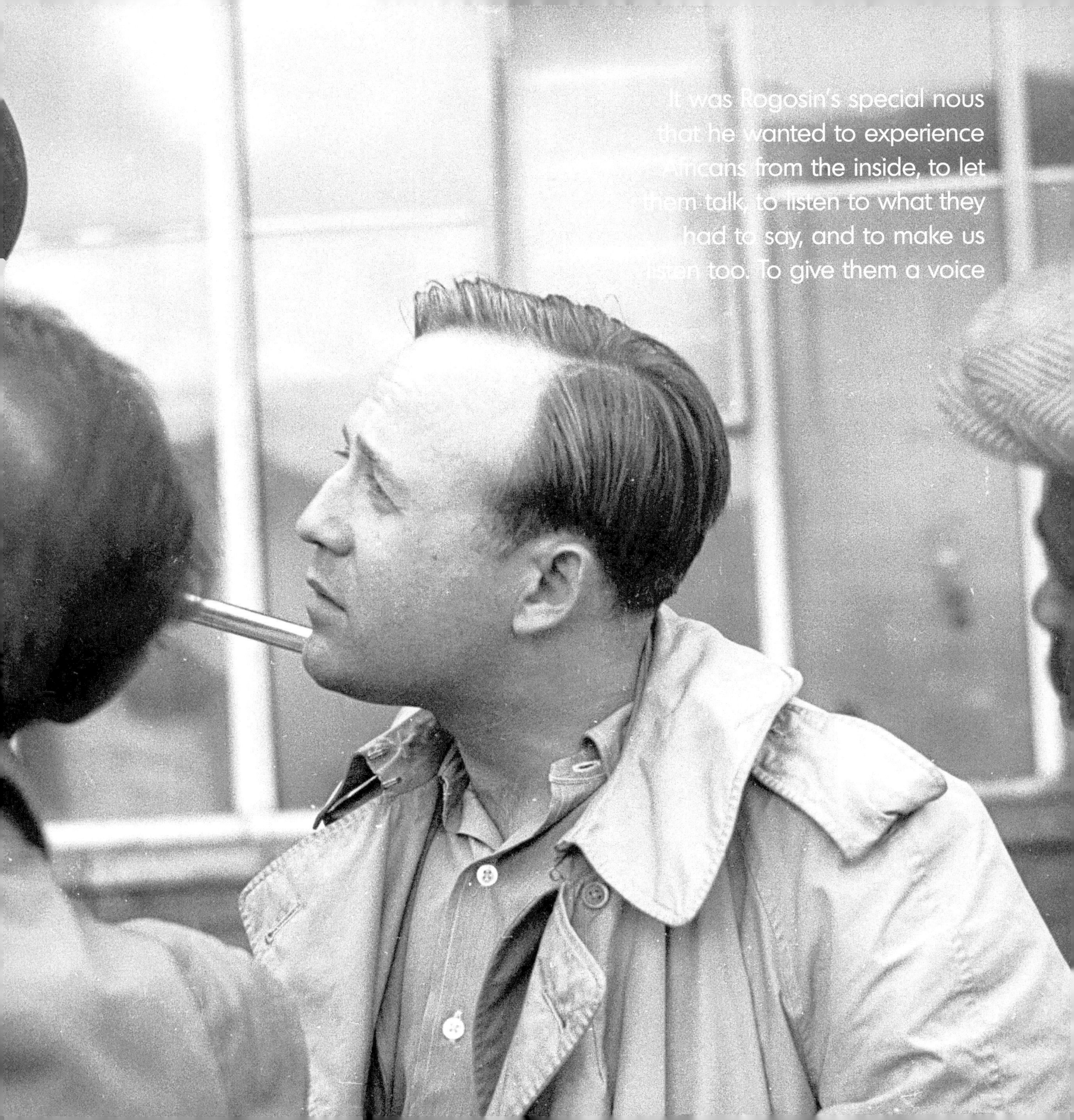

It was Rogosin's special nous that he wanted to experience Africans from the inside, to let them talk, to listen to what they had to say, and to make us listen too. To give them a voice

playground, its people and animals, its mineral wealth, there for the taking.

Consider that while Africans were portrayed in films many times, almost invariably as cliché warriors or background servants, they usually did not speak. They were iconic, and so voices for them were superfluous, other than to sing from time to time. Africans, like the animal inhabitants of the continent, were exotica, and did not need to explain themselves; in fact for them to do so would be a negation of the exotic. Being either exotica or backdrops, Africans had always been seen from the outside. White film-makers did not want to hear Africans talking about their situation any more than a big game hunter wants to hear a lion complain about being shot at. The film-makers were making films for white audiences, and what they showed them was their interpretation of African life, which was invariably primitive, sensationalist, the myth of a dark continent inhabited by dark people ruled by the darkness of ignorance and superstition. It was Rogosin's special nous that he wanted to experience Africans from the inside, to let them talk, to listen to what they had to say, and to make us listen too. To give them a voice.

In South Africa, he made contact with a group of writers associated with the crusading magazine *Drum*, men whose names have since achieved near-mythical fame — Can Themba, Bloke Modisane, Lewis Nkosi. Because he was willing to listen to them, ask their advice, value their judgments, he earned their respect. As Lewis Nkosi said, "Suddenly there was a rapport." Rogosin had a vague outline of what he wanted: "A very simple story from the point of view of an African, to show simply what life was like for an African, what pressure he's under, what humiliations, what pain, what suffering Africans have under apartheid." He got together with Nkosi and Modisane, and in one brainstorming afternoon the three of them talked the story through. As Rogosin said, it was "a piece of cake".

The "piece of cake" was the story of a migrant worker who comes to Johannesburg to look for work. To find his chief actor, Rogosin and Modisane went to bus queues, pulling astonished men out for a screen test (the men thought they were being arrested). He was looking for a particular face, and he found it in the migrant worker Zacharia Mgabi.

Rogosin takes his migrant worker Zacharia through a series of jobs — mine-worker, house-boy, hotel cleaner, auto-mechanic — that constitute a microcosm of the African experience during the past century, not limited to South Africa, of the mass movement of people off the land and into the cities. Drawing on the intimate experience of Modisane, Themba and Nkosi of township life, Rogosin gave us the first, and probably the greatest, depiction of the confrontation between unskilled labour and industrial society, the breakdown of traditional values, complicated by the trauma of apartheid. Everywhere, in his job-seeking odyssey, Zacharia is tyrannised by the doom of the pass laws, which control where he can live, where he can go, where he can work, and even forbid him from sleeping with his wife.

Although the film shows none of the momentous political events taking place at the time, this is an intensely political film. The society revealed in *Come Back, Africa* is one where racism is endemic. There is the black-on-black violence of township crime, but principally what one remembers is the violence to human dignity of being treated as an inferior, and the mundane torment of seeking work in a system of exploitation. These experiences are by no means confined to blacks, but to be defined by colour makes it infinitely more humiliating. In the microcosm of the experience of one despised individual is subsumed the macrocosm of a society that will soon resort to shooting down unarmed civilians. To this film, Rogosin gave the title of the great rallying cry of the dispossessed of the fifties — Mayibuye i Afrika, "Come Back, Africa".

Rogosin filmed in Sophiatown at a time when it was being torn down around their ears, and it constitutes the most detailed record we have of what life was like in the suburb that has since achieved legendary status as a cultural mecca. The vital street life, the crime, the impassioned conversation of the shebeen (the back parlour drinking den), the very personalities of Modisane, Themba and Nkosi, the first screen appearance of Miriam Makeba, are here captured in a document beyond valuation. *Come Back, Africa* is an essential part of South African history, the only record on film from that time not only of what the African reality looked like, but what Africans felt about it.

I first saw *Come Back, Africa* in 1960. Although I was not ignorant of the meaning of apartheid, the film had a power beyond the words of description I had read, the photos I had seen published in newspapers. It hit you in the gut. On screens around the world it had tremendous impact. One British reviewer wrote

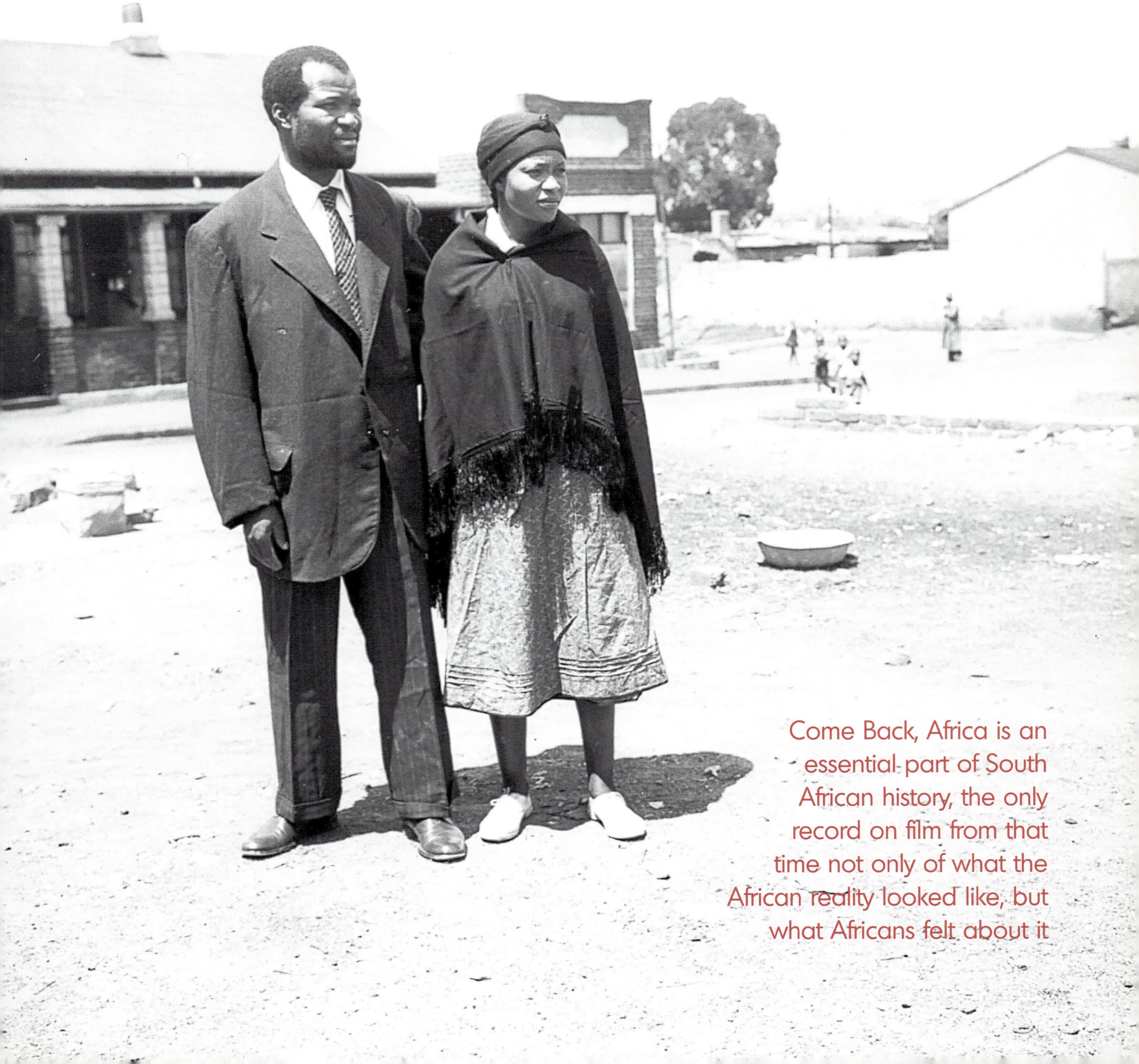

Come Back, Africa is an essential part of South African history, the only record on film from that time not only of what the African reality looked like, but what Africans felt about it

that "[it] makes me ashamed of being white". The South African government embarked on a massive campaign of vilification, tarring Rogosin with the communist brush. This accusation and the spirit of the times (areas of the Unites States were certainly as repressive and racially vicious as parts of South Africa) made it impossible for Rogosin to find an American distributor. But Rogosin was not a man without means — he came from a well-to-do Jewish family — so he purchased the Bleecker Street cinema in New York's Greenwich Village, and for years crusaded to make available an alternative cinema beyond Hollywood, a cinema not afraid to challenge the establishment.

By a coincidence, his film opened in New York close to the date of the Sharpeville Massacre of 1960; significantly, this watershed moment was also captured on film, and appeared in newsreels around the world. After that, no-one could claim that *Come Back, Africa* was an exaggeration.

What distinguished *Come Back, Africa* from every other fiction film about South Africa — certainly from every film out of Hollywood — up until the time of *Mapantsula* (1988), was Rogosin's willingness to place blacks at the centre of the apartheid experience, as opposed to mediating that experience through well-meaning whites, as in *Cry, Freedom* or *Dry White Season*. In the course of time, thousands of documentaries would be made about South Africa. It was even, at one point, and far too late, the flavour of the month in Hollywood, for a very brief period of time. *Come Back, Africa* came early, and its message was enduring. For decades it served as a valuable anti-apartheid learning tool. Since the fall of apartheid, it has been rediscovered as a record of black South Africa's "lost culture", and its images are in constant demand.

Rogosin was especially interested in the black experience. His *Black Roots* (1970) featured Flo Kennedy, Reverend Frederick Douglass Kirkpatrick, Reverend Gary Davis, Jim Collier and others, and music from Leadbelly to Sly and the Family Stone. *Black Fantasy* (1972) was about the psycho-sexual relationship between musician Jim Collier and his white wife, and their precarious standing in society. *Woodcutters of the Deep South* (1973) was about the struggle of black and white workers against the pulpwood companies that ruled their lives.

Rogosin made films into the seventies, but could not make any inroads into what should have been his natural outlet, television, which was becoming increasingly politically conservative. In his own country he was largely an unjustly forgotten figure. But he continued to be honoured abroad, notably in Britain, France, Holland and Germany. After his death, his accomplishment increases in stature.

THE LOST MANUSCRIPT

After Lionel Rogosin died in December, 2000, his sons Michael and Daniel, in sorting out his papers, discovered an unpublished manuscript. This was his account of the making of *Come Back, Africa*. It was in two parts that were probably written at different times, with the chronology of the two parts often overlapping or unclear. It was typed not by Rogosin himself but by a typist transcribing from a quarter-inch tape that Rogosin had most likely recorded on a tape recorder as he expressed his thoughts. The many misspellings and lacunae indicate that the typist was not familiar with South Africa nor with the people involved, and Rogosin seems to have had time only to partially correct the many errors and fill in some of the gaps. Because of my knowledge of South Africa and its history, and because of the familiarity I already had with the making of the film (my book, *In Darkest Hollywood*, and documentary of the same title, made in conjunction with Daniel Riesenfeld, had brought me into personal relationship with Rogosin), Michael Rogosin approached me about preparing his father's manuscript for publication.

It presented a challenge, not only because of the errors and gaps, but because it mentions numerous people of whom I had no knowledge. So trying to track these down — where it seemed worth the trouble to do so — was something of a quest of detection. In this, I had signal assistance from Emil Knebel, Elinor Rogosin, Lewis Nkosi, Reverend Paul Singleton and Tom Karis. These people were all in some way associated with the making of the film, and were able to correct errors of memory on Lionel Rogosin's part, and to help fill in gaps. Above all, the work was rewarding in itself because the manuscript reveals so much about how a dedicated film-maker went about his craft, and how he operated in difficult circumstances; and it gives us insight into a particular place and time that was seminal in South Africa's tortured progress. It is a vivid slice of film history.

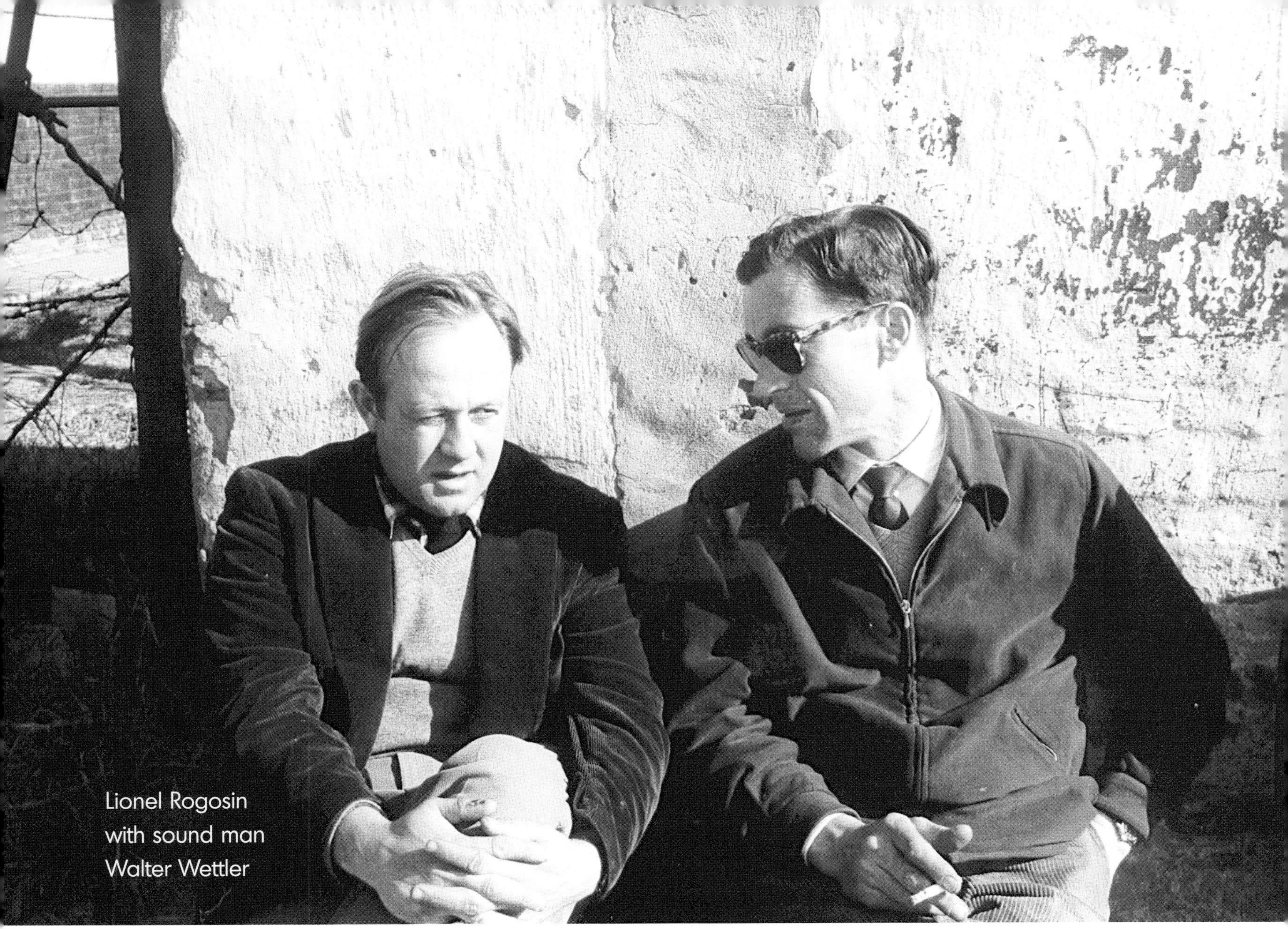

Lionel Rogosin with sound man Walter Wettler

In editing the manuscript, my principal concern has been with the main body of the narrative, which describes the trials and tribulations involved in the making of the film. There was a section on Rogosin's travels through Central Africa, which I have omitted for this reason, and there are other omissions. The manuscript was never thoroughly proof-read, so it was filled with errors and gaps which I have corrected or filled in. Since the manuscript was dictated, and not written, it contained numerous repetitions, which I have ironed out. Rogosin would certainly have reworked his own text. At the same time, the very fact that it was dictated means that Rogosin's voice can be clearly discerned behind the written word, and I have tried to maintain that immediacy.

Rogosin's text contains words and phrases that today would be considered politically incorrect — his reference to "Negroes" and "Boers", for example. In his attitude towards Afrikaners he could even be accused of being racist. But these words and attitudes were of the time. Less excusable is his unquestioning acceptance of a supposed psychological problem inherent in the status of being of mixed race — in South Africa, designated as "coloured". This prejudice either supported, or was supported by, his unstable relationship with Morris, a member of his crew. As Emil Knebel has pointed out to me, the very suppression in Rogosin's manuscript of the full extent of the friction between them implies that Rogosin had an uneasy conscience about his treatment of Morris, however much Morris might have provoked him.

Intriguing for any student of film is Rogosin's exegesis of his craft, which in this case includes the aesthetic he evolved for his actors. He often admits that due to the extreme conditions under which he was working he cannot get from his actors the results he desires. So even for himself, *Come Back, Africa* was a flawed work. If this is so, the film nevertheless soars above its faults.

The manuscript reveals Rogosin's punctilious dedication to research, beginning with Walter White of the National Association for the Advancement of Colored People in the United States, through Father Trevor Huddleston and Michael Scott in London, and the months of immersion into apartheid South Africa, where he found the sympathetic whites and key blacks who would help him along. It is worth pointing out that this major investment of time is not a luxury accorded many modern makers of documentary, where the bottom line is more important than the final product.

The manuscript also reveals the atmosphere of fear, even paranoia (completely justifiable) in which the film was made: fear of the police, of having the film confiscated, of being expelled —- a daily terror of "discovery" that had to be endured. Rogosin himself draws a parallel between this kind of underground film-making and the condition of a spy. But a spy is accorded time to learn his craft; for Rogosin, this was on-the-job training, where any mistake would lose him his job. Undoubtedly the most debilitating, the most oppressive factor was the cat-and-mouse game played with him by the bureaucracy over several months, which left Rogosin in doubt the whole time as to whether he would be allowed to bring in his crew to make the "unlikely travelogue" that he had decided on as his cover story. How much this struggle against an apparently immovable object consumed his energies is reflected in the space he devoted to describing it.

But if you are going to make films in impossible conditions, it helps to be an obsessive. Rogosin was driven by the compulsion to make a statement against apartheid, to draw the attention of the world to the contempt for human rights in one country. Every obstacle, he writes, only made him more determined to go on. It is a measure of his obsession, for example, that he only mentions in passing that his wife Ellie is pregnant — which doesn't prevent her from working on the film — and only when they are leaving South Africa does he acknowledge the presence of baby Michael, who was born some weeks previously.

This was an obsession not without ruthlessness. Of course, he has to deceive the authorities, but he also has to con other people into helping him. Near the end of the manuscript he inveighs against South African "liberals" who refuse to help him finance the film, grudgingly recognising that they might believe that they would put themselves in danger if they did so. He lies to a business friend of his father's. While it has to be admitted that it is not unusual for those who work with documentary film-makers to put themselves in jeopardy to get the truth out, decency requires that they at least be allowed to choose to do so. Rogosin did not allow this choice to those he suspected of not being sympathetic to the anti-apartheid cause, and whom he tried to use. At the same time, there don't seem to have been any serious repercussions against those involved in the film, which can perhaps be explained by Emil Knebel's rationale at the end of the book — although I think that the risk that the authorities would shut down the film was substantial.

This all-consuming passion to complete the film, which involved deception; which demanded the constant exercise of an alert cunning; which drove his crew and himself to exhaustion; which neglected family niceties; and which, under the strain, exploded in the end in a fist-fight with one of the crew, were manifestations of — as Rogosin described himself — "a man possessed" in the crusade against apartheid.

Peter Davis
Vancouver, Canada, 2004

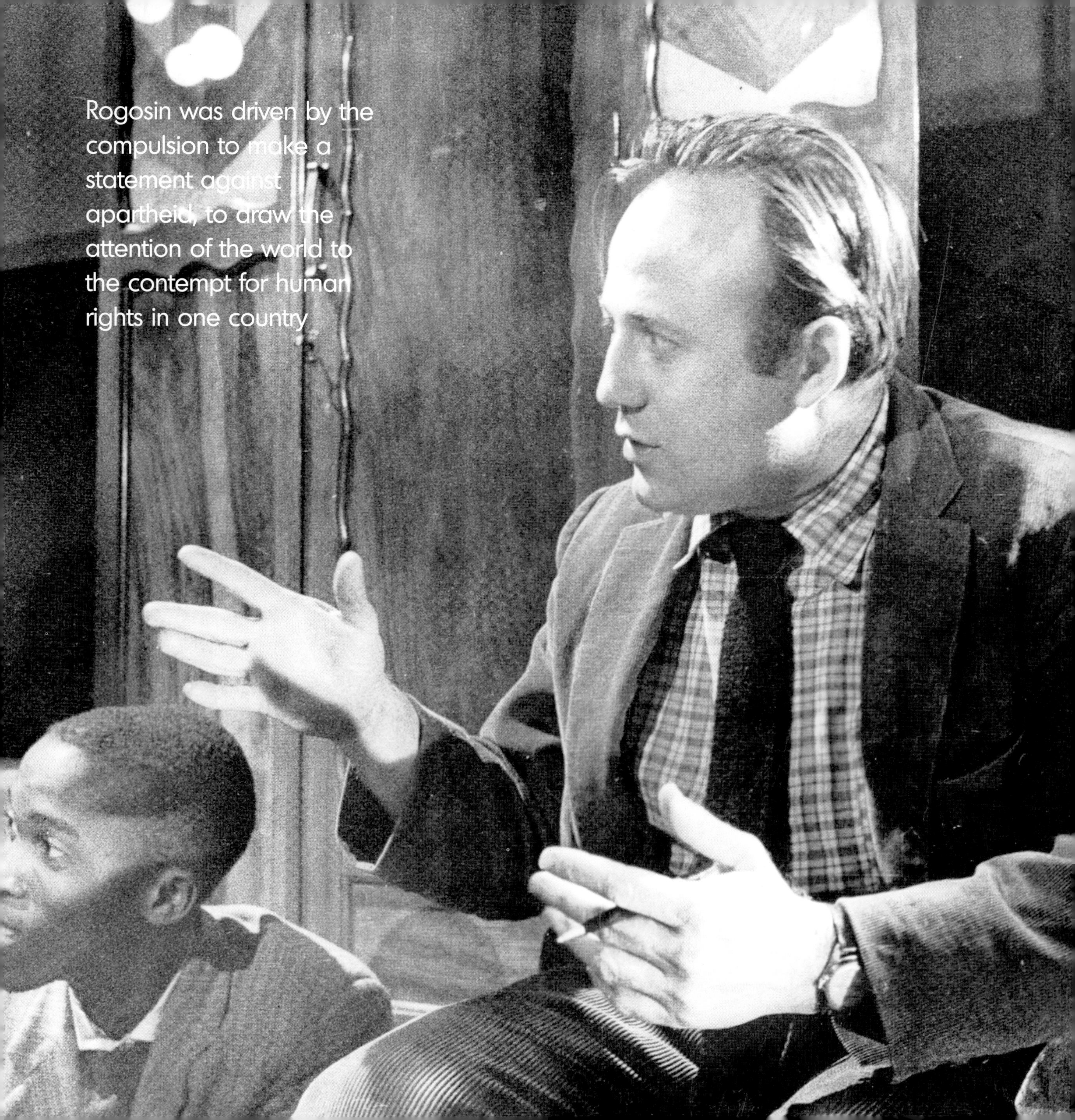

Rogosin was driven by the compulsion to make a statement against apartheid, to draw the attention of the world to the contempt for human rights in one country

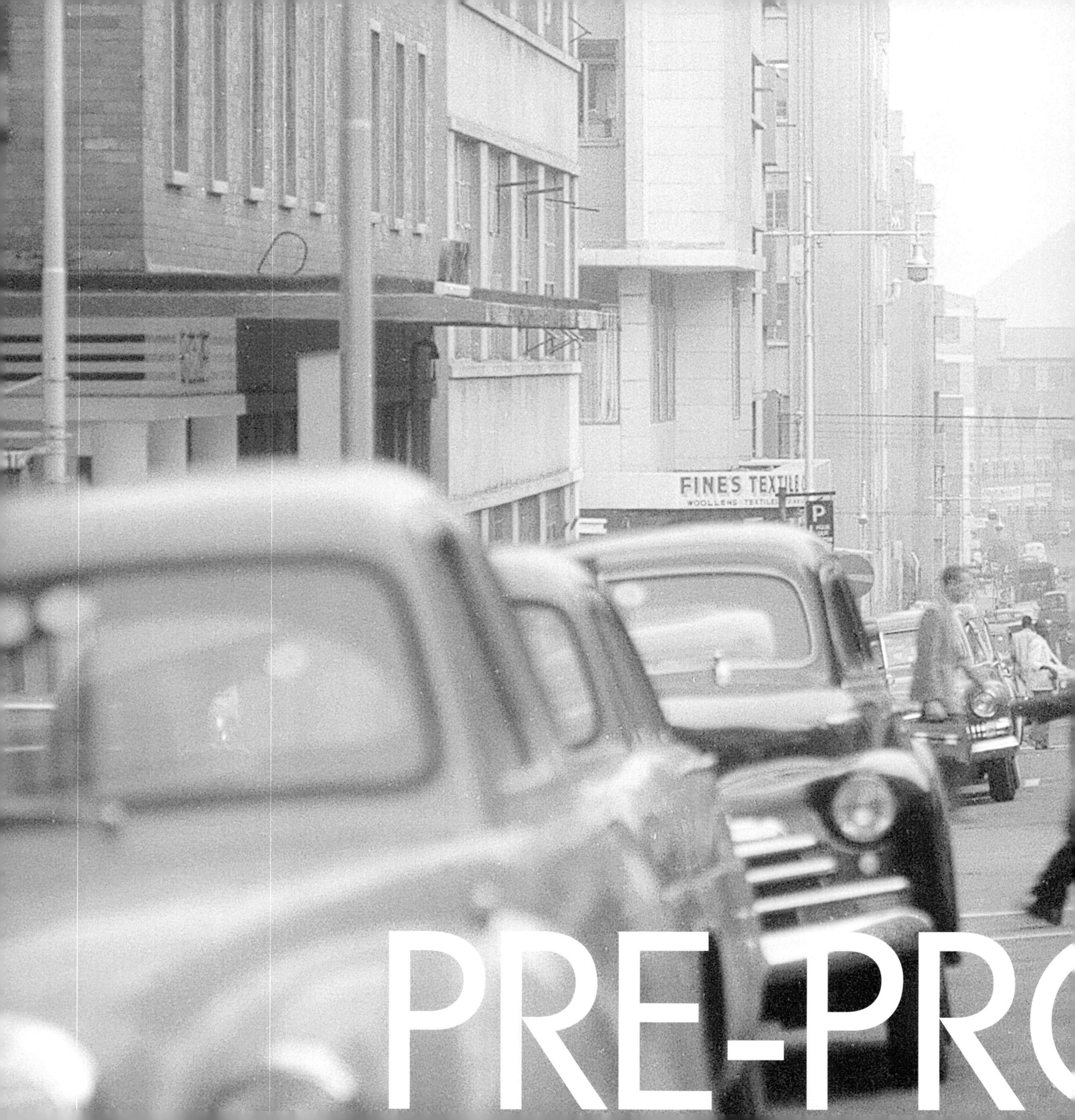

PRE-PRO

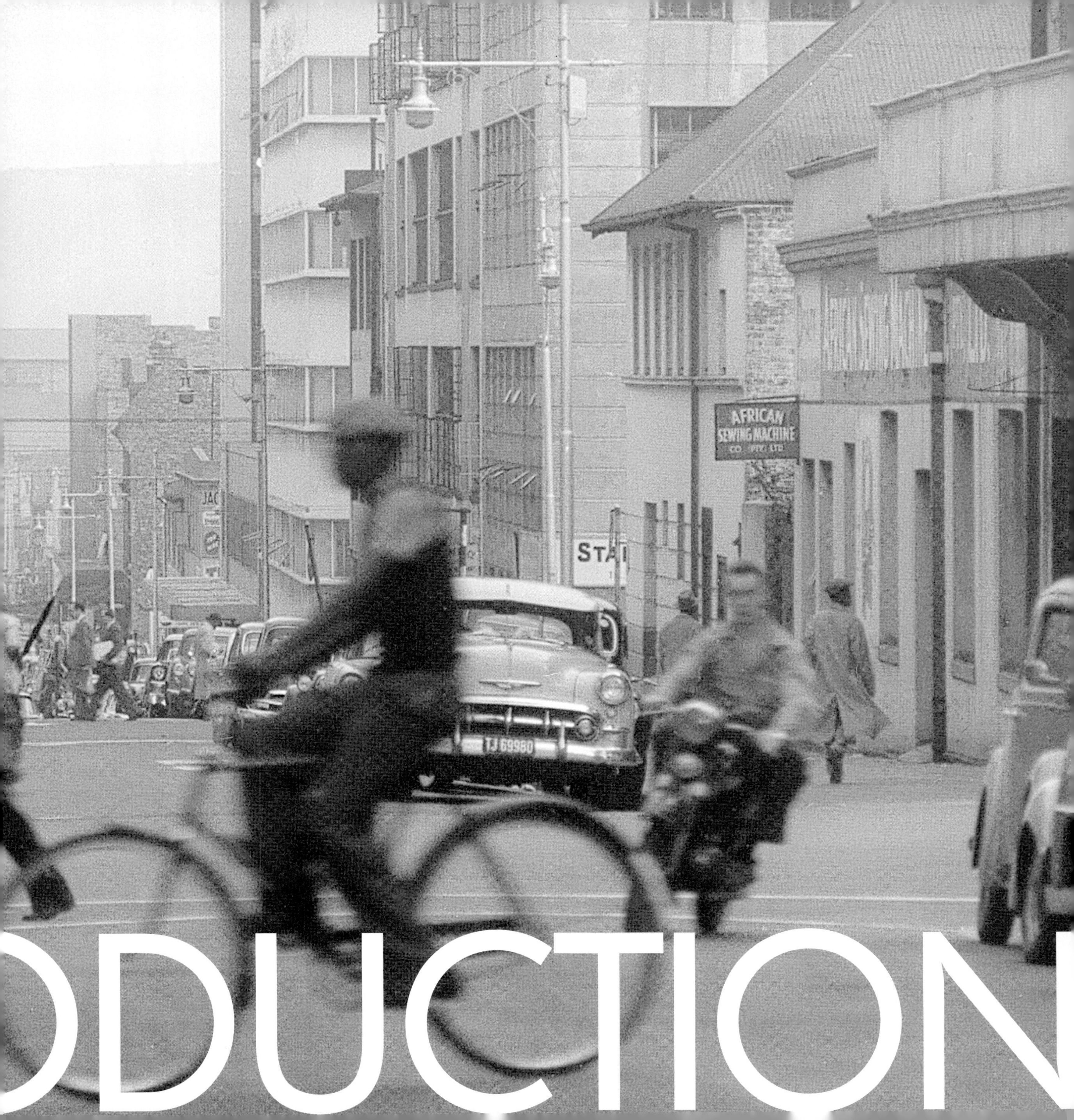

ODUCTION

WHY SOUTH AFRICA?

After the war I had the conviction that anything remotely resembling fascism had to be fought with all the energy that one could possibly muster. It seems remarkable how unfashionable this attitude appears today. Particularly remarkable considering that it was less than two decades ago that the Nazi barbarians nearly crushed civilization and made the world a nightmare to live in. This was the conviction that caused my anguish and indignation about apartheid in South Africa and racism in the United States. I felt some desperate need to communicate to people everywhere the disastrous effects of such unchecked primitive behaviour. When I was making the film about the Bowery in New York, I conceived of a large universal epic in the form of a trilogy on racialism in the United States, South Africa and Asia. Since 1948, stories about South Africa had been coming through of such monstrous proportion that I felt the imperative need to fight this ill-conceived ideology with the most effective weapon available to me, cinema.

After having produced *On the Bowery*, I was ready at the beginning of 1957 to start my film in South Africa. I sent my wife, Ellie, to get the visas at the South African consulate. We decided that it would be better to apply as tourists. We were both very nervous that the South African authorities would not grant the visas. Our anticipation was well-founded, because they immediately wanted to know if it was my intention to make a film, but Ellie was well schooled and told them that we wanted to go as tourists to see the country. Because of this, obviously I was not able to enquire about the customs or currency regulations, which was to lead to difficulties later on. This was a kind of film that was a great financial risk, and needed support from a group of people. However, I was not able to try and raise the budget in the usual way since I could not tell anybody what the subject was. Obviously a film made underground was not the kind of film that one could disclose to a large group of people. I took the precaution of telling only one or two people in New York and London, including the anti-apartheid campaigner Michael Scott, of my intention, in case things should misfire and I might be in need of their help.

Early that spring we took *The Constitution* to Italy, and as the boat cut through the water, I felt that I was being carried inexorably to my fate. The boat docked in Italy, and after seeing a few friends in Europe and getting on to London, we were soon on the *Edinburgh Castle* bound for Cape Town and points beyond. Our only stopover in the two weeks of that interminable journey was the Canary Islands. It seemed to be one long round of agonising shipboard games in which neither Ellie nor I participated. I spent practically every day reading about South Africa, and in those two weeks I ripped through enough books to give me a pretty good picture of the country, although I had been reading about South Africa for many years. I remember one particular fellow aboard ship who came up with his tongue hanging out in desperation and said, "Aren't you glad you're not British? You don't have to participate in all these games."

We arrived in Cape Town on a miserable cold evening before Ascension Day, 29 May, 1957. It was raining, and with no heat in the rooms we were freezing. It was now the beginning of June, and of course this was winter in South Africa, where we had been told that the weather at the Cape would be the Mediterranean winter. We groaned when we heard that everything would be closed for three days. Fortunately, however, everything wasn't completely closed and we were able to rent a car and drive around the area of Cape Town. The next day we started out early and drove down the length of the Cape and back. It was magnificent — rocky sea-coast, with cliffs and heavily wooded hills. Somehow or other during all this driving my finger had become infected and on the following day I found a doctor, who with the usual antibiotics gave me a quick cure. Dr Gruenther was, like most South Africans, very friendly and he invited me home to dinner. Dr Gruenther was soon going to America and he was anxious to hear something about the country. We spent a very pleasant evening with him and found him to be likeable and friendly, and although not strongly outspoken, he seemed to deplore the present government. He and his wife and children told us many things about South Africa and we began to get a feeling of the country.

Dr Gruenther seemed to be particularly upset about the fact that the school that his children were forced to go to spoke Afrikaans as the first language. He was anxious for them to learn good English. From the general tone of his conversations we had the feeling that he liked the African people. This was a rare reaction among white South Africans. Dr Gruenther, like many South Africans one met, seemed to have a foreboding of tragedy, as if one could not tell what would come of the situation there. He said that

I must read a very important book entitled, *When Smuts Goes*, by Arthur Keppel-Jones, who wrote, years back, about what would happen when the Smuts government was overthrown. His predictions had proved fatefully true.

We moved on to Johannesburg, where we planned to spend only a few days, since we would be coming back later. I ran around immediately to find out the facilities for film-making. In my cursory investigation, I discovered that it would be difficult to rent equipment, and that perhaps no laboratories would be available. I had given a great deal of thought to how I was to do this film and there were many problems that one anticipated. First of all the laboratory: it was almost imperative to develop this film and print it in South Africa in order to see the rushes since it is rather difficult to make a film without seeing your daily progress, and how one scene fits into the other. On the other hand, if I should develop the film in the Johannesburg labs, there was always the danger that somebody, seeing the rushes, would guess our intentions. There was another problem as well. How would I ever get into the locations (townships) in order to film, since these were prohibited by law to whites without a permit?

I felt that getting a permit would be quite difficult for a foreigner. I kept going over and over in my mind how these problems could be solved, creating fantasies of what might happen, in order to plan out methods of counteracting and outwitting the authorities.

It had been my intention to spend six months touring Africa before starting my film in South Africa. I wanted to take the opportunity to see that great continent and at the same time I felt that somehow or other it would be my insight into South Africa.

LOOKING FOR A CREW

During my travels I had been wondering how I would develop my film in South Africa and where I would do the editing. I had thought seriously of India, and when I heard Satyajit Ray (India's greatest film director, best known for his Pather Panchali trilogy) would be in Italy at the Venice Film Festival I decided to fly there from Nairobi, where we now were. I was also concerned about my film crew. After having passed through Johannesburg, I was quite

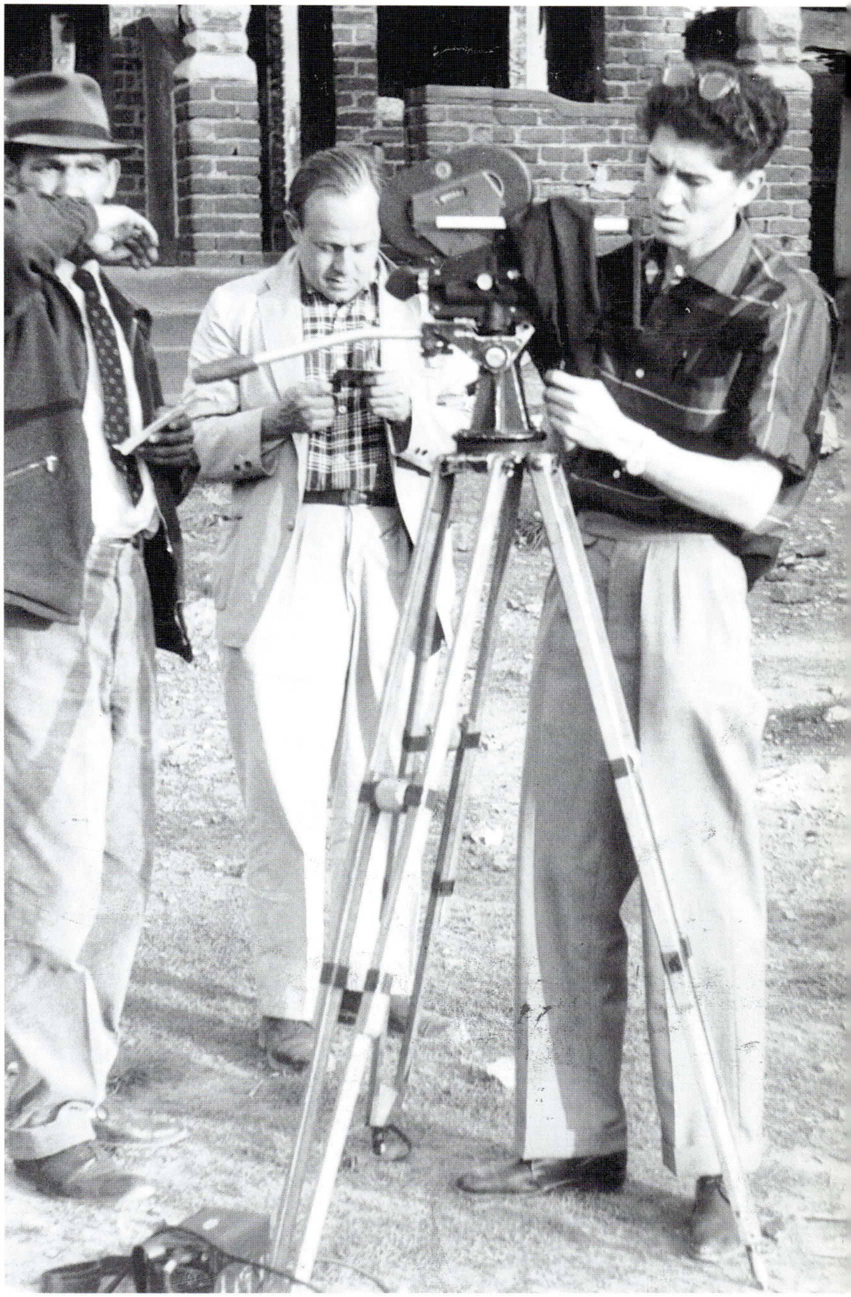

I saw 10 or 15 documentaries, but there was only one photographer whose work I liked, Emil (Milek) Knebel

sure that I wouldn't get the proper people there, that they would be racist in their attitude and dangerous to work with on such a film at this. I would have to go to Europe to find the crew I needed. At the Venice festival I found that Ray was very amenable to my project. I also spoke to a few photographers in Venice to find out if they would be interested in helping. I wasn't able to find anybody suitable, or willing, to undertake it. I then flew to Israel and continued my search. I saw 10 or 15 documentaries, but there was only one photographer whose work I liked, Emil (Milek) Knebel. I met him as soon as possible and, uncannily enough, he was perfect in temperament and attitude for this film. One always knows this immediately, and it is strange how quickly it happens. He was full of excitement and enthusiasm as soon as he heard of the project. I was very happy to finally find someone who was not only right but extremely enthusiastic and willing to make any sacrifice necessary for such a film. He leapt at the chance of going. I now had chosen one man, but I needed two cameramen for the kind of dialogue I wanted to shoot, and a soundman. In Europe I had already talked to Fred (Walter) Wettler and Ernst Artaria who agreed to come to South Africa, so I had the minimum crew necessary to make the film. I returned to Nairobi and flew directly to Johannesburg.

JOHANNESBURG

Elinor and I arrived early in the morning in Johannesburg, and I will never forget my first impression as I stood outside the air terminal office in the centre of the city. I noticed a group of Africans standing talking near the airline bus. They looked and dressed so much like American Negroes that I was quite startled when they started to speak Zulu. It seemed completely wrong to my sensory perceptions, it was as if I had come to a dubbed movie, and everybody was speaking the wrong language — like seeing a Western in Rome with all the cowboys speaking Italian. I expected to hear American slang, the hipster language of New York.

We arrived from the airport at the Carlton Hotel with great trepidation. We entered the ornate lobby, and just as I was about to speak to the bell captain, the floor beneath us gave way with a tremendous shudder. I exclaimed: "What was that?" and the bell captain smiled with self-satisfaction. "Oh, that's just one of the minor earthquakes that goes on here." I later found out that these earth tremors, and some of them were shattering, were a result of the mining that had gone on underneath the city. Sometimes buildings would sink several inches. The first few months we were there, after we had found our flat, every once in a while during the night the floor would suddenly give way with a tremendous crack, and one's heart would leap to one's mouth.

I was afraid even to talk to anybody, since I had no idea of exactly how things worked in South Africa, or how the police checked on foreigners, or how much of a police state South Africa was. I started to walk the streets of Johannesburg trying to see as much of the city as possible, down one street and up the other in absolutely geometric pattern. I visited the museum and tried to find out as much as I could about the history of the city, taking stills wherever I went.

Perhaps it was previous conditioning, but my first impression of Johannesburg was one of foreboding violence. It may have been because of all the reading I had done about South Africa and the high crime rate, but the whole aspect of the city was one to inspire dread and gloom. We had been warned not to go out on the streets alone, and we were told that somebody had been cut to pieces a few yards from the hotel several nights before. There was one fairly untravelled street in the city which was given the name of Murder Alley. To make it worse, when we arrived it was Sunday, and Johannesburg is a strange city that on Sundays, as well as the evenings and nights, is almost completely deserted except for an occasional African. At these times it has the stark gloominess and despair of Wall Street on Sunday and the old City of London. The reason for this is that almost no one lives in the city itself. The standard of living for whites is so high that nearly every white has their own automobile, and transportation out of the city is quite easy. Almost every European lives in the suburbs and comes into the city at eight o'clock in the morning, leaving again at five or six o'clock in the evening. Africans are prohibited by law from living in the city, except a few servants as caretakers for each building, who live on the tops in little houses. I spent a lot of time on these rooftops, finding them a good place to take shots of Johannesburg. It was rather strange to see the living quarters on the top of the skyscrapers where the Africans have their charcoal braziers, clinging to their tribal customs.

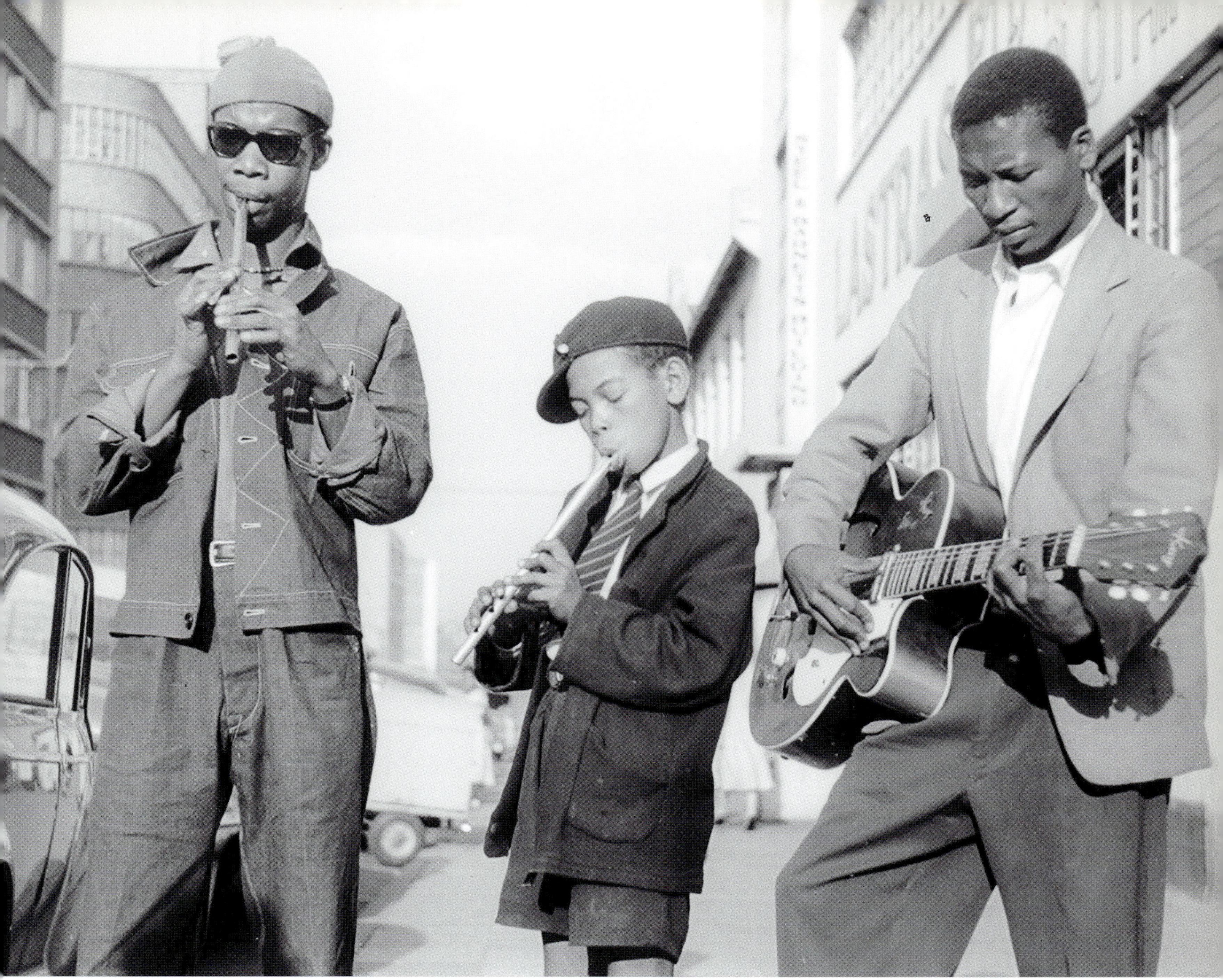

"Suddenly music seemed to be all around us ... a group of wonderful African children dancing in the streets to the accompaniment of their own whistles"

One of the first Sundays that we were in Johannesburg we walked around the city, which was almost completely empty, until suddenly we heard music in the distance. Walking on, we found a band of African children. Here and there throughout the city we found similar groups, and suddenly music seemed to be all around us, people playing guitars walking down the street, a group of Africans marching to church hymns, and a group of wonderful African children in colourful silk costumes, red and yellow, dancing in the streets to the accompaniment of their own whistles which they played with an extraordinary African rhythm. We soon found out that it was Guy Fawkes Day, the English festival, and the children were dancing for pennies. However, there were very few Whites at all to be seen. Suddenly, an enormous parade of African Boy Scouts, playing drums, appeared. They were filled with elan and pride as they came marching on with signs such as: "Africa belongs to us." This walk through the city gave me a vision of what I would like for my opening sequence for the film. This gloomy city gave form to a kind of architectural sequence, buildings dissolving into each other in this death-like silence, and suddenly from nowhere the discovery of a band of joyous Africans singing and dancing in the streets. There was music everywhere in the streets of Johannesburg. It was strange, because Johannesburg was a ghost city, and it was music in a ghost city.

ANTI-APARTHEID WHITES

Since I had made no contacts as yet, I started to walk around the streets of Johannesburg to get a feeling of the city, taking stills as I went along. As I was standing outside a department store, taking a shot of a drunk staggering on the street, somebody who looked like one of the homeless men I had filmed for *On the Bowery*, I suddenly heard my name called. I turned around and there were two women in a car behind me, one of them waving to me. Coming closer, I suddenly saw Mary Benson, whom I had met only once or twice in London for a few minutes, but I recognised her and she was quite excited to see me and I was pleased to see her. She knew what I was there for, and being connected with the Africa Bureau was certainly sympathetic to the film. She asked where we were staying and shortly afterwards called to invite us to go to dinner at her friends' house, the Levsons. I accepted with some hesitation since I did not really know yet how the system in South Africa worked, how closely people were watched. I had heard that licence numbers were taken down and cars were followed. Considering that Mary Benson was with the Africa Bureau and pro-African, I was afraid that perhaps some of her friends might be watched. However, I decided that this might be innocent enough, and we took the chance with great apprehension. When we drove up to the house, the eternal African watchman was sitting outside in front of his fire. He looked very suspicious, and he greeted me with a kind of feeble grin, and I thought he must undoubtedly be a police spy, which I heard existed almost everywhere. As it turned out he was not a particularly pleasant fellow but certainly not a spy, otherwise I would not be writing this book now, because I never would have completed my project in South Africa. The truth of the matter is that although South Africa is somewhat of a police state, it would be impossible financially to watch every single tourist and foreigner who comes into this country night and day.

I found it to be quite true in South Africa, particularly amongst people who are against the government, that there is always a kind of excitement or tension at parties or gatherings, as if one belonged to a grand conspiracy. At first it is a little bit frightening, but after I think one actually got to enjoy it. I certainly think that the people who live there and who had the courage to stand against the government, with all of the discomfort, got a certain pleasure and enjoyment from the danger, as if they were living more intensely, and their lives had more meaning than the ordinary person's. I think it is quite true that people who are involved in a real cause admittedly can suffer great hardships because of it, but somehow live fuller and deeper lives. That's why I have such nostalgia for South Africa and would like to go back there. Once I got over my depression due to the fear of the city and its possible dangers, I began to be involved with a group of wonderful people. It gave one a feeling of one's life being worth something. Of course there was again some peculiar quality of Africa, which I'm not sure exactly what it is. Many people have written about it: I think it may be a combination of the country, the scenery and the open spaces without clutter, pure nature, African music, dancing and this additional quality of excitement and achievement.

We had a marvellous evening with the Levsons that night, but at the same time we were a bit fearful as they told us more about the system there and we got a clearer picture of South Africa. However, they warned us not to be too nervous and cautious since one could do quite a lot, particularly if you were not too fearful. The problem for me at that point was knowing what I could do and what I couldn't, since the society was completely strange to me. I decided to go slow and feel my way carefully, and I think it was this that in the long run enabled me to accomplish my purpose.

I spent nearly nine months in the country before I started shooting. By this time I knew every pathway of danger, and I knew the geography of the society so well that I could feel my way away from pitfalls, and when I found myself in danger, I knew how to handle it according to the mentality of the authorities. The Levsons were anxious to help me in any way they could, and Leon Levson himself being a still photographer was quite excited about the idea and wanted to discuss it more fully with me, perhaps even help in the production.

In the next few days I started meditating very carefully as to how I was going to succeed in this project, and how I was going to continue undiscovered. I came to several basic theoretical conclusions which I think helped me in finding a procedure. First of all I felt that I had to know the culture completely, the laws and the police, the way the bureaucracy functioned, how businessmen behaved, how laboratories reacted, how technicians worked, the mentality of everyone, so that I could know how to proceed exactly, without creating suspicion. And to me this was the key thing. If I didn't create suspicion I could probably get away with almost anything. And suddenly I began to feel what it was like to be a secret agent in any society, and I suddenly realised that the regime is far less aware of whom the agent is than the agent is aware of the regime. Actually, the regime has no way of knowing without some suspicious act, unless of course they have a complete police state like the Nazis, when it becomes a little easier. But even then there must be some suspicious act.

For example, if an agent were to sit in his room in the city and do nothing but go out to eat, visit people socially, etc, there would be no way of the regime knowing he was an agent. It is only when he begins to work and try to find out things that he can be discovered. And even then, the discovery can have no proof until he actually transmits information, and it is at that point that he can be caught. Therefore I realised that I was in the same position, and until I committed a suspicious act of some kind there was no way of the government of South Africa knowing what I was up to, particularly since I was an American citizen, a tourist, a film-maker, none of the things which would ordinarily make one suspicious. I had no past political affiliations or associations. To their knowledge I was just a kind of semi-freelance playboy. That was exactly the way I liked it to be thought of. There was no question about it, I could go for months travelling around the country, absorbing material, watching things without creating any suspicion whatsoever. However, there would be a point at which I would start to create suspicion. That would be when I started to develop my film in the laboratories (unless I sent it to America), when I started to meet Africans and talk to them and meet them socially, and worse yet, go into the locations, which was prohibited. This was a more serious problem. And finally the actual shooting itself. But in the meantime I would spend months absorbing knowledge about the country before I made any serious moves. And of course I had to take risks.

The Levsons suggested that I see Bloke Modisane at the *Golden City Post*, a weekly African newspaper. They thought that he would be very helpful. I went to see Bloke, and I told him I was anxious to make a film on South Africa. I remember my first meeting with him, his cheerful smiling face and happy grin, and I knew right away that this was the man who would be of great help to me and my best liaison with Africans. I was to learn later that this smiling face was a cover-up for a great deal of hostility towards the world and the white race in particular, a hostility which I cannot, with all I have witnessed, accept as inevitable and natural under the circumstances. We talked quite a long while about many things. Bloke was extremely amiable and outgoing. He gave me all the information about things that I would see and suggested that I come out to Sophiatown and visit him in the near future. I said that I would be very happy to do this. Before I left him, he invited me to a party that coming Sunday, at the house of a young English couple.

Ellie found an ad in the paper for an African talent show called *African Jazz* which I decided to go to. It was both a disappointment and a pleasure. A disappointment because it was such a mixture, of African and American pop, jazz, commercial, etc, that it lacked pure authenticity. Yet it did have something very African about it. There were some numbers that were very good and also there were the Africans themselves, and there were Indians as well with them, and coloureds. It was full of vitality, and the show had a spirit of exuberance that was marvellous. During the entire show, watching all the performances, I said to Ellie, "There are only two people here who are worthwhile." One was Miriam Makeba, the African girl, and the other was Sonny Pillay, a South African of Indian descent who had a marvellous voice. I realised then that Miriam would be great in the film in some way, but I didn't know how I would use Sonny, as the film would essentially be about Africans.

On Sunday night we rushed ourselves off to the party wondering exactly what it would be like. It was quite a pleasure to see a party that was mixed. The room was full of Africans, whites, people of all races enjoying themselves thoroughly. It struck me that even with all the restrictions, legal and social, of South Africa, when there is mixing there is far more than there is in the United States. Those people in South Africa who are committed against the regime really have a great deal of friendship towards the African, far more than their American counterparts. It struck me even more forcibly when I arrived back in New York and found that so few of the white progressives and intellectuals have many Negro friends, and the parties are either all Negro or all white, with a sprinkling of the other race. Perhaps two or three whites in a Negro party, or the same thing in a white party, but never real complete mixing of people. These mixed parties I went to in South Africa were some of the best parties I'd ever been to in my life. They weren't forced gaiety and drunken liberty, but the African exuberance brought all of us whites out of our shells and enabled us to enjoy ourselves. There was always music and dancing, which adds a lot to any gathering. But the Africans really danced — I've never enjoyed dancing very much, but I always did at these parties, because their dancing seems to be the real kind of thing, not a pretence to cover up some other motive.

The party was for a young English couple called the Harts, who were going back to England because they had gotten into quite a lot of trouble in South Africa because of their friendships with Africans and such parties as these. Of course, a party like this was a bit dangerous, and one was always afraid of raids. The serving of liquor to Africans was illegal and we could have all had our names taken. In addition, such a party would be frowned upon seriously by all the neighbours, and there might be some complaints. We were all a bit noisy. There were a lot of people that night, and everybody seemed quite friendly. Particularly, we met some people named the Bermans, whom we both rather liked, and they invited us to come out to their house early the next week. During the evening with the Bermans, Monty Berman got talking about films, and we discussed the sort of things that I would do in South Africa. Suddenly he asked if I had ever heard of a film called *Cannery Row* made in the United States. As he talked, I thought he might have been talking about my film *On the Bowery*, but I wasn't quite sure, and said that I'd never heard of a film called *Cannery Row* but that it sounded like a story by Steinbeck. He then said to me: "You must have heard of it, how could you not have heard of it — it was very famous." I then began to feel slightly chagrined and said "Could you possibly mean *Skid Row*? and he said: "Yes, that's it," and I said, "Oh, that's a film that I made," which was quite a surprise to everybody. *Skid Row* was the original name we had for *On the Bowery*. Monty had read an article written for the magazine *Sight and Sound*. Monty and Myrtle were both people who were dedicated to the African cause, and became good friends of ours, and were very helpful to us during the long months ahead.

At about this time I met again with Leon Levson, who offered to help me as much as possible. I discussed with him the technical problems of having the film developed and also of bringing in the crew. I told him that I would need some device to give the Government as a reason for bringing in the crew and making a film. I suggested that perhaps if I could find some company to say that I was making a travelogue for them, this might be one method of doing it. Leon said that he would help in this matter, so after various introductions I finally found myself having lunch with the head of Finches Travel Agency. He seemed to be very interested and was definitely anxious to have a film made, so I let him do all the talking. He made me an offer which, under normal circumstances, wouldn't be very good, and that was that I should make the film that I thought would be successful as a documentary, and give them some publicity or credit. For that they would bring in my entire crew, and pay for transportation and all living expenses during their stay in South Africa.

Of course, the film itself would cost a great deal more than this, and normally no film producer would accept such an offer. However, all I wanted was a front, so I was delighted to accept these terms. Through other sources I finally got an appointment with the publicity manager of the Chamber of Mines, Mr Kolig. We had lunch together, but he seemed much colder. There was no

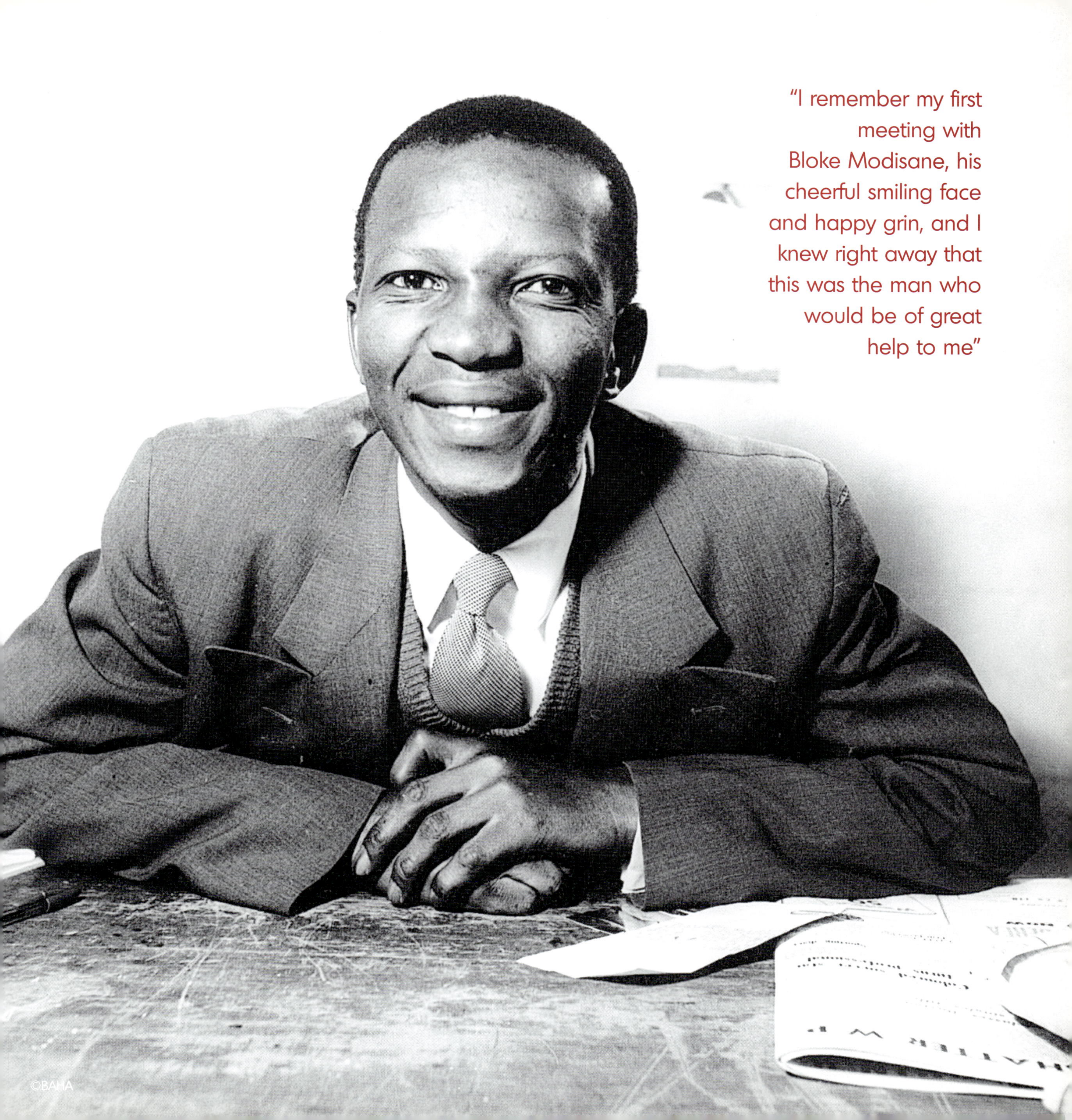

"I remember my first meeting with Bloke Modisane, his cheerful smiling face and happy grin, and I knew right away that this was the man who would be of great help to me"

enthusiasm on his part. He said that he would consider it, and we left it that I would contact him again. In the meantime, I had one possibility that I could pretty nearly count on, or so it seemed.

A VISIT TO THE MINES

In Johannesburg, the Chamber of Mines runs a tour of the mines for tourists coming to South Africa. I sometimes wondered why they did this, since I hardly think that it is a good advertisement for them, but apparently they thought it was good public relations. I suppose they are able to fool a certain number of people. Shortly after we arrived in Johannesburg, around February, 1958, I decided to take the tour. I found the mine at East Geduld very interesting. There were a lot of little touches that impressed one. For example: every African you met there saluted you. There was something that made you feel very strange about this.

Our tour included the mine school. There was a scientific programme of films, aptitude tests and training programmes, obstacle courses to find natural leaders, all very modern, fascinating. African and white trainers who teach thousands of illiterate Africans to become miners in a matter of several days. They had Africans putting together red blocks and working mechanical puzzles. As I watched I wondered what was the reaction of the tribal African to all of this? Did he think it was mad, ridiculous, mysterious? Perhaps it was. After the tests they are taught various mining occupations: shovelling, making pipes and how to set charges for blasting. The school is very modern, but diabolical. It is a machine: precise in its organisation and inhuman in its impersonality.

This testing went on continuously because every few months thousands of raw recruits pour in. There was a huge amount of manpower used on the mines. Actually it was the biggest labour force in South Africa, over 350 000 Africans in the one occupation. Since they were practically all there for fairly short periods, the turnover was enormous. Our guide was proud to tell us that they were recruiting and flying in Africans from as far away as Kenya and Tanganyika. The constant turnover is costly, but a permanent labour force has greater dangers. Continuous stability might lead to unions and political organisation. Under the present system, before the raw recruit can become a little sophisticated his contract is over and he is back in Swaziland or Basutholand.

The Chamber of Mines presents the mines as a wonderful opportunity for the African. Tourists don't probe too deeply, so the Chamber can cleverly present a case favourable to itself. Their polemic is as follows: "The African earns far more than he could earn in the tribal reserves. They are anxious to come to the mines. They are given a nutritious diet and gain weight during their contracts. They have nice living quarters and companionship. In the reserves Africans are starving to death and in the mines they get a chance to earn a little decent money."(It is amazing how happy the Africans are to be doing work and living under conditions that would horrify the whites.)

What they say is true, but they don't present the entire case. The South African regime demands that the migrant worker lives in a compound completely separated from his family for long periods of time. Often it leads to the complete break-up of a family. It can only be considered an advantage by those who regard the African as an animal and a chattel who will not suffer when separated from his parents at a tender age. Furthermore, the conditions of famine in the reserves have been caused by the whites themselves. Successive governments have continually expropriated the land owned by Africans. Today, Africans represent 85% of the population and retain only 13% of the land.

In the mines and on the farms the wages are between two to four pounds per month, whereas in factories an African can earn five to ten pounds a week. When tribal Africans become aware of this they are reluctant to work in the mines or on the farms and there is a labour shortage in these industries. Forced labour from Mozambique alone brings 100 000 men to the mines.

I went on the mine tour with an ordinary group of tourists and at lunchtime we were all herded together with the various white foremen who had been conducting the tour. I was sitting together with an English-speaking type who had rather a nice face. With us there was a woman from Rhodesia — pinched face, sharp nose, a shrewish type of woman whom one finds almost everywhere, who was complaining about Africa and the Africans and how barbaric they were and how difficult and how bad they were as servants. The man shook his head in agreement, but thoughtfully said, "It's a pity, it's really a pity, I don't know what's going to become of it, I don't know what's going to happen. The situation is very bad. It's because

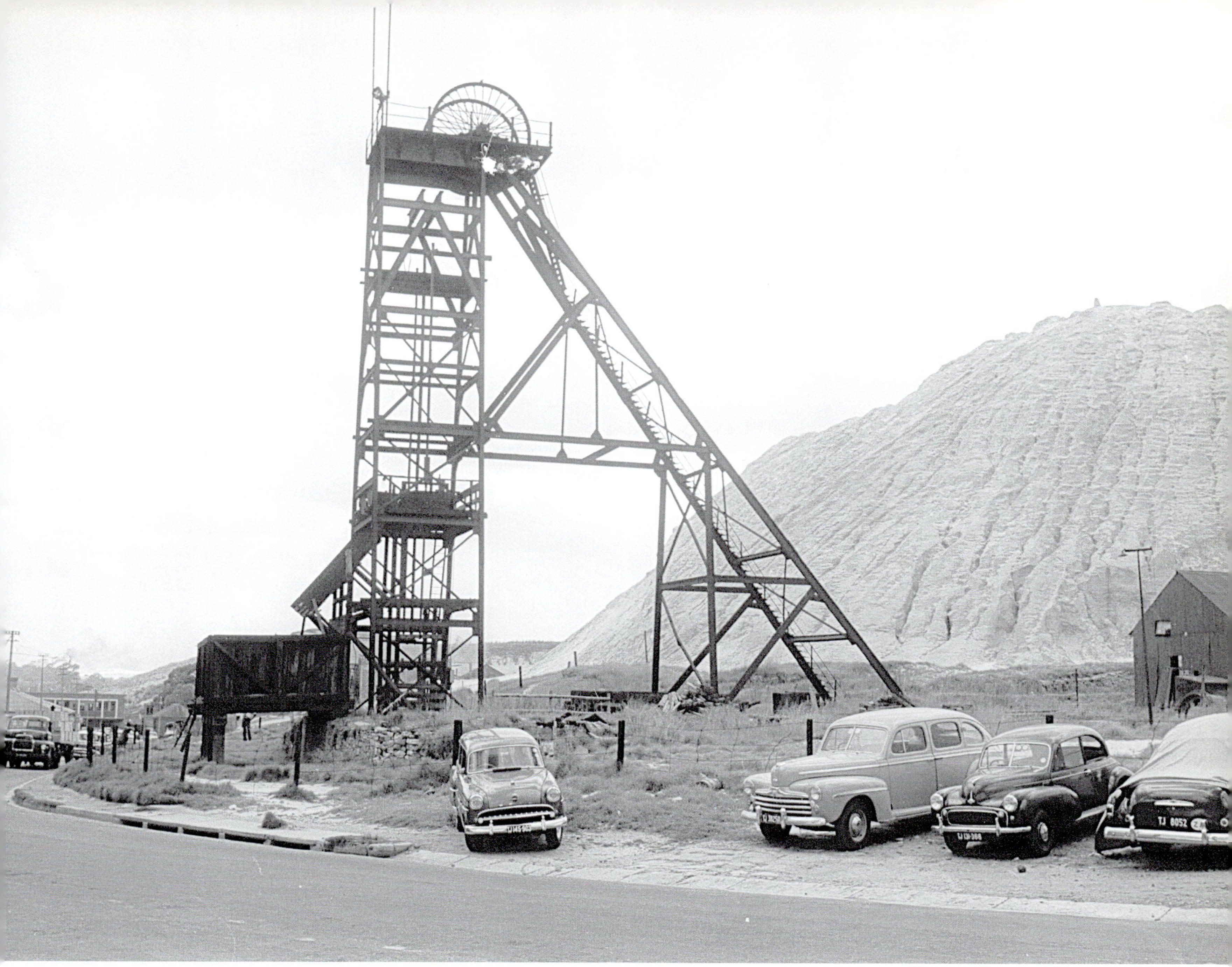

The Chamber of Mines presents the mines as a wonderful opportunity for the African. Tourists don't probe too deeply, so the Chamber can cleverly present a case favourable to itself

we are greedy. We exploit the Africans." And then of course he had to add the rationalisation for himself, "Not here, of course, in the mines, but everywhere else."

He was an English-speaking South African and he talked about how he had been in England two years ago. He talked with great nostalgia about England and the richness of its culture and how things were well done there compared to South Africa. All this conversation was started by our discussion as to how we had gotten to the mine and how we could have had difficulty finding it because of the road sign which was very poor. It was rather surprising at first to hear South Africans, particularly English-speaking South Africans, talk this way, but I shortly realised that South Africa is not really a nation. Most of the people don't consider themselves really South African. A nation can't be made up of groups of isolated clans that have no loyalty or connection with each other, and in this sense South Africans are different from Americans who, although they may have conflicts and group differences, essentially all feel American, whereas in South Africa there is only one small majority of the whites, the Boers, who feel any sense of belonging and have an independent culture. But of course for them everybody else counts for nothing, and therefore the others consider the Afrikaner-dominated government completely alien to their interests. Millions of Africans constitute the exploited majority. The coloureds are a buffer between Africans and privileged whites, but are certainly not even second-class citizens. The English-speaking group still feels tied culturally and patriotically to England. Therefore, I think that it is true to say South Africa is not really a nation in the sense of a cohesive cultural force made up of people who, although varied in culture, have a loyalty to the state.

But as this English-speaking South African spoke at lunch, I found him very decent, human and likeable. He certainly seemed to have an awareness of the injustice of South African life, but unfortunately he was confused and bewildered himself and did not seem to have any clear ideas as to what it was all about, certainly not how to change it. He was common of a certain minority of white South Africans, those people who seem to have some conscience and awareness of the evils and flaws of the society but have neither the strength nor the possibility nor the imagination to do anything about it. I found him rather typical not only of people in South Africa but of mankind to a large degree all over the world. In our discussion he told me that there was very little social contact between the Boers and English-speaking South Africans at the mines. They worked together but hardly ever saw each other socially. What a depressing state of affairs, when even white men in the same country cannot meet for fear that the conversation will touch on areas that they can't even discuss together! I thought that I would definitely like to use such a type in the film, and I considered using him. I felt that it would give the film a well-rounded picture.

Not all whites were monsters and unthinking human beings. There was a considerable number who seemed to realise that everything had gone haywire in South Africa. When you lived in South Africa and talked to so many whites who were blinded by racism and obsessed by fear about the subject so that they could not think clearly, so that they could not make any changes to avert the situation, you realised that most people are thoroughly conditioned by their society, and that if one's childhood is indoctrinated with a certain idea, there is no escaping it. It takes some kind of profound shock to get people to start analysing what their position is, whether it is good or bad, or right or wrong. It makes me realise how rare is the individual who speaks out against injustice and oppression within his own society. The people that I knew in South Africa made me speculate as to what creates such an individual. Rather than thinking this is the way all people should be, I found myself thinking, why is it that there are such people? The irony of it is that although such a person is quite an asset to society he is almost inevitably hated because essentially he is trying to make people look at their own corrupted images for the sake of changing them. What is it that makes these rare individuals? We must find out what it is so that we can have more of them.

THE TYRANNY OF THE PASS

Every African male is required to carry a pass on his person at all times. Recently the government has started forcing women to carry passes as well. Naturally, the Africans detest these passes, which they refer to as "the Bible". The police can stop an African at any time and ask him for his pass. The different stamps in his pass-book an African must have are infinite, and every month his pass must be signed by his employer. If he loses his employment, he is liable to arrest if he does not return to his place of origin within 72 hours.

The pass system itself is a system of forced labour. Tribal Africans who want to work in the cities have difficulty in obtaining the proper passes and because of this they are forced instead to seek work on the mines or on the farms. In the mines they get their two to four pounds, which has not risen more than 10% in 40 years, but the most crucial shortage is in farm labour. Pass violators often end up not in jail but on the farms. Approximately one million Africans are arrested per year for this petty offence. They receive penalties up to 90 days' imprisonment and the law allows them to be sold to the farmers at the rate of one shilling per day. The farmer, who is the backbone of the white Nationalist Party, is as a result prosperous, and the African is shackled.

Under the Group Areas Act, the husbands and wives of domestic servants are not allowed to live with them on their employers' premises. With this Act you have the ludicrous situation of husbands and wives being arrested for living together. Thousands of night raids take place in Jo'burg every year, giving the police plenty of chance for the abuse and mistreatment of Africans. In the cities there are numerous pass regulations and restrictions regarding the locations where Africans can live, and it is difficult for the men to bring their wives with them. In my visits to the reserves (rural "homelands") I saw that they were depopulated of men. It was as if some great war had called all of them away. The women remain home, exerting themselves to raise the children, but malnutrition and its companion diseases are rampant. From the mines the men bring home tuberculosis; infant mortality is about 50% and pellagra and malnutrition are common.

Because of the pass system there is a large army of unattached men in the urban areas, separated from their families. Crime, prostitution, syphilis and illegitimate births have steadily increased. Many of these children are deserted and actually grow up on the streets, destined to end up in the "tsotsi"gangs (bands of criminals who roam the African locations terrorising the populace). The urban African has been demoralised by this process, which has been going on for over 50 years. Migratory labour is a ruthless system which has fractured the social structure and emotional life of the African people. South Africa is a classic sociological case of tribal society disintegrating under the impact of the machine age, brought to its most extreme form and exacerbated rather than alleviated by the regime. Whites call the Africans primitive and barbaric, but such exploitation and indifference to suffering can also be considered as barbaric. Jo'burg does have the highest crime rate in the world, but Africans from the rural areas behave according to a strict code and there is very little crime in the reserves.

AFRICAN FRIENDS

We were now about ready for our first visit to Sophiatown. The Harts came and picked us up and cautioned us generally to be careful about going to Sophiatown. They said that their licence plates had been marked down on going out there to parties. This really worried me. I was afraid that somehow we would be noticed, and then the first suspicious act would have taken place, and the film would never be completed. Finally we arrived at Bloke's in one piece. It was a small party, this would go without saying in Sophiatown because the houses were seldom more than one small room, sometimes two or three. There were ourselves, Bloke and his wife, the Harts and Hazel Futa, a very attractive girl, and her boyfriend Nimrod. Hazel had a provocative face, she was gay and vivacious as well as attractive; she didn't have the dignity and appeal that I would want for the main woman in my film, but I was sure I would have a part for her somewhere.

The food and drink were good. Local food, from what I've sampled, is somewhat simple. This was actually curry, and Africans in the city seemed to be turning to curry from the Indians. There was lots of music, and pretty soon people began to pile in. No invitations were necessary. This is typical of an African party, people just seemed to come in from all over, and this of course is something quite different from our way of life. There are no telephones in the villages, and no invitation is necessary. People just come and go as they please. As a matter of fact, one hardly has much privacy due to the coming and going, but there is something quite wonderful about the warmth of life and the lack of formality. This carries over to the whites as well. I must say that I rather liked it myself. I very often do it now, I pop into somebody's house at the last moment, and I always feel that they enjoy it. Pretty soon the room was filled with people, and there was the dancing and gaiety of a typical African party. I still wasn't quite used to the situation, particularly since I was afraid of the police, and it was my first acquaintance with Sophiatown.

Suddenly, through friends, I heard that the Johannesburg Film Society wanted to meet me. Something like this, which ordinarily I would most likely welcome, in South Africa caused me consternation and confusion. I didn't know whether I should meet the film society, I certainly didn't want publicity at this point, and I didn't want too much known about my previous work. So I didn't quite know what to do. After quite a lot of thought, I decided to meet with them, since they already knew I was there, and I made an appointment to visit Neal Smith, the treasurer of the film society. At our meeting with the film society they asked me if I would be willing to bring in *On the Bowery* to be shown to their film society, and I was surprised to learn from them that the United States Information Service was bringing out a film that I had made for the United Nations called *Out*. I was a bit startled by this news, considering that it came suddenly from nowhere, and particularly with the South African attitude towards the UN, which was one of animosity.

I didn't know what effect it would have on the authorities' attitude towards me. At the same time I was aware that any publicity would probably be an advantage for me, with the exception of a statement that I had come to make a film about apartheid. But *Out* was on its way in and there wasn't much I could do about it without creating suspicion. It finally arrived and was introduced to the film society by David Dubois of the United States Information Service. He was quite pleased to have the film, and while I listened to his introduction I had a mixed feeling of annoyance and gratitude. I gave a short talk at the film society, I can't even remember what about. Shortly after this *On the Bowery* received a nomination for an Academy Award for documentary films. News of this reached the film society and they had it published in the Johannesburg papers. So I started getting some publicity, which I felt was all to the good. Later on, when we were filming, I always carried a few such press cuttings in my pocket in case we should be stopped by the police. I thought it might be some favourable method of introduction as to who I was. There was another showing of *Out* at the United States Information Service, which I attended, and staff members of the *Golden City Post* were invited. Bloke and Lewis Nkosi were there. I had met Lewis before at the offices of the *Golden City Post* and as soon as I saw him I was struck by something unusual about his face. He looked extremely young to be working on a newspaper. At that time he looked very much like a teenager, and although he was an African from Zululand originally, there was something in his appearance of an American prep school boy, something about it in his manner also. At the same time, his first appearance seemed sullen and angry. Until that point I had had almost no contact with Lewis because there was something about his looks that put me off him. During *Out*, as he watched the film, which was about the Hungarian refugees from the uprising of 1956, he became quite excited, and there were certain moments of the film where he exclaimed "Beautiful, beautiful". Actually, the film to me was never a success. It's a film that I don't feel is completely mine by a long shot, since I only worked on the directing of the film and not the editing, so it was not under my control. However, there are some good moments in the film. There was something very sensitive about Lewis, and we became very strong friends from the moment that the film ended.

Bloke and Lewis from that time on used to come to dinner at our house very frequently. It was always very enjoyable having them, and conversation was interesting and exciting, about the situation in South Africa, always tainted by the fear of the neighbours, that they might see Bloke and Lewis coming to our flat and object and complain to the police. Lewis was an excellent reporter who had a lot of courage. Not only was that necessary for his job, but he showed it against every form of racism that he encountered. He went up to Zeerust at the time of the disturbance there and questioned some of the people, and he and another journalist were locked up in a hut by the chieftain and severely beaten. He stuck his neck out on several occasions like this. One time, reporting a court case, he refused to sit in the African section, and had an altercation with the judge, and believe me, in South Africa that takes a bit of courage to do. Sometimes one felt the courage was a bit reckless, and yet one couldn't help admiring his fight against injustice.

Every day the Johannesburg press carried headlines about the coming national elections. The Africans were depressed because everyone thought Strijdom and his misanthropic crew would win

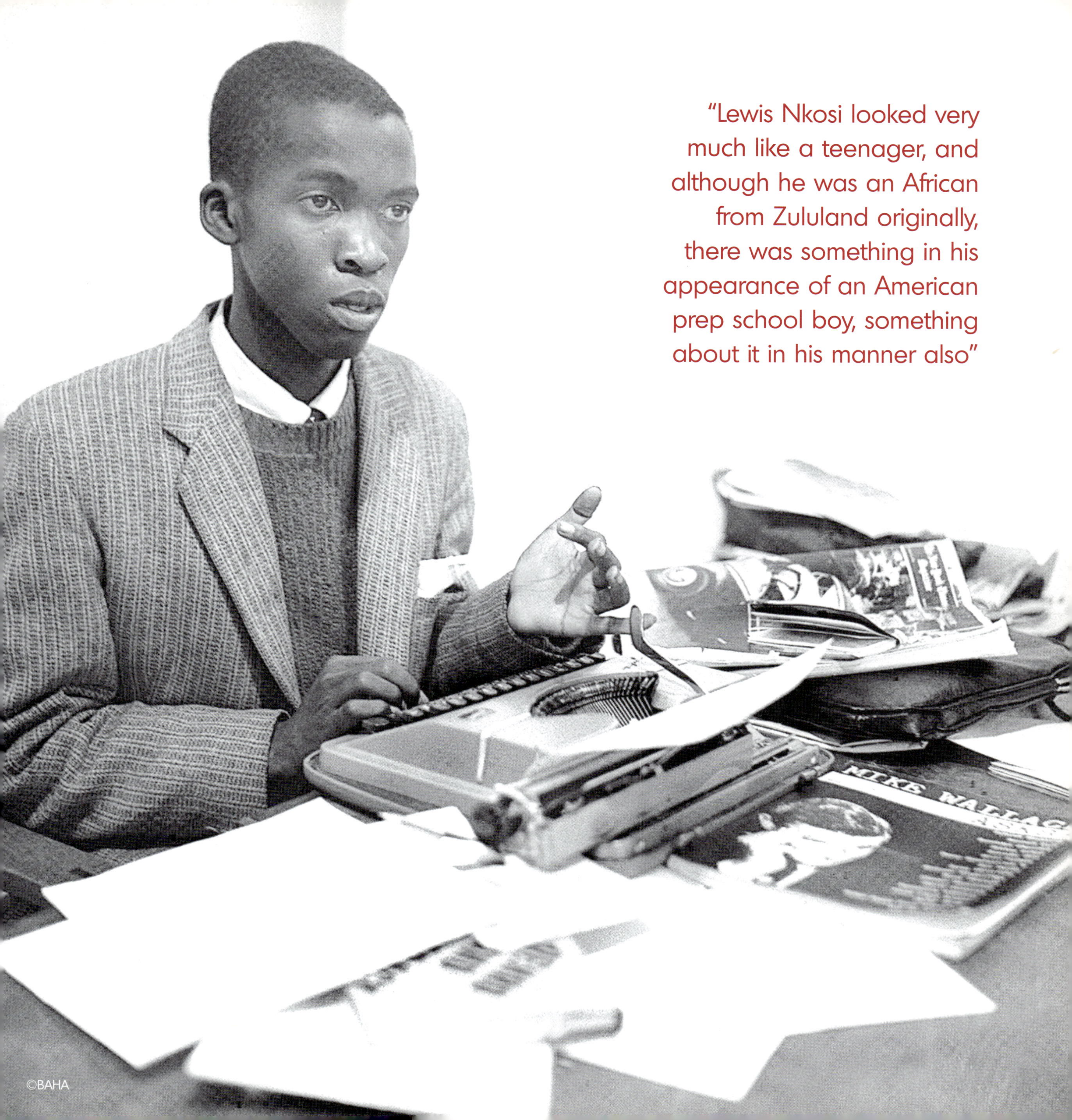

"Lewis Nkosi looked very much like a teenager, and although he was an African from Zululand originally, there was something in his appearance of an American prep school boy, something about it in his manner also"

again. The African National Congress proclaimed a stay-at-home, a unique political device, both as a protest and a show of strength against elections in which they had no vote. The stay-at-home was invented to circumvent a South African law which prohibits Africans from going on strike. In the past, Africans have been beaten, terrorised and arrested for attempting to break this law. Staying at home from work en masse is not illegal in South Africa, unless it can be proved that there is a conspiracy between all those participating. As the election date approached, the government threatened to break this mass protest with police force. The authorities justified this illegal action with the claim that they intended to protect those who wanted to work. The ingenuity of evil men is infinite.

Excitement reached a climax the afternoon before the elections. I was with Lewis Nkosi at that time and he asked me if I would drive him home. I didn't understand the danger this involved. I agreed willingly, but as we drove on towards Sophiatown I realised the consequences of this action. Lewis gaily mentioned that the police were already active in Sophiatown. He treated the matter as if it was a lark, but I could sense that he was nervous. I wanted to back out, but I didn't want Lewis to think that I was running out on him. I began to get extremely uneasy as we approached Sophiatown. With great trepidation I drove through the streets, keeping an eye out for the police. Finally we arrived at his digs, and with a sense of relief I turned around immediately and drove back. I was annoyed at Lewis for leading me into such a vulnerable situation. Completing the film would be a weapon against apartheid and if this action was a test, a lark, or just thoughtlessness, he had exposed me to an unnecessary and dangerous risk. To be stopped and questioned by the police would have been disastrous for me.

The next day the phone rang. It was Lewis: "Man, it's really hot out here; the police are raising hell — they are going into the houses and pulling people out and beating them in the streets." I was shocked and angered by this ruthlessness and arrogance. The Africans were acting within their legal rights, unjust as the law is. The (Afrikaner) Nationalists control the government and police. They make oppressive laws and then break them when these have operated to their disadvantage. An infuriating technique when one is the victim of it. The stay-at-home has become a common occurrence in South Africa. It could be a powerful political weapon for the Africans if it could be sustained, because the entire economy of South Africa depends upon African labour.

I was extremely touched that Lewis had called. With each incident I witnessed, I became more deeply involved in the African cause. Since Lewis had looked to me for a small measure of moral support, it appeared that he considered me a friend.

It might have been a little foolhardy on my part to invite Africans to our flat rather than meeting them someplace else, since it exposed me to some danger and could jeopardise the film, which was far more important to the African cause than whether we met them at our house or not. Although it was not illegal for them to come, it was something that was so uncustomary and against the habits of South Africans that it would have caused a great deal of resentment amongst the neighbours. We must have had some pretty cosmopolitan neighbours, I think, who were not South African, because we never had any complaints. After all, having Africans was not illegal, what was illegal was serving them liquor, and for this you can be charged. A friend of ours, John Goldblatt, had been jailed recently for serving alcohol to two Africans, and they were sent to jail as well. John had had a colourful career in South Africa. He had been caught with an African girl, which is also against the law, an infraction of the Immorality Act, so-called. Of course anything like this causes enormous scandal in South Africa, and he was called in front of his boss and accused of being a communist. Shortly after that he lost his job. But John seemed to have a particular liking for African ladies — in fact one might call it an obsession — and this experience with the police didn't stop him. Just after that, he had a very intricately contrived labyrinth of doors and curtains made to protect him from intruders, and from that time on he was always careful to pull the curtains.

Now that I knew Bloke and Lewis, I began to spend practically all my time in Sophiatown. I felt that I was really getting into things thoroughly. This of course was the subject of my film, but in any case I enjoyed completely this experience and relationship. Through Bloke and Lewis I met a third member of the group, Morris Hugh, with whom Lewis lived. Morris was not an African, he was "coloured". His father was a European and his mother was an African. Like many of the coloured South Africans, Morris didn't know his father. He may have known who he was, but he had no acquaintance with him, and Morris had all the peculiar qualities of a man with such a background. As I got to know Morris and to hear about coloured people, I realised that in human terms, in psychological terms, the coloured people of South Africa were the really great tragedy of the country, because the African, although he may have been economically exploited and suppressed politically, psychologically he was extremely strong. Africans were not a beaten people, they were not warped people essentially, although in the urban areas there was a percentage of fractured personalities, criminals, etc. The Africans were a majority in their country, they knew that eventually they would be on top, they knew, whether consciously or subconsciously, that they had the power, they felt this, and they were essentially a happy people, even in their poverty. But the coloureds seemed to have a misery and an inferiority.

It was quite obvious that they really didn't know where they belonged or what they were. They were outcasts from both groups. They were set up originally by the British like a buffer between the Africans and the whites by giving them special privileges, that crazy old system of "divide and rule", and with this system it caused the complete breakdown of a people psychologically, because they were hated and regarded with suspicion by the Africans, and by the whites with contempt. Since they had special privileges due to their race, and yet not enough privileges to be accepted, they became the worst racists of all. They still refuse to mix with Africans on buses, in theatres, etc. This is now breaking down somewhat since the Nationalists, foolishly, have started to take away some of their privileges.

In reading the wonderful book *Tell Freedom* by Peter Abrahams, himself a coloured writer, I remember being forcibly struck by his description of the school he went to as a child, in which the lighter children amongst the coloureds oppressed the darker ones, and he made the statement that he realised that the oppressed oppress the oppressed. This is something I suppose I was aware of before, but it was crystallised by this statement of Abrahams. Certainly it explains the anti-Semitism of Jews, and the fact that persecuted minorities look down upon other minorities more persecuted than themselves. It is part of the bitter price of self-hatred paid by the victims of the hatred itself. This is the terrible injustice of persecution. There is a threefold price the victim has to pay. Firstly, the persecution itself, political, economic, social, etc. Secondly, the self-hatred that develops within himself and the destructive qualities to his personality. Thirdly, the bitterness that it brings forth against the outside. Some Africans had a bitterness like the American Negro had which, although justified, is in many ways self-destructive.

SOPHIATOWN

I was by now a frequent visitor to Sophiatown, and we had constant bull sessions at which Lewis and Bloke and Morris talked about their feelings towards society and life in general in South Africa. In many ways they were very bitter, and I myself began to be affected by their feelings. I found myself so involved with their attitudes that I would sometimes get into a fury about the situation that existed there. It was easy to do, it was so absurd. Sometimes we would drive along and see the most hair-raising sights, suddenly a policeman would be pulling an African off the sidewalk and beating him for no reason. I remember one particular Sunday when Lewis was particularly upset, although he covered it up with laughter. James Ambrose Brown, a well-known writer, had written in an editorial in one of the South African newspapers: "The Africans are cruel to animals, they have no kindness towards them". It was really quite an absurd article, considering the situation in South Africa and the treatment of Africans by whites. Lewis couldn't seem to get over this, and he kept talking about it over and over again. It was a Sunday afternoon and we were drinking a bit. Lewis got a big high and started making a parody on the article, saying: "Africans should be kinder to animals, they should treat cockroaches better and bedbugs too," and so on. It was quite amusing and he had us all laughing very much.

What struck me, though, was that at the same time there seemed to be a tremendous excitement and enjoyment of life despite all these hardships. There was an almost magical quality about Sophiatown, filled with music and dancing. There was hardly any night that life wasn't full of interest and every house was open to any neighbour who cared to drop in and chat. I don't think that anyone who has ever visited can fail to be caught up in this spirit. I have often felt desperately that if people on the outside, the whites who had such fixed attitudes about the Africans, could spend some time in Sophiatown without fear and terror, perhaps a new understanding would be reached. I realise that many people would not — their minds would be shut off — but there would be many who could, and it was this that I hoped to accomplish through the film. I didn't want the film to be a pure polemic on political terms "about" the wrongs and injustice of apartheid, I wanted also a communication of human spirit so that the people on the other side of the barrier could feel emotionally what Africa really is like and not what their particular mentality has created for them — the stereotype image.

While we were filming, Sophiatown was being destroyed by the authorities to make room for a white suburb. There were many protests about this, and there were fights in the courts. The government actually claimed that they were destroying Sophiatown because it was a slum in order to move the Africans to better housing. This was not true, since Sophiatown had some very good housing, and was of a far higher standard than other places such as Pimville, Moroka and Senoane. I visited those areas and the conditions were absolutely deplorable. They were pulling down much better houses in Sophiatown and leaving those worse areas untouched. John Gunther, the American author of *Inside Africa*, describes Sophiatown as an African middle class area with the highest standard of living and the highest educational level of any African location in the Transvaal.

There seemed to be two main reasons why the government was destroying Sophiatown. One was the fact that Sophiatown was one of two areas in which Africans had freehold rights, that is to say that they had the right to own their own land. Secondly, Sophiatown was an area in which most of the political action started, since the Africans in Sophiatown had been urbanised longer and were more politically conscious. In addition, since it was a freehold area, all groups of South Africans could live there — Africans, coloureds and Chinese all mixed together, which of course was against the basic policy of apartheid.

If you pass through Sophiatown quickly you might wonder why people would fight so hard to stay there. There were many good houses, as well as others that were small but well-built, and nicely kept, but most of it was broken-down shacks, slum areas. But if you spent time in Sophiatown, even just one Sunday, you would find a spirit that was highly contagious. It was one of those places where people were always on the street, moving and milling around full of activity, life and music. On Sundays, weddings were taking place. Music, brass bands, penny-whistlers and church

If you spent time in Sophiatown, even just one Sunday, you would find a spirit that was highly contagious

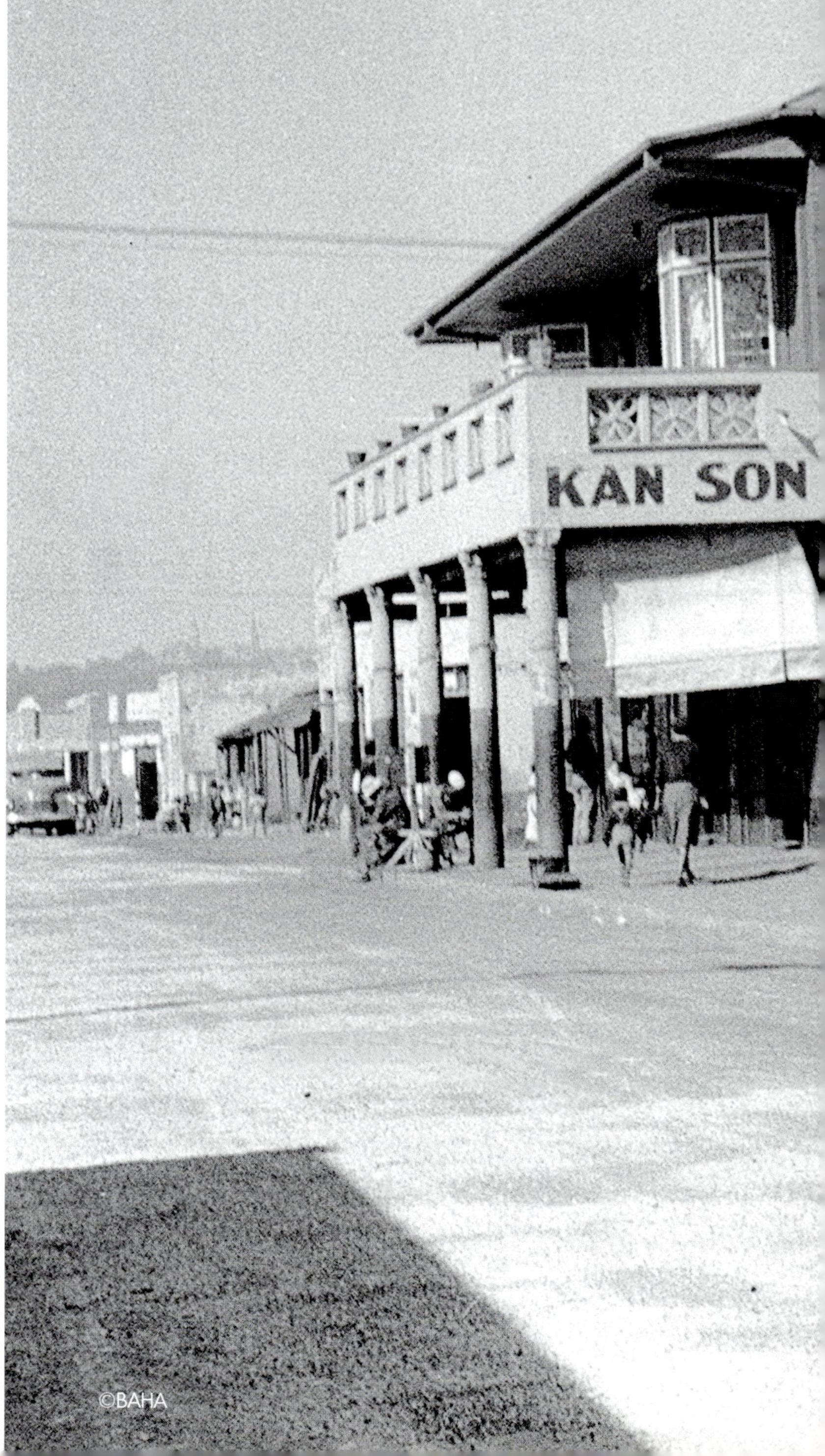

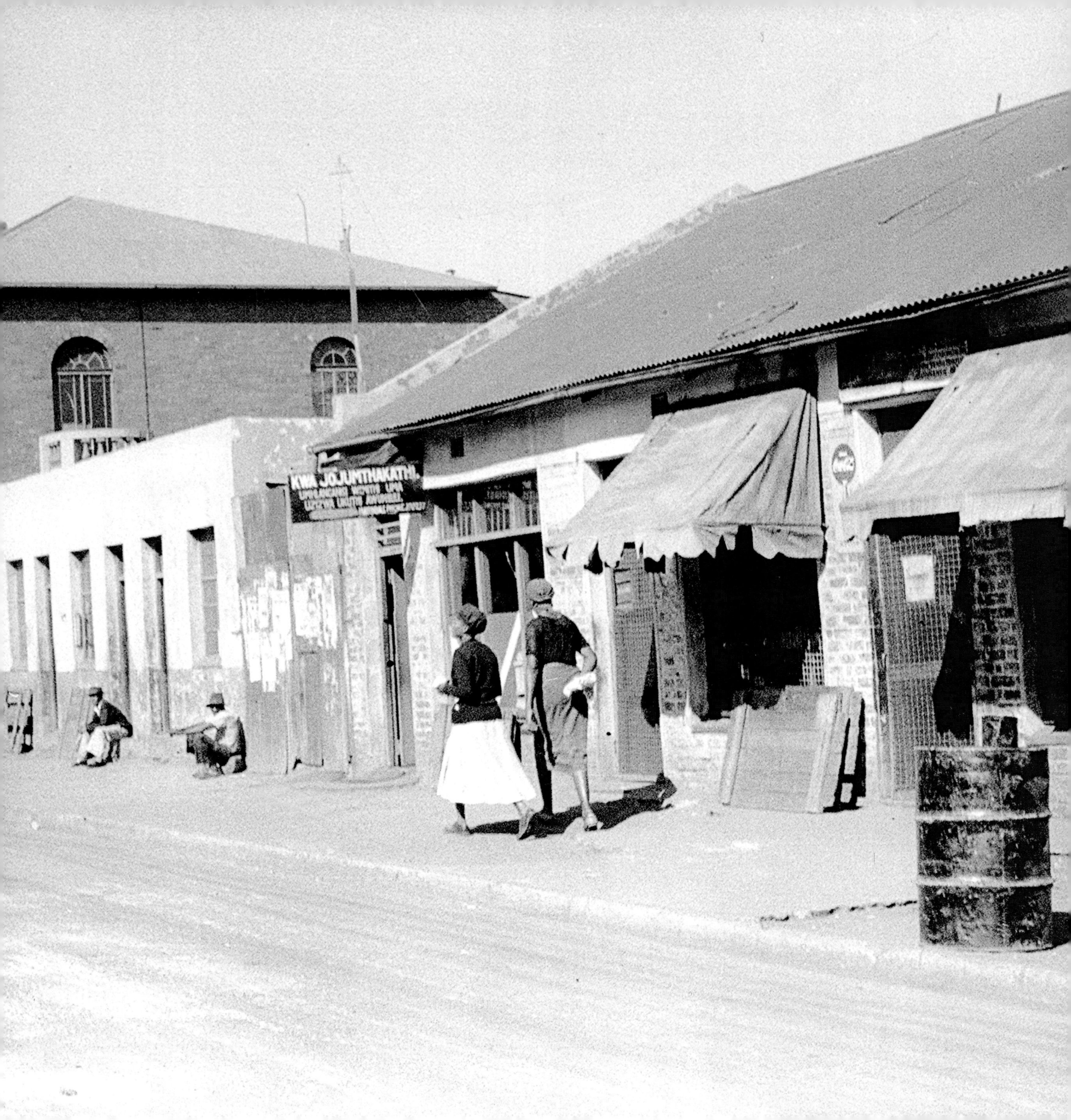
KWA JOJUMTHAKATHI.

choirs filled the air. The contrary in the townships. Nothing was happening there on a Sunday or in the evening. The streets were dead.

I recall the first evening I went out with Bloke. There was a boy who was leaving Sophiatown, and we met him, and he insisted on buying us all drinks. There was something quite touching about that boy that made me realise what an extraordinary place Sophiatown must be. Everybody who lived in Sophiatown seemed to love it, and leaving it was a very moving experience for this boy, so much so that he had to make a special occasion of his last night in this place. We went to a shebeen, which is an illegal drinking den and pretty soon it was crowded with Africans who were drinking beer and whisky, and the singing started. It was amazing how well they harmonised without any previous rehearsal or acquaintance with each other.

This was one of the best nights I've ever spent in Sophiatown. The rapport between us was so good, and the whole feeling was so natural and uninhibited that one felt completely at ease, you just seemed to float along without any sense or consciousness, everything seemed perfectly right. It was a marvellous scene, the faces all in shadow, singing by lamplight. It was one of those rare moments when one doesn't realise what a wonderful time one is having until after it is over, and we were being gently shoved out of the door into the night.

The first night Ellie wasn't able to come with me, but the next night we went out again together. This time we went to a different shebeen, and I brought my tape recorder and started recording some of the songs and music. Of course, I always realised that there was danger that the police might come. This was a chance I had to take. I could hardly do a film without going into African areas. Suddenly, that night the police did arrive. I wasn't quite sure whether we were in trouble or not, but I left Bloke to handle it. Luckily they were African police, and were as much overawed by my presence as I was nervous about theirs. But their attitude was quite obvious and it put me at ease. African police apparently will never molest a white man. They had with them some prisoners in handcuffs, who, I gathered, had been caught drinking whisky, which is illegal, and they were on their way to jail with them when they stopped by to see what was going on with us. Bloke and the others didn't pay too much attention to them, so I started to play the tape recorder back because it had music on it and I thought that might divert their attention. The police stood by very quietly watching the whole procedure. Finally we started to sing again and suddenly the prisoners in handcuffs started to dance. This rather annoyed the police who rebuked their carefree charges, and we all had a good laugh.

THE TOWNSHIPS

Life in the African townships was in stark contrast to life in Sophiatown. I must say that it gave me a very strange feeling every time I visited them. In South Africa according to the law, all Africans living outside of the tribal areas must live in locations, or townships. This was true except for two townships — Sophiatown and Alexandra.

No African is allowed to live in the townships without permission and a pass from the government. He is not allowed to own his own land and the house he lives in is on land that doesn't belong to him, and therefore he can be moved at will by the government. In addition to this, the location is surrounded by barbed wire. There is a white superintendent guarding the township, and no guests, relatives or friends are allowed to spend the night without permission from the superintendent. No whites are allowed to enter the area, for business or pleasure, without the permission of the superintendent. At some of the townships I visited, the Africans were allowed a radio which had one station, government-controlled.

The townships outside of Johannesburg stretched for miles and miles on barren tree-less land. There were several of them but they all ran into each other: Orlando, Meadowlands, Moroka and Senoane. The houses were built in barrack-like rows, giving the impression of an army of 700 000 Africans camped around the white city of Johannesburg. I found it a terribly depressing sight, somehow symbolic of the isolation of the twentieth century and the machine age. This was like an extreme end of it. It was one of the most soulless places I had ever seen. It did have something, without the extreme, of Auschwitz. It was such an enormous contrast with African tribal life or, on the other hand, with Alexandra Township and Sophiatown, despite the fact that these latter were designated as slum areas.

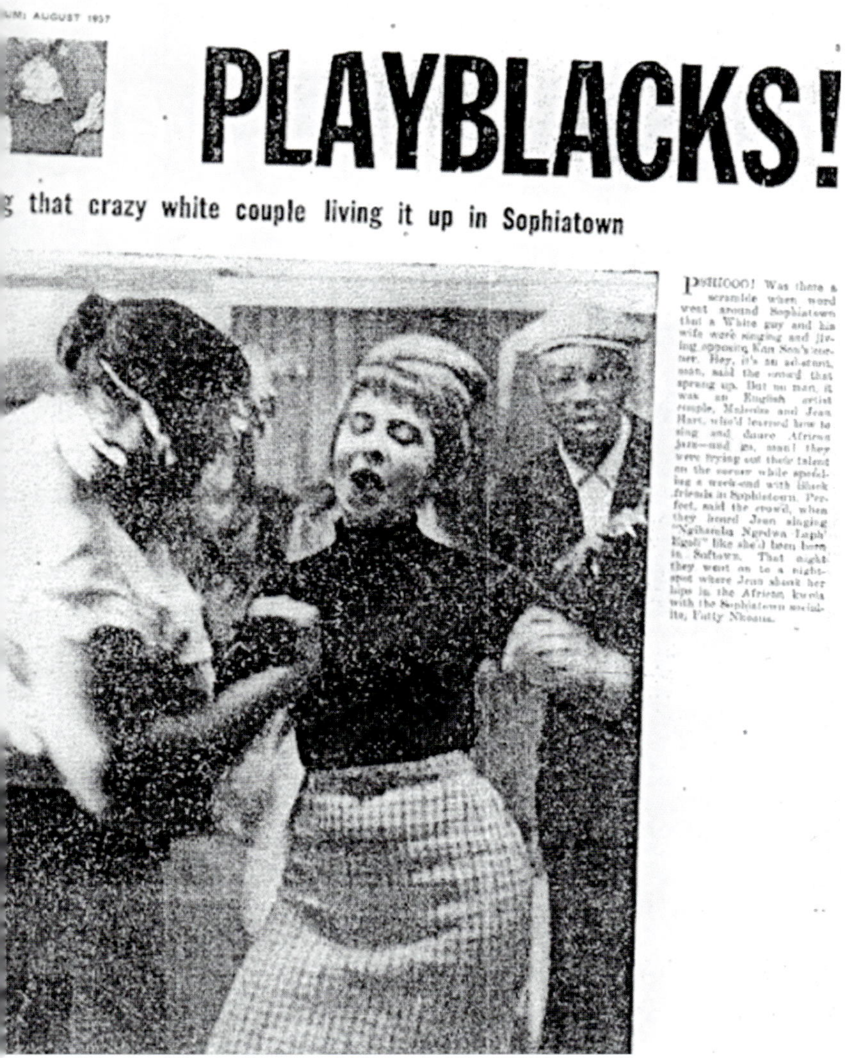

AUGUST 1957

PLAYBLACKS!

... that crazy white couple living it up in Sophiatown

PHEEOOO! Was there a scramble when word went around Sophiatown that a White guy and his wife were singing and jiving opposite Kan Son's corner. Hey, it's an adventure, man, said the crowd that sprung up. But no man, it was an English artist couple, Malcolm and Jean Hart, who'd learned how to sing and dance African jazz—and go, man! they were trying out their talent on the corner while spending a week-end with Black friends in Sophiatown. Perfect, said the crowd, when they heard Jean singing "[illegible] Ngedwa [illegible]" like she'd been born in Softown. That night they went on to a night-spot where Jean shook her hips in the African kwela with the Sophiatown socialite, Fatty Nkoana.

"I have often felt desperately that if people on the outside, the whites who had such fixed attitudes about the Africans, could spend some time in Sophiatown without fear and terror, perhaps a new understanding would be reached"

In the townships, Africans could not own their land. They must pay a monthly instalment for the houses, but they could be moved at any time the government saw fit, and the government of South Africa had often moved the people bodily en masse from one area to another without appeal. There was also a rumour that by concentrating Africans all together in one area completely isolated from the rest of Johannesburg, they would be easier to control in case of an uprising. When you drove through the area you suddenly felt that this apparently absurd reason was quite plausible. They were so condensed that they would be easily open to strafing and bombing.

Later when the film was finished there were some attacks from the South African press that my film was biased, that I had shown the slums of Sophiatown rather than the townships as a place where the Africans lived. It really is unbelievable that they could think that the townships are an ideal place to live in.

LIBERALS

I started to do tape recordings of the conversations I had with Bloke, Lewis and Morris. I had been with them long enough to have a good idea of the way they thought, and I started getting it down on tape. All their attitudes and feelings about the situation. They seemed to be particularly bitter about "the liberals" which they were to articulate so passionately in the film's shebeen scene.

Their main complaint was that the liberals talked about these principles of equality, but didn't do anything at all about it, and actually were pretty unreliable when it came down to the real situation. They considered Alan Paton as one of these people, despite his enormous international reputation. He is not particularly liked by the Africans, as a matter of fact he is considered rather patronising. In Paton's famous book, *Cry, the Beloved Country*, the African who emerges as the "good African" is the old priest who behaves himself and causes no protest and the "rebellious African" falls in with bad company, murders someone and is sent to jail and executed. As Lewis says in the film; the moral of the story is that the old priest, Reverend Kumalo, the gentleman who thinks the world of the whites, goes back to the reserve, and what does he do, he builds a church. "I tell you what — the liberal just don't want a grown-up African, he wants an African he can still patronise."

In South Africa, the African position on the liberal seems to be essentially justified. It is also I think rather indicative of the liberal position generally. It is at best the well-wishing of sincere people who do nothing, and at worst a salve for one's conscience. Liberalism seems to have no probing sense that society must be profoundly changed in order to eliminate some of the worst evils that mankind suffers from, and just behaving like a gentleman and talking nicely doesn't help anything, unless you're willing to do something about a system as awful as apartheid. I really could hardly blame the Africans for being fed up with the liberals, and it made me sceptical about myself, having considered myself a liberal at one time. In a way, I am beginning to think that the liberals are worse than the reactionaries, who at least state what they believe in clearly and make themselves a target that can be fought. The liberal is a more amorphous entity, since he takes ideals that people cannot quarrel with, and although he doesn't live up to them, fools many people into believing that the right thing is being done.

If we are not going to do something about the great social problems that exist in our society, if we are going to delude ourselves into thinking that we are all nice people, then eventually we will cover it up until it cracks apart. It is an attitude which is ebbing away the whole dynamic of western society, and unquestionably giving communism not only the political but the moral lead in the world. Some of the methods of communism may offend the sensitivities and sensibilities of many of us. However, if we are not ready to do something, then we should keep our mouths shut, because how do we expect people to live in such agony and suffering without lifting a finger, and then expect them to believe that our system is the greatest one that ever existed? The fact is that if we can allow these things to exist it is proof that it is not the greatest system. I think that this situation gives the American radical the right to say that he is totally dissatisfied with American society, which may have been advanced at one point but which today is at least 50 years behind the times. To take concrete examples, we can discuss the American Negro. I think that we can say that if this problem cannot be solved, then democracy is a failure. The biggest task of a writer, an artist, is to remain objective, certainly an analyst of the political situation must remain objective, and I think for an American to be objective he cannot be concerned with all the obsessions and chauvinism that grips the ordinary citizen. He has to be able to say: This is wrong, this is right, this is better, and this is what must be done.

THE RACIST MENTALITY

I don't remember how I was introduced to Patrick O'Malley, however, he worked for the South African Broadcasting Corporation (SABC) and we met for drinks. He wanted to help me find subjects for filming in South Africa and we made arrangements to go out together and see certain things around Johannesburg. Also he had connections with some of the studios and he said that he would be willing to introduce me to the people at the Irene Film Laboratory.

O'Malley was a very large florid man, with a round beefy face, and the characteristics of speech and manner and appearance of an alcoholic. He refused to take any alcohol when we met, which was rather a sign in itself. There was something a little crude and rough about him. We started out in the morning driving to one of the African locations where he had to get some information for a story he was doing. We drove around and at first I found him quite congenial. At the African locations we had some African beer, which he seemed to like. He appeared to be sympathetic with the government position. Naturally, he would be, working for the SABC, which was government-controlled, but I thought that perhaps this was merely on the surface, that he was going along with it since they paid for his bread and butter. I found it a little uncomfortable talking to him because I could not express myself freely and had to nod my head knowingly whenever he made some absurd statement supporting the government's policy. He was quite well known and we went into various bars on our way. I began to find him a bit irritating. When he was in the bar with his cronies, his language turned vulgar. It wasn't the obscenity of the language so much that bothered me but the constant use of it, in such a lewd and dirty sense. As the day went on I found it more and more disagreeable to be with him. It turned out to be a very long and miserable day. I began to realise more and more that he seemed to hate Africans, which I found strange since he was not a man born in South Africa.

He was not indoctrinated with the attitude and probably had very little contact with Africans one way or another. His hatred seemed to be stronger than that I found amongst the Boers or English-speaking South Africans. It was really very extreme in its form. After the morning rounds we started to drive to Pretoria. Along the road a dog suddenly jumped out and I nearly hit it. I had to make a great effort to swerve and miss the dog. He was very bothered by this and kept harping on it, making a big issue of the entire matter. I had done my best to avoid the dog, and it was not my fault that the dog had jumped out in front of the car, so it hardly needed such an involved discussion, but he seemed to be quite a rabid dog-lover, and there was nothing that I could do but to patiently wait until he had finished his tirade. We went to another tavern where he had an appointment with one of the Air Force generals, and he discussed military aircraft, on which he was somewhat of an expert, as he told me. We left the tavern and drove on, turning off the main road towards Irene, where the laboratory was located. Suddenly in a glade, in a slight dip in the road, covered by trees with the sun coming through the other side, I was momentarily blinded by the light, and when I was able to see again clearly I saw a group of African children playfully jumping and dancing in the road. I blew the horn frantically and swerved, fortunately missing them as they scattered in all directions. O'Malley's reaction was, "You should have hit them, they are nothing but kaffirs."

I remembered that when we had almost hit the dog he said, "I would rather hit a kaffir than a dog, any day." He again made the same remark. At this moment I was filled with complete disgust with this man. His reaction was grotesque, whether one liked Africans or not. There was something so marvellous about these children in their playfulness, to think that a grown man could have the desire to see them destroyed was incomprehensible to me. It made racism take on a new and almost unthinkable quality. It made me realise that the hatred within must have been enormous and must be there by itself, having nothing to do with the subject. It wasn't the Africans that he hated, it was merely that he hated and had to have something to hate because one cannot normally or rationally hate a child. There was something very warped about this man. Something terribly dirty and slimy. Sick. A man who felt his own inadequacies and inferiority and had to hate to cover it up, who could only survive by hating Africans, whom he did not even really know or understand, who were an abstraction to him. Alcoholics of course are known for being a classic example of men with a sense of inferiority, a sense of shame and inadequacy about themselves. It was the kind of attitude that I ordinarily would not let go unchallenged. However, I did not dare provoke him since I needed to appear uncommitted. In addition to this personal idiosyncrasy, he was not a very charming individual in any case. He was full of bombast. His character fit his big-boned, greasy, red-faced appearance very well. I had never seen such a clear example of the mental functioning of racial hatred. Patrick O'Malley was to me the perfect example of this psychological type.

I am absolutely convinced that racism is a deranged mentality. In its milder form one of the flaws of human personality, in its extreme form, a form of psychosis. Racism itself is not the essential problem. It is merely the target for the disturbance, a screen onto which to project the individual's in some cases abnormal hatred, in other cases normal hatred. I think that there is a threshold of hatred in almost every one of us. This of course is exploited to a greater or lesser degree by the society in which we live. A racist society uses this to mobilise and lead public opinion. If Jews, Negroes, Armenians and other persecuted minorities did not exist in societies, they would have to be invented. We have to find ways to release any aggression in fairly harmless ways or we have to find ways of reducing it.

The intensity of hatred amongst outsiders in South Africa was often greater than the normal South African's. I found this amazing, because I knew that people outside of South Africa, Englishmen, Dutchmen, etc, generally deplored the South African policy, but those people who came to visit South Africa seemed to be a special breed. They seemed to be made up essentially of people who are either misfits or inadequate to meet the demands of their society back home, but here they found a haven, a place where they could be members of the "super race". The worst racists are often the most inferior whites rather than the most superior. I often found that it was the middle class, ignorant housewife who had the most exalted opinion of the supremacy of the white race rather than a highly educated, intelligent professor of anthropology.

The white immigrants certainly were attracted to life in South Africa. In addition to feeling superior, their standard of living was far higher than it would have been in Europe and possibly America. They all had cheap African labour as servants for around five pounds a month. Many whites at the level of skilled labour had as many as two or three servants. Some of the questions we were asked at times were very amusing. I remember somebody once asked us how we wax our floors every day in America if most people didn't have servants. I looked at Ellie slightly perplexed, and said that we just don't wax them. They waxed their floors every day and therefore they assumed it was a necessity. I was often told, "We have a better life here even than the Americans, we have more cars, have a higher standard of living and cheaper, and have more servants." The only problem with this idyll was that it took no account of the possible explosion to come which might wipe out all of this in less than a lifetime.

It was common at gatherings and parties for Africans to make joking references to the coming revolution. They did this for shock effect upon the white audience. Newcomers of a more timid nature would be quite disconcerted to hear remarks that when the revolution came, no white would be safe, because friends would not be able to be distinguished from enemies, and that it would be a bloody massacre. Of course we all made a joke of it, but at the same time, deep down we knew it was quite true and tragic.

STOPPED BY POLICE

One night Lewis and Morris and I were on our way from one shebeen to the next when we were stopped by the police. This time I was really frightened. I thought for sure that I would be discovered and that information regarding me would be sent to Pretoria and ruin all chances of my completing the film. The police got out of their car, shone their flashlights in our faces, and there I was sitting with Morris and Lewis in the front seat. I had no story thought up because I was sure that Lewis would be able to give the proper answers as to what we were doing. The police asked us what was going on and where we were going, and Morris and Lewis, instead of giving the proper answers in such a situation, were absolutely mute. There was I, without having enough background, having to give myself away. The police were quite rough and crude, and I realised that I had better do some talking, and so when they said, "Who are you?" I got out of the car and told them that I was an American film producer. I was sure that was the wrong thing to say. They pushed Lewis around a bit but he still said nothing. They looked at my passport, saw that I was a film producer, and asked me to open up the trunk of the car. On opening it they searched it thoroughly, apparently looking for liquor, because a lot of whites drive to Sophiatown to bring in illicit liquor. When they saw there was nothing they politely sent me on my way. I was quite upset, and was pretty sure that they would report me. However, they didn't write down the licence plate number and didn't seem to take much notice, so I hoped they would pass it off as an insignificant incident.

I was spending as much time as possible now with Bloke in Sophiatown. One Saturday night when we were sitting quietly in Bloke's place, suddenly a little African came in, bubbling over with personality. His name was Eddie, and he was quite a comedian. He kept on making jokes, and horsing around. It is known that this kind of African and American Negro uses humour as a weapon against whites. Often their over-solicitous behaviour, the "yes baas" drawled out in an exaggerated way, is part of their defence to play the clown and ridicule the "master" to his face. I decided that Eddie was such a marvellous African type and so typical and symbolic of the racial situation there that I must use him in the film. It seemed to me that such a film should be a portrayal of the forces, the characters, the people, rather than a mere plot, and therefore I was building my story from such things and for such reasons, thinking up the characters of the film before I had my plot.

CAN THEMBA

Bloke really was a big help at this point, and on Sundays he would take me around Sophiatown and visit with the people from house to house. The people were generally very friendly, perhaps guardedly polite, but I felt very little hostility, I suppose because I was with Bloke and they assumed therefore that I was not sympathetic to the regime. This was the kind of thing I could never have done alone — Bloke was absolutely indispensable to help me to get to know the people and the place. One night at about this time, we went to a shebeen with Can Themba and Jenny, a young English girl. I had heard a lot about Can. He was regarded with mixed feelings as a sort of legend in Sophiatown. At that time he

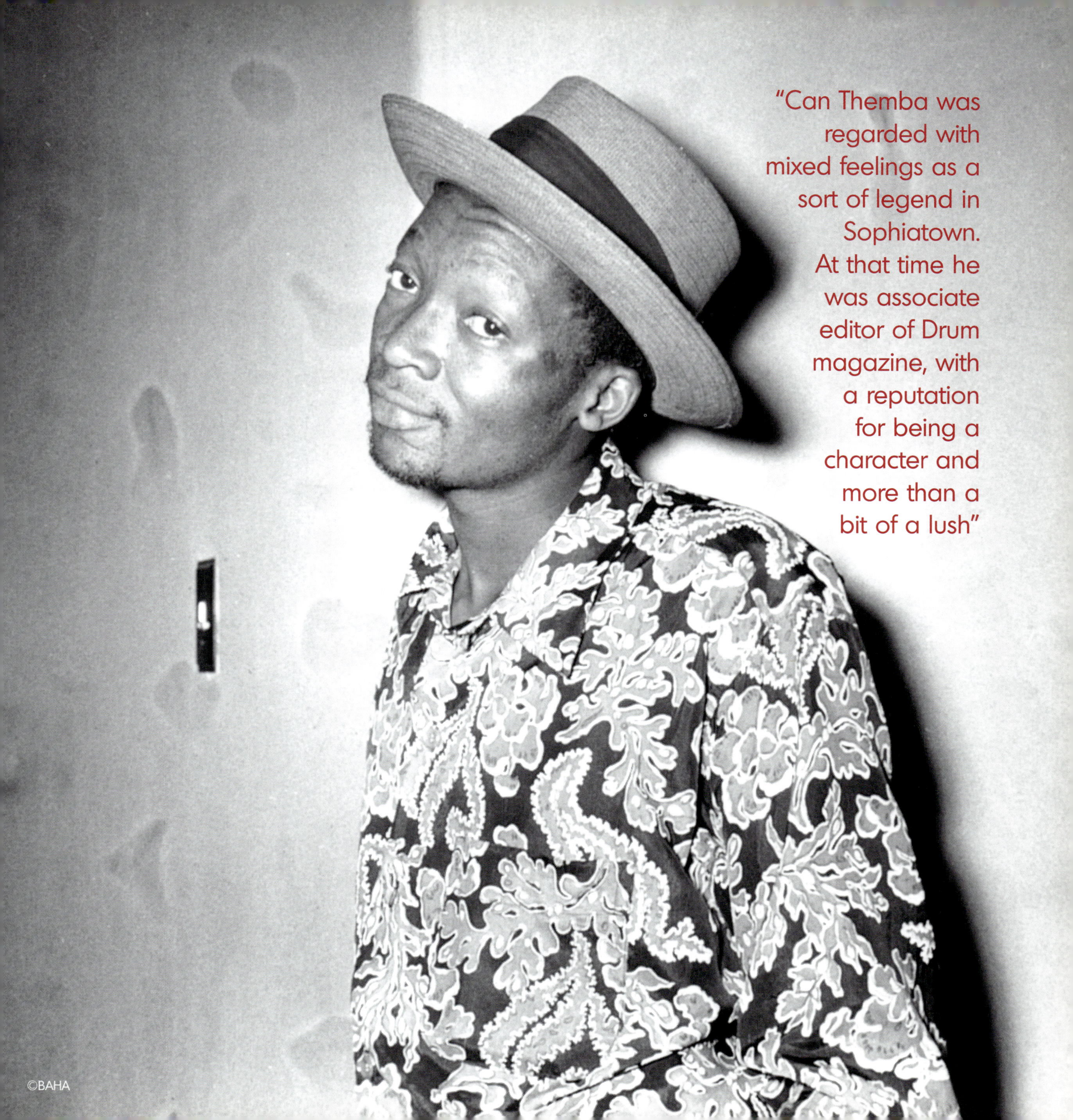

"Can Themba was regarded with mixed feelings as a sort of legend in Sophiatown. At that time he was associate editor of Drum magazine, with a reputation for being a character and more than a bit of a lush"

was the associate editor of *Drum* magazine, with a reputation for being a character and more than a bit of a lush. I took an immediate liking to him, which I think is the reaction of most people. There was no question about it, this man was exceptionally keen, although dissipated and in some ways unable to cope with life in South Africa. His language that night was full of bitterness, and his disillusioned drunkenness seemed to show a disgust with life in general. He was fed up with the whites, and to me he seemed to be a kind of symbol of what many Africans who were aware of what was going on must have felt; an extreme form of it no doubt, because of his own personal dissatisfactions, but nevertheless a kind of nihilism of our age. There are, of course, many young Africans who are not beaten, who are struggling for freedom in South Africa, but these I would say are rather exceptional men in any society, and not typical either of the masses or the intellectuals.

I did not want the film to reflect political leadership and the political leaders. I wanted it to be more a picture of African society, and South Africa generally, and also I felt that the effect of racism on the intellectual was to create this kind of bitterness far more than political action. And in South Africa the situation does seem particularly hopeless since the whites have such military power and seem not at all hesitant to use it in the most ruthless manner. There was something in Can's manner of speaking that was almost poetic. I was extremely impressed by this man, and moved by him emotionally. It wasn't a matter of whether he was right or wrong, politically or socially, it was more a matter that one could feel deeply for his reactions to the life around him, and I felt that he would express this in the film better than any other group of intellectuals. I decided to use him for my discussion in the shebeen scene, and it turned out to be the right choice.

COVER STORY AND PUBLICITY

People kept badgering me about what film I was going to do in South Africa. I was using the line that I was going to make a documentary on native life, wildlife, etc, but this seemed to be wearing a bit thin, and I was afraid that it might not go down too well with everybody. Finally Neal Smith of the film society, who had been asking me for an interview for several months, pressured me into it, and reluctantly I gave in. He came up to my flat, and by this time I'd been thinking about my story for weeks and weeks, until I had finally worked out quite an elaborate tale. I told him that I was going to do, if possible, a film about the Boer War classic by Deneys Reitz, called *Commando* — quite a good book, by the way, and it would make a wonderful film. The Boer War was a major incident in Afrikaner history, one which they hold in great reverence, and I felt that this was a theme that would please the authorities. I told Neal that I was casting for this film, although I was actually casting for my apartheid film. He put this in at the end of the article, and I got a few enquiries. Also, since I had been telling people that I wanted to make a travelogue, I had to answer this situation.

The rumours started to spread quite rapidly about my film, and I started hearing stories I'd never even told. Friends of mine told me that they had heard that I was making a film about a Frenchman. This rumour about the Frenchman was quite amusing, and that came about because at a moment of expansiveness, probably at some party, I suddenly began to elaborate on the idea of a travelogue and said that I was going to do a new kind of travelogue with humour, about an American, an English and a French tourist, using Danny Kaye, Fernandel and Alec Guinness, who were at the time the most famous American, French and British comic actors. This was what had gotten back to my friends. I gave this story to Neal as a second possibility for a film. It was a rather touchy moment, as I really didn't want to give him a story like this, because it would make him look rather foolish when the true situation came out. However, I had no choice, since he was badgering me persistently for an interview and I didn't want to turn him down flat.

I had forgotten completely about it, when suddenly one fine morning I got telephone calls from friends telling me to get hold of the *Sunday Times*, and there was almost a full page spread about the film, and about making *Commando*. It was pretty hilarious for all of us. I kept meeting people on the streets for a couple of days who said, "Oh, I hear you're making a film about *Commando*, the Boer War classic", with knowing winks and grins. Later, after *Come Back, Africa* was finished, Neal saw it in New York and later in South Africa, and reviewed it. It was a curious review because reading it, one would want to see the film very much, and he gave it some great praise but at the same time attacked it, and I wondered if my previous interviews had anything to do with his attitude.

COMMUNITY OF THE RESURRECTION

On passing through London I had met Father Trevor Huddleston, who gave me the address of the Community of the Resurrection, and suggested that I see Father Jarrett-Kerr on my arrival in South Africa. I had not contacted any of the people whose names I had been given abroad for fear that they might be watched, but felt that Father Jarrett-Kerr might be somewhat safer and worth taking a chance with. Finally I went to see him at the school in Rosettenville. He was quite friendly, and seemed to be very willing to co-operate when I told him that Father Huddleston had sent me. I told him that I was trying to make a film. He was one of the few people, and one of the first, to be told. Bloke, the Bermans and Father Jarrett-Kerr, Lewis and Morris, were about the only people who were in on the situation. I wanted to tell almost no one, but there were a few people that I did have to tell in order to gain their confidence — a risk I had to take.

Father Jarrett-Kerr suggested that I go to the mission in Sophiatown and spend some weekends there in order to get an idea of what was going on. He suggested that I contact Father Singleton, whom I had already met at the Levsons' house. I went to see Father Guinness at the mission in Sophiatown, the Community of the Resurrection, and he invited me to spend the weekend. When I told him that I was with my wife, he said that she could stay at the Cloisters across the street. The mission was certainly a different world from anything I had ever experienced before. There was no talking at certain meals, and in the Cloisters where Ellie stayed the nuns were not allowed to talk at any time. Generally speaking, the clergy in South Africa are certainly not strongly against racism, but these Anglican monks certainly had done a great deal and had sincerely tried to help, from Father Huddleston right down to the last one of them.

Of course, the significant thing is that almost none of them are South African, and they have not been conditioned by hatred. I understand that there is a tradition among the Anglicans of social reform, which does not exist in the Church generally. During Father Huddleston's time in Sophiatown, and before, the Anglicans ran mission schools which they finally closed down, since they refused to comply with the Bantu Education Act. They took the very courageous and proper stand of saying that before they would teach such a distorted curriculum, they would shut down the schools altogether. Under the Bantu Education Act, the government of South Africa shut down many mission schools or forced them to teach a very watered-down kind of education, mainly emphasising African languages and handicrafts, with a minimum of education, more or less to comply with their policy of keeping Africans as labourers, since with such a curriculum no African would ever be prepared for anything beyond a most elementary education.

VISIT TO ZULULAND, AND THE BARKERS

I felt that we had been seeing enough of the city, and that we should really try to see some African tribal life in rural areas. In Johannesburg we had met the Barkers, who ran a hospital in Ngutu in Zululand. It was the only hospital in an area of about 800 square miles, with a total population of about 40 000 people. We drove down there one day to see the Barkers at work. Their hospital slept about 300 people, and with their small staff their work went on night and day without cease. There was no phoney patronising attitude about the Barkers. They were absolutely devoted to their work, of giving help and alleviating suffering of the Africans.

The countryside in the surrounding area was magnificent, not what you would could beautiful, but rather strange and quite mysterious, as if it had some unnatural quality. The hills were nearly barren, they rolled away like a sea and occasionally one would see strange earth formations such as at Isandhlwana, which was the site of the great battle of the Zulu war, and certainly an impressive setting for such an historic event. We drove off with Dr Barker one afternoon, and he took us to some of the kraals of the Africans who were his patients. Late in the afternoon we came upon a family group, the grandfather and the children, the father and mother, all of them living together as they do, having a beer party to which we were invited. The beer was African beer made from "kaffir corn", which is actually sorghum, and passed around in gourds from one to the other. It is quite bitter, but I rather liked it. Everyone was feeling quite gay, and the party was very friendly. After a while it became obvious that there were very few young men at these kraals. The tribal areas were nearly depopulated of young men, who were mostly working in the mines, on farms or in the cities, since it was nearly impossible to earn a living with a family in the restricted areas of the tribal reserves.

I originally thought I would begin the film with life in the tribal area, and show the background from which the Africans come. I found out in Ngutu that I must get permission from the local magistrate in order to even visit Africans in the reserves. I went to the magistrate in Ngutu and was told that I would have to apply to the Ministry of Native Affairs in Pretoria for final permission. I finally decided against doing such a section on tribal Africans, partly because of the difficulty involved and the shortage of time, and also because I felt essentially it was not necessary to the film and would destroy its unity. South Africa today is essentially a struggle of races in urban South Africa, and the rural African, although he exists, is rapidly changing under this impact.

Dr Barker took us to see some traditional houses. On the way back we ran out of petrol. Dr Barker and the others went to get petrol and I stood there by the road waiting for them to return. It was just before dark and there was a magnificent sunset. We happened to stop just alongside an African kraal, a group of three or four huts in which one African family lived. I stood there watching as the people moved from one hut to another with the food and cooking utensils, back and forth, very slowly. It was a beautiful scene, the background of Zululand, the sunset, and there seemed to be a great sense of tranquillity in their way of life that made me feel how dehumanised we are becoming. Their houses fit in so perfectly with nature and perhaps their lives fit in so perfectly with nature as well.

Of course I am aware that African tribal society has great problems and evils in it — malnutrition, disease and of course enormous fears and superstitions. It has that side of it too, but I think essentially "primitive" man is generally more integrated within his society and suffers far less conflict. I am sure that much is to be learned from the study of the life of "primitive" man because I am convinced that in our society we have gone wrong in many ways and will have to find out how to disentangle ourselves from our slightly schizoid world.

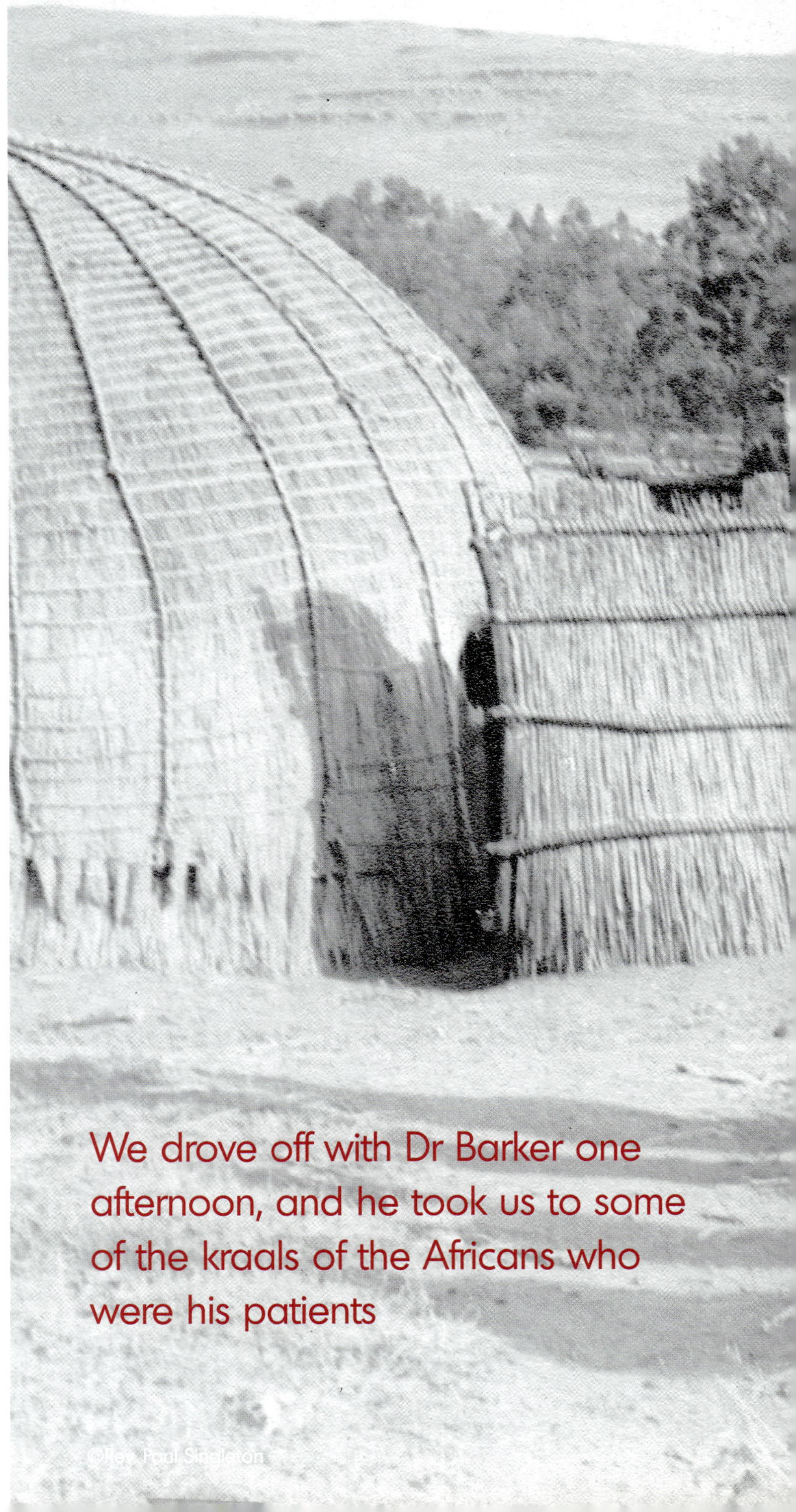

©Rev. Paul Singleton

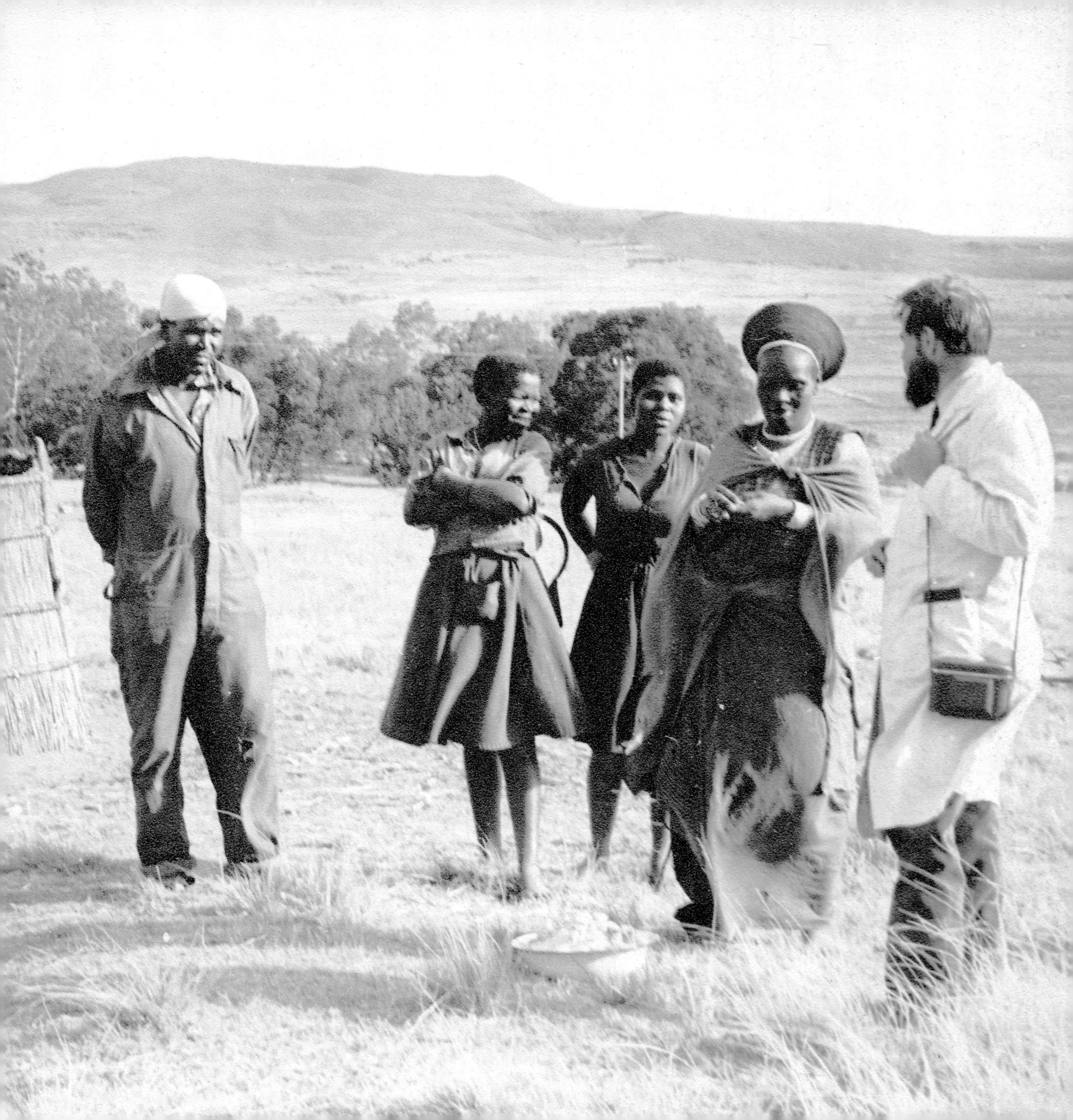

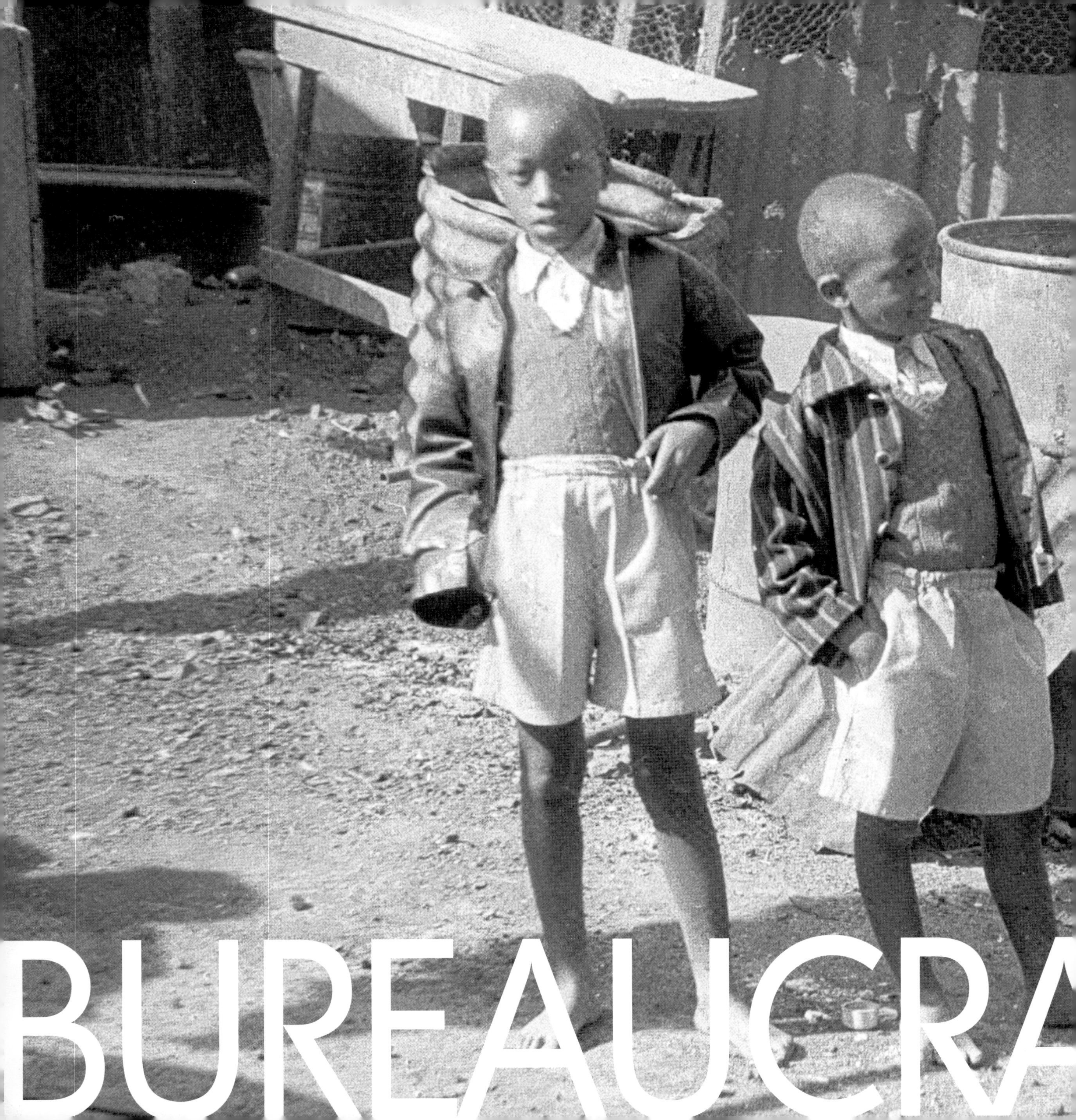
BUREAUCRA

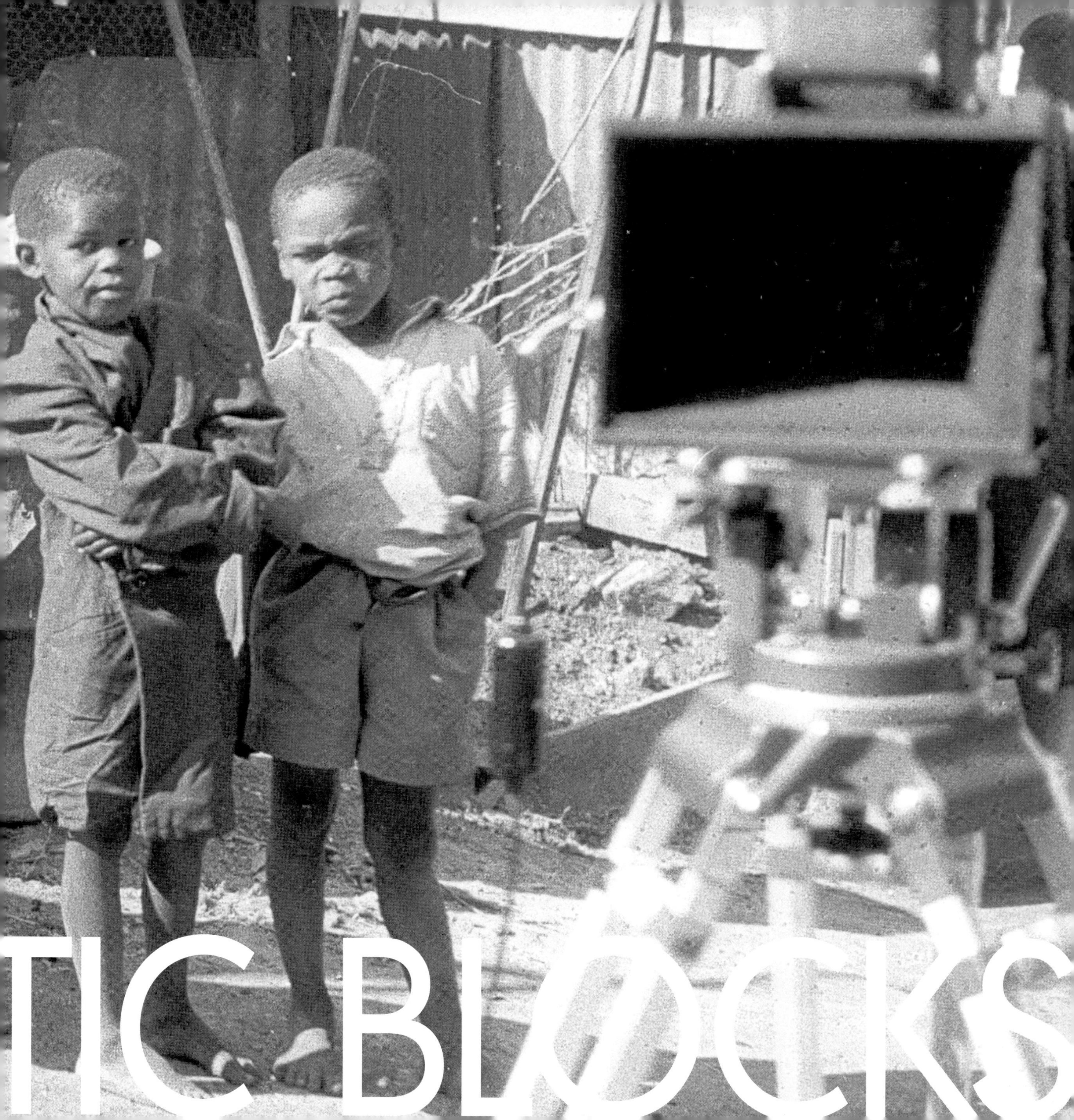
TIC BLOCKS

I was going around the streets of Johannesburg taking stills, and getting to know the city. I was exploring Sophiatown. It was about time that I now tried to get an extension of my visa since I had Finches Travel Agency as a client for my "travelogue". I went to the immigration officer in Johannesburg who told me that I would have to go to Pretoria. It seemed odd that one had to go all the way to Pretoria merely to extend a visa, but actually everything had to be done in Pretoria. There were no offices in Johannesburg to take care of these matters, and it meant travelling back and forth dozens of times for me in the next few months. After wandering around the immigration offices in Johannesburg and the streets of Pretoria, I finally found the proper office in Pretoria, and walked inside and made my first contact with the man who was to make me miserable for the next few months. His name was Mr Mitchell. My first impression of him gave me quite a shock, because I knew that this was a man who wouldn't be easy to deal with. He had a cadaverous head, with pearly-grey fish eyes that always seemed slightly watery. The man almost never smiled, his emaciated thin mouth practically stuck to his teeth.

I explained the entire situation to him, that I wanted to extend my visa, and that I also was planning to make a film for a travel agency and would want to bring in a crew. His first question was: Why did I not get a work visa in the first place? This I thought would cause a problem. My explanation, which had been thought out clearly and gone over many times, was that I had really not known where I would work, and as a film producer I had come to Africa to look around and see where there would be possibilities for making films. I had been to many other parts of Africa, the Congo and Kenya, Tanganyika and Rhodesia, etc. and South Africa appealed to me the most and had the best facilities for making films, so now that I was here I would like to apply for a visa to make a film and to bring in my crew. He said that he would have to check with the higher authorities, and he then left the room. He came back a few minutes later and said that he would extend my visa until 30 June ,1958. I asked him how I would go about getting a visa for my crew and he said that I should write a letter requesting visas for them, and that there should be no difficulty, that it would only take a few weeks to receive a reply.

David Dubois of the United States Information Service invited us to a cocktail party where we met many people of all kinds — American diplomats, some Afrikaner intellectuals, officials, newspapermen, etc. It was all very gay but made me a bit nervous, considering the fact that I was now closer to my enemy. These Afrikaner officials wanted to know what sort of film I was making and suggested that I come and visit them, which I cheerfully agreed to do, at the same time wondering with great trepidation what I was getting myself into. Dr Schneider, who was head of the United States Information Service, invited me to come to Pretoria and meet some of the heads of government departments in order to facilitate my work at a later date.

Schneider's invitation caught me a bit off guard. I was in a quandary as to what to do. If I didn't accept, it might seem very odd for a film producer not to take such an opportunity, but on the other hand I didn't feel like walking into the lion's den voluntarily. The situation demanded a snap decision and I agreed to come to Schneider's office the following week. I then went with Schneider to see Prinsloo, the head of Native Affairs, with whom I had one of the most extraordinary conversations one can imagine. Prinsloo had that broad, rather open and yet slightly brutish face of an Afrikaner farmer. He was a big, coarse man, who seemed to have some background of sociology, but, as I have learnt from anthropologists, South African academics are at a very poor level because all their thinking is warped by their strange racism. His theory was the theory of a half-educated man, a mixture of knowledge and prejudice and warped ideas, and distorted by defending an untenable position.

He started off in a hale and friendly manner, saying: "We Afrikaners are just like the Americans. We also have a rising birthrate, which proves that our attitude is optimistic, and we believe in the future. We are not like decadent people who are dying out and have a declining birthrate. You see, we have the Bushmen here in South Africa who are nearly extinct. There are also the Maasai in Kenya, who cannot adjust to modern civilisation and who are dying out. It is a pity, because these are noble people, but unfortunately it's inevitable." It was extraordinary to hear someone take such a facile attitude about a whole people. He went on to say that Africans were not ready for the industrial revolution. The tribal African was completely unable to cope with modern life, with urban society, with the breakdown of his customs and culture. This was his rationalisation for the exploitation of Africans, and for the system of apartheid. The facts may have been correct but the conclusions were disastrous. There is no question that people who have grown up in a tribal culture are not adequate to survive in modern urban society. It is true that the impact of such a society causes a breakdown in the moral structure, but it seems quite obvious that the solution is to help them make the adjustment through education, and not by the harshest kind of political methods, not through a pass system, and through constant arrests and imprisonment, not through the separation of families by migratory labour. Such people should be helped to make the very difficult transition and not be destroyed. They should be prepared to fight, as Dr Barker of Ngutu so beautifully called it, "the lonely battle of the twentieth century".

Prinsloo advised me of some books to read, sociological, etc, and lectured me that I must respect the customs of the country. His manner was quite arrogant, and I must say that he used very little tact and diplomacy. He said, "We will not, of course, restrict you in any way in what you want to do." There was always this attempt by South African officials to create the illusion that it was a free country. Prinsloo then proceeded to give me a list of admonitions and prohibitions on my behaviour in South Africa, indicating that too free an association with the Africans would not be advisable. He said that some Europeans who came paid no attention to these important considerations. There was the case of a white who bathed in the river nude, which was very much frowned upon. It seemed extraordinary that an official of the government would talk to a foreigner in such a way.

After he had thoroughly aired his views on racism, South Africa, etc, I gave him a brief outline of what I wanted to do, claiming that I was going to make a travelogue about tribal life, animal life, etc, all the glories of South Africa. I then asked him if he would give me a permit to enable me to visit the tribal reserves. Prinsloo was very clever. He replied, "No, you will have to find that in Pietermaritzburg. See Mr Steyn in this office, and he will contact our department in Pietermaritzburg." I asked for a letter from him, knowing that without it I would have difficulties. He said, "No, see Steyn." I then went with Schneider to meet Mr Hynes of the State Information Office, who received us cordially and we had a pleasant chat together. As soon as possible, I went to Steyn's office. We had a very nice chat, talked about things in general. I explained my situation and what Prinsloo had said, and asked him if I could have a letter enabling me to see the tribal reserves. His answer was very much the same evasion: No, he could not give me the letter,

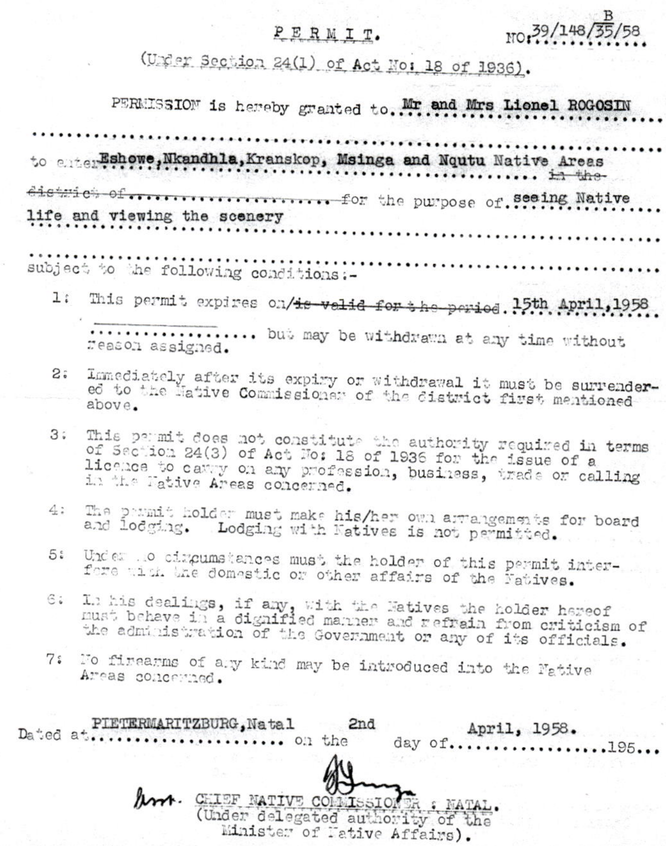

PERMIT. NO: 39/148/35/58 B

(Under Section 24(1) of Act No: 18 of 1936).

PERMISSION is hereby granted to Mr and Mrs Lionel ROGOSIN

to enter Eshowe, Nkandhla, Kranskop, Msinga and Nqutu Native Areas ~~in the district of~~ .... for the purpose of seeing Native life and viewing the scenery

subject to the following conditions:-

1: This permit expires on/~~is valid for the period~~ 15th April, 1958 .... but may be withdrawn at any time without reason assigned.

2: Immediately after its expiry or withdrawal it must be surrendered to the Native Commissioner of the district first mentioned above.

3: This permit does not constitute the authority required in terms of Section 24(3) of Act No: 18 of 1936 for the issue of a licence to carry on any profession, business, trade or calling in the Native Areas concerned.

4: The permit holder must make his/her own arrangements for board and lodging. Lodging with Natives is not permitted.

5: Under no circumstances must the holder of this permit interfere with the domestic or other affairs of the Natives.

6: In his dealings, if any, with the Natives the holder hereof must behave in a dignified manner and refrain from criticism of the administration of the Government or any of its officials.

7: No firearms of any kind may be introduced into the Native Areas concerned.

Dated at PIETERMARITZBURG, Natal on the 2nd day of April, 1958.

Asst. CHIEF NATIVE COMMISSIONER : NATAL.
(Under delegated authority of the Minister of Native Affairs).

Finally, after a great deal of persuasion and argument and a request for him to call Pretoria, he agreed to give me a tourist permit. It would not allow me to do any work or filming, but would allow me to see the tribal areas, which was all I wanted at that moment but he would call Pietermaritzburg. He asked me to call back. Finally I called Steyn again and he said that he had not called Pietermaritzburg yet, he would call them next week, but that in the meantime I could go down any time. When Ellie and I arrived in Pietermaritzburg, the man I had been told to see was on leave, the usual story of bureaucracy. Apparently no word had been left of my arrival, and no word had been received from Steyn. I was told to come back the next day, when the man I spoke to had received no word about my permit, which I found exasperating. Finally, after a great deal of persuasion and argument and a request for him to call Pretoria, he agreed to give me a tourist permit. It would not allow me to do any work or filming, but would allow me to see the tribal areas, which was all I wanted at that moment.

NATAL

That afternoon Ellie and I drove to Durban, which I found quite exciting, the beautiful sea and the streets swarming with Indians. (Durban, and Natal in general, is the population centre of the Indians, who came there in about 1860 to work as indentured labour on the sugar plantations.) The next day I decided to try the back roads through Zululand and really get into the interior as I wanted to see, at least geographically, the tribal areas as much as possible. From my experience of driving in Africa, we felt that the road would be too rough for Ellie, who was pregnant. The next day I started out early, going first towards Durban and then up the coast to Stanger, passing through swarms of very black Indians. All along the road one saw hordes of Indian children with their schoolbags, going to school. This was really almost entirely Indian country, as opposed to Johannesburg, which was mostly African. The Indians here also seemed to be different, of the labouring, coolie class, people who work on sugar plantations. As we drove through miles and miles of sugar cane in the same area, the Indians here were poor, as opposed to the fairly prosperous traders in the Transvaal.

At Stanger I turned inland, away from the coast towards Eshowe, the capital of Zululand, through winding mountain roads. They were quite narrow and unpaved, almost only wide enough for a single car. I was surprised at how untouched this country was, considering how close it is to Durban and how developed South Africa generally was. We saw very few cars as we travelled along the road, luckily. The countryside was a little more wooded than the area around Ngutu. The African population wasn't very dense. One saw Africans scattered here and there in single-family groups. In this part of Africa, as in East Africa, the Africans had never lived in cities, or even in villages, living together as separate individual family units, rather than as tribes. The drive was quite marvellous, and I was enjoying it although it was a bit nerve-racking. I kept looking for a petrol station until I practically ran out of petrol. By a lonely farmhouse I saw a pump and was able to fill up again. At this point I started having some kind of engine trouble, it seemed like something in the fuel line, and finally when I got to one of the towns in the mountain pass, the car broke down, fortunately only about 20 minutes from the outskirts of a town. Very shortly after that the rains started pouring down. Somehow I managed to get to the police station to get some help.

This experience was a bit of an omen of what was to come shortly after. Ellie and I got back to Pietermaritzburg quite late that night, and the next day we made a fairly late start and decided to drop over to see the Barkers at Ngutu. It was late in the afternoon by the time we left them. I told them how the plans were shaping up and tried to make arrangements for the shooting which would probably take place in the near future.

CAR ACCIDENT

We started back late that afternoon. As we drove along and it became dark, we found that coming towards us in the opposite direction was a steady stream of cars, driving at almost breakneck speed, and recklessly passing on this two-lane highway of which the shoulders of the road were not in good condition. We had not realised that it was Good Friday and a very bad time to be driving on this Johannesburg-Durban road, which was being repaired in many spots. And people seemed to like to leave Johannesburg after work on Thursday and drive down to Durban for the weekend. Driving became so difficult, with the lights constantly pouring from the opposite direction so blinding, that I found the driving very unnerving. I had just decided to stop at the next town when

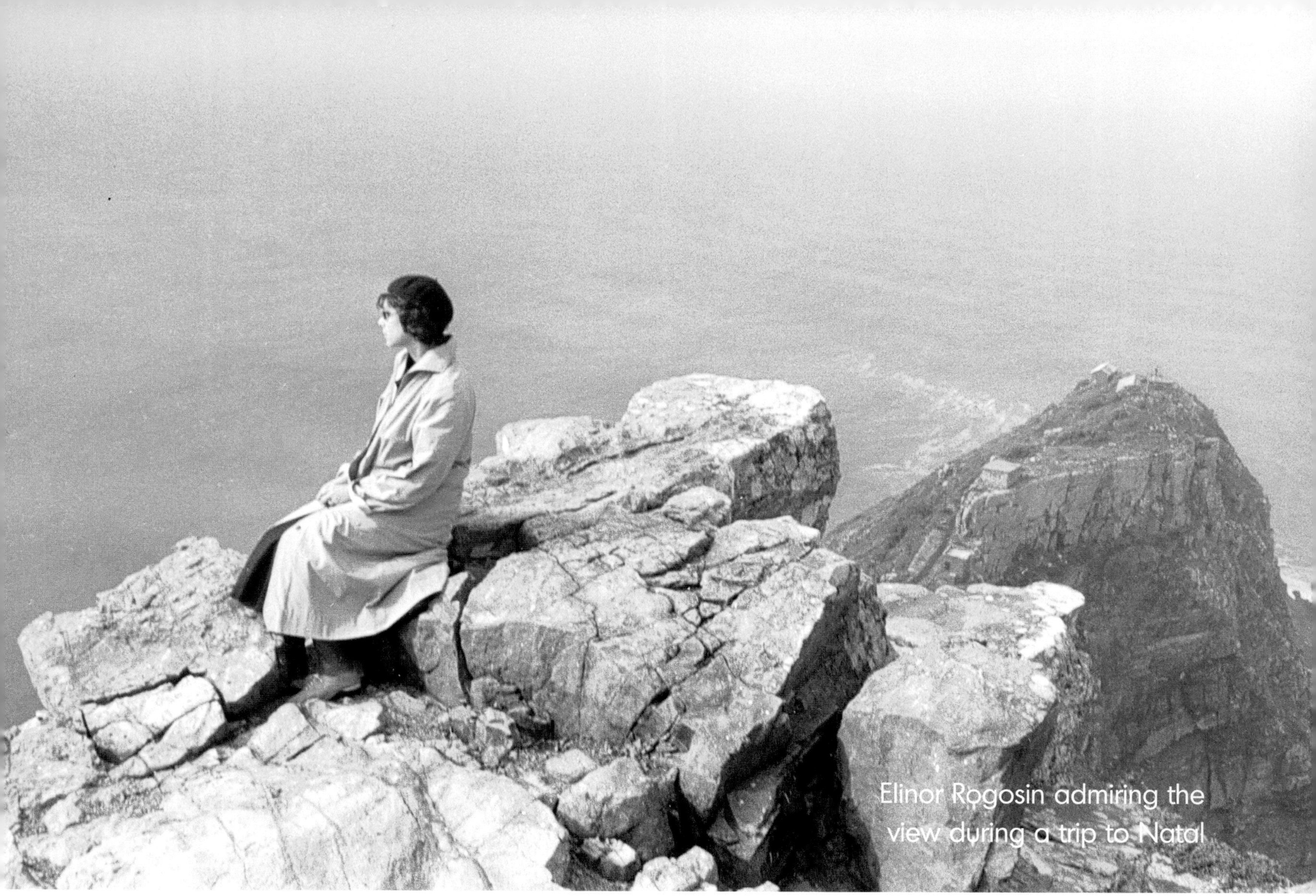

Elinor Rogosin admiring the view during a trip to Natal

suddenly I saw a car from the opposite lane coming right at us, and before I had a chance to swerve out of his way, a collision took place. There was a tremendous impact, and for the first few seconds one didn't quite know whether one was mortally wounded or just shocked. I felt a bit bruised, but realised that I was not badly injured. Ellie seemed to be absolutely terrified and hysterical and grabbed me to see if I was all right, and kept saying "Oh, you're all right", and at the same time I tried to find out how she was. Apparently nothing was broken and there were no serious injuries, although her legs were a bit bruised and cut. I was rather afraid that she might have a miscarriage, being in the third month of her pregnancy in a crucial period. The windshield was completed gone, smashed to a thousand pieces and lying all over the seat and floor of the car. The other car was smashed up quite badly. Fortunately my swerving had caused him to sideswipe us, rather than hitting us head on. He was in a smaller car, a Volkswagen, and therefore didn't do much more than surface damage to us. The car had stopped many feet away and I saw that it was packed with people. I went over to talk to the driver, who looked like an Afrikaner farmer. He seemed completely incoherent. I tried to talk to him and all I got was a kind of mumbling. I said to him, "Look what you have done, you almost killed us!" and he just looked at me with a dazed expression on his face. He seemed either drunk or overcome by shock. I was quite calm, although rather shaken up, but in complete control of myself. I didn't seem to be affected by shock to any great degree. I was able to see what had happened. Apparently the driver had come to the turn-off in the road to his home, and had turned right into my car without even looking, so suddenly that it was impossible to avoid a collision. It was the action of a man who was either a complete fool or drunk.

By this time one or two cars had stopped and somebody was giving first aid. Finally the police arrived in a police van, and after one look at them I felt very apprehensive. They were in their undershirts, not in full uniform, their hair was messy as if they had either been sleeping or were drunk. They came with a crude, harsh manner. They seemed to know the driver, and they came right up to him, slapping him on the back as if he were an old friend. I immediately sensed trouble, and felt that I had very little chance to make any kind of complaint against the driver. I decided not to press the matter too strongly, considering they were personal friends and knowing the Boer mentality of xenophobia towards outsiders. Charges could be pressed at a later date. The police did not offer to take us to a doctor or bring us to a hospital. I said, "You must take us some place where we can get help. My wife is pregnant and I'm afraid the shock may cause a miscarriage." When Ellie spoke to them they said: "We are not American police, madam." They said that our things should be left in the car overnight, and George, our African driver, should remain with them. To me it seemed extraordinary to think of leaving a man out alone on the road in a car all night, particularly since we were not sure, without examination, if any of us were seriously injured. George did have some injury, and so did Ellie. I said, "I can't leave all my things in the car overnight because I can't lock it, and I am not going to leave the driver here." At that point they made some remark in Afrikaans about "He's just a kaffir". Anyway, after quite a bit of argument I got them to take us and our luggage to the nearest hotel. We were dumped off there at about midnight. No attempt was made to bring us to a doctor or a hospital.

The accident took place in Greylingstad. At the hotel there was only an African servant on duty and a drunk wandering around the lobby. The place was very depressing. The nearest hospital was in Heidelberg. We telephoned for an ambulance, which took us to Heidelberg. We were all badly bruised, and the long ride straight into the lights again was a bit of a nightmare. It would have been better if we could have stayed at the hotel, but we were both concerned about Ellie's condition. At the hospital there was no one except a nurse on duty. I insisted that she call a doctor, although she was very reluctant to do so. Finally she called a doctor and spoke to him on the phone. He asked a few questions, but refused to come. The nurse finally made an examination of Ellie, and assured us that she was quite all right. I insisted that she examine George, and she gave him a perfunctory glance and let it go at that. We were told to come back in the morning.

Since we all seemed to be all right, I decided to stay over in Heidelberg, because it was quite late at that point. We drove to the nearest hotel in the ambulance. It was dark and no lights were on, and it seemed to be completed deserted. Finally, after we had been knocking for a long time, an African opened up and told us that there were no rooms available. From there we went to a police station. The reception there was one of cold hostility, and I finally had to shout at them to get them to do something. They then merely took my name and seemed quite indifferent. I still wanted to try to get a doctor, and also a room to stay the night. They were no help with either of these, and all they could offer was to get us a taxi to Johannesburg at a charge of five pounds. Again we had the same drive against the lights coming at us in a constant stream without end, the same as we had before the accident. I told Ellie to turn her head away from the traffic and to put her head on my shoulder, which she did. But driving against the lights this way, with these maniacs cutting in and out of their lanes, was nerve-racking. Finally, very late, after 3 am, we arrived home and climbed into bed badly bruised. I lay down, and I felt for the first time as if my chest had caved in. I was almost sure that I had broken a rib. The next day when we woke up we were still terribly shaken by the experience. It was like having gone through a nightmare — the accident itself was only a small part of the horror, the real thing being the long trip back and all the brutality and lack of sympathy we had encountered.

Our treatment certainly warranted a protest by the US Embassy, but I felt that it would probably be one of these situations which would be ignored. We called the Bermans and told them what had happened, and they were quite wonderful. We went immediately to their house and spent the afternoon there in a state of shock and nerves. Both of us seemed to suffer from a terrible emotional hangover from our experience, which I think was due more to the ordeal of getting home than the actual accident. Some time that day the doctor examined Ellie, and said that there were no symptoms and that everything would be quite all right.

CASTING CHARACTERS AND FINDING THE STORY

Five months had raced past since we arrived in South Africa, and the choice for the leading role had eluded me. The garage mechanic I met had a beautiful face, but he was too naïve and fled in terror from Bloke's and Lewis's rebellious ideas. I had met several marvellous characters, like Eddie, but casting the two leads, the tribal African and his wife, was long overdue. I planned to choose all my actors before I wrote the script, the reverse of accepted procedure. This idea occurred to me as I was editing *On the Bowery*. It was only at the end of shooting that I began to understand these men. Gorman and Frank were the most real characters in the film because I had had a constant association with them for about six months before filming commenced. I decided that for my next film I would spend several months getting to know the performers before writing the script. Since they were amateurs who were to portray themselves, I had to understand them thoroughly to guide and direct them. They would teach me about South Africa as I was learning about them. Directing would be an analysis of personalities and creating the conditions to enable the actor to express himself in front of the camera. One of these conditions is that the dialogue is not to be memorised. The performers have to be guided by the director to improvise on the themes of the plot.

I had the theme of the film and a rough idea of the form in mind, therefore I knew who I needed to portray the major roles. If I discovered additional types who were symbolic of South African life I would recruit them for the cast as well. The script was growing out of my daily experiences in South Africa, however, certain sections came to me in intuitive flashes; the idea of the deaf mute and the ending had emerged from my subconscious before I arrived in Johannesburg.

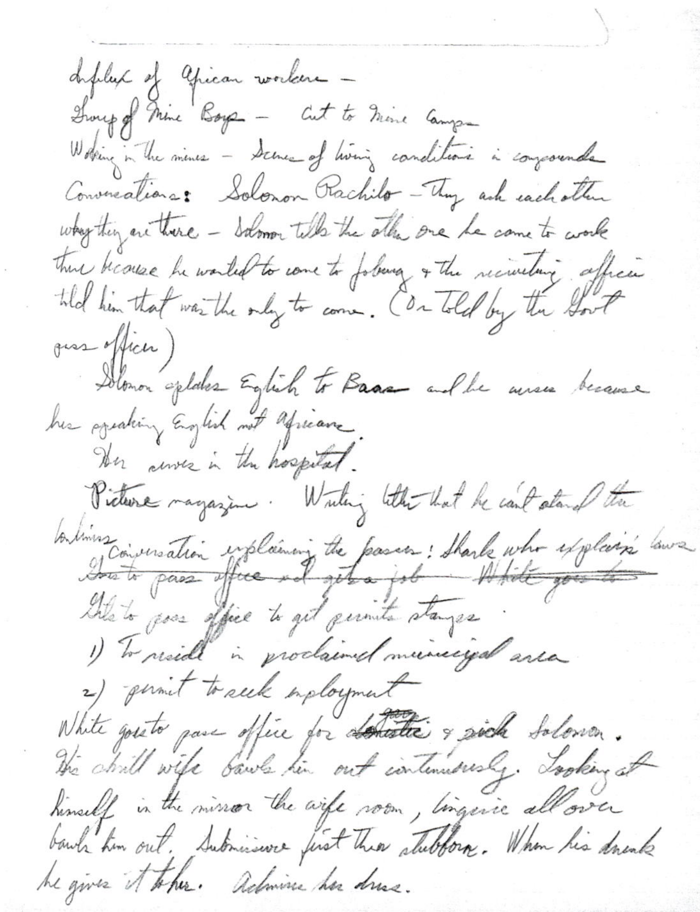
Influx of African workers –
Group of Mine Boys – Cut to Mine Camps
Working in the mines – Scenes of living conditions in compounds
Conversations: Solomon Rachilo – they ask each other why they are there – Solomon tells the other one he came to work there because he wanted to come to Joburg & the recruiting officer told him that was the only to come. (Or told by the Govt pass officer)
Solomon speaks English to Baas and he curses because he's speaking English not Africans.
His cures in the hospital.
Picture magazine. Writing letter that he can't stand the loneliness
Conversation explaining the passes: Sharks who explain laws
~~Goes to pass office and gets a job – White goes to~~
Gets to pass office to get permits stamped:
1) To reside in proclaimed municipal area
2) permit to seek employment
White goes to pass office for ~~domestic~~ [illegible] & picks Solomon.
His shrill wife bawls him out continuously. Looking at himself in the mirror the wife room, lingerie all over bawls him out. Submissive first then stubborn. When he's drunk he gives it to her. Admires her dress.

I told Bloke and Lewis that I wanted them to help me write the script and I wanted them to give me the story. And so the three of us sat down on a Saturday afternoon and I made notes. It took about six hours, and that was it. That was our story

There weren't enough weeks left for the time-consuming process of writing the script, rehearsing and preparing for the production before the crew arrived. What I didn't realise then was that I would lose nearly six weeks trying to persuade the authorities to grant permission for the crew to enter South Africa. I hoped that Ernst Artaria, the other cameraman besides Emil Knebel, would arrive a month before the others, so that I could rehearse the actors while he made the necessary preparations for the production. I had allowed four weeks to rewrite the script and plan camera angles, in conjunction with the rehearsals. These six lost weeks eliminated these preparations, and I was forced to begin the film with a script that was written in ten days. Actually, it was little more than an outline for shooting. I told Bloke and Lewis that I wanted them to help me write the script and I wanted them to give me the story. And so the three of us sat down on a Saturday afternoon and I made notes. It took about six hours, and that was it. That was our story.

Although I didn't want written dialogue, I wanted to record the rehearsals on tape. Playing back this recording, I would have a guide to modify the next rehearsal. In this way I would evolve the proper dialogue and still maintain spontaneity. This would have been a great asset. Improvising on the set was more difficult than I had imagined. The Africans were marvellous actors, but not as facile at improvisation as the Bowery men. This was due to the fact that English was not their native tongue, and also to psychological characteristics. The Africans were not as glib, nor as prone to make use of alcohol as an aid to acting.

I consulted my African advisory board, Bloke, Lewis and Morris, of which Bloke was the senior member, regarding my problem of finding the leading performers. Bloke suggested that I advertise in the *Golden City Post*, the *World* and the Johannesburg *Star*. I resisted this idea, because I didn't think that I would find the right amateurs with professional casting methods. I was also reluctant to publicise my activities when it was necessary to conceal my purpose. Finally I agreed to Bloke's suggestion after realising that being brazenly open was the best defence. It was impossible to go into locations with 35 mm equipment without being seen, but favourable publicity now might help in the future. Bloke helped me to phrase some innocuous copy in the appropriate showbiz journalese, "Would you like to be a film star?" etc. This advertisement motivated 36 cats to propel themselves up four flights of stairs to an office on Jeppe Street for a try-out. I wanted two qualities — the proper appearance and the personality that suited the role. There were nine women and approximately three times as many men. Ellie and I were surprised at this unbalanced proportion, but attributed it to the reticence of African women. The women were striking; the men didn't look promising. The interviews reinforced this impression. Out of nine women, four were beautiful; any would have been adequate for the roles. Hazel we had already met at one of Bloke's parties. Miriam Makeba we had seen on the stage as a singer of African jazz and also met her at a party. Vinah Bendile was a domestic servant who had a queenly grace. She had beautiful Hamitic features, high cheekbones and the slightly oval eye. These three were Xhosas, who are famous for their beauty. The name of the fourth, of delicate and beautiful features, came as a surprise. Instead of an African surname hers was Klein. She was a coloured girl. Her features were not African enough for any of the roles.

These four girls and six of the men were asked to come to an audition next Saturday at Bloke's house in Sophiatown. We had seen one of the men, Steven, before in an amateur play. To my knowledge he was the only one who had any previous experience, but he was far from a finished actor. He had developed bad habits, but he had marvellous assets — a resonant voice and a handsome, sympathetic face. He was more self-conscious than Zacharia, the man I eventually selected, and therefore not as natural or as easy to direct, but with work and experience, and if he is not ruined by hacks, he could become a fine actor. Steven was Jo'burg-bred and much too sophisticated for the main role of a tribal African. He was perfect for the role of Zacharia's friend.

Vinah, Miriam and Hazel arrived. Perhaps Klein had an intuition about my reaction to her because she didn't show up. Hazel's acting was poor, but she was so suitable as a siren that I took the risk of using her for this minor part. Miriam was expressive of deep and powerful feelings in her singing, but she was painfully shy and unable to ad-lib. She had previous experience in films and was disappointed when I told her that she would have to act without written lines. I was tempted to use Miriam as the lead because she had deep resources of emotion and might be marvellous, but I was afraid that she might demand an enormous amount of my time and I couldn't risk it. I recognised great artistic qualities in this woman. However, there was another contradiction in her playing the lead. I was determined to have her sing in the film, and for the

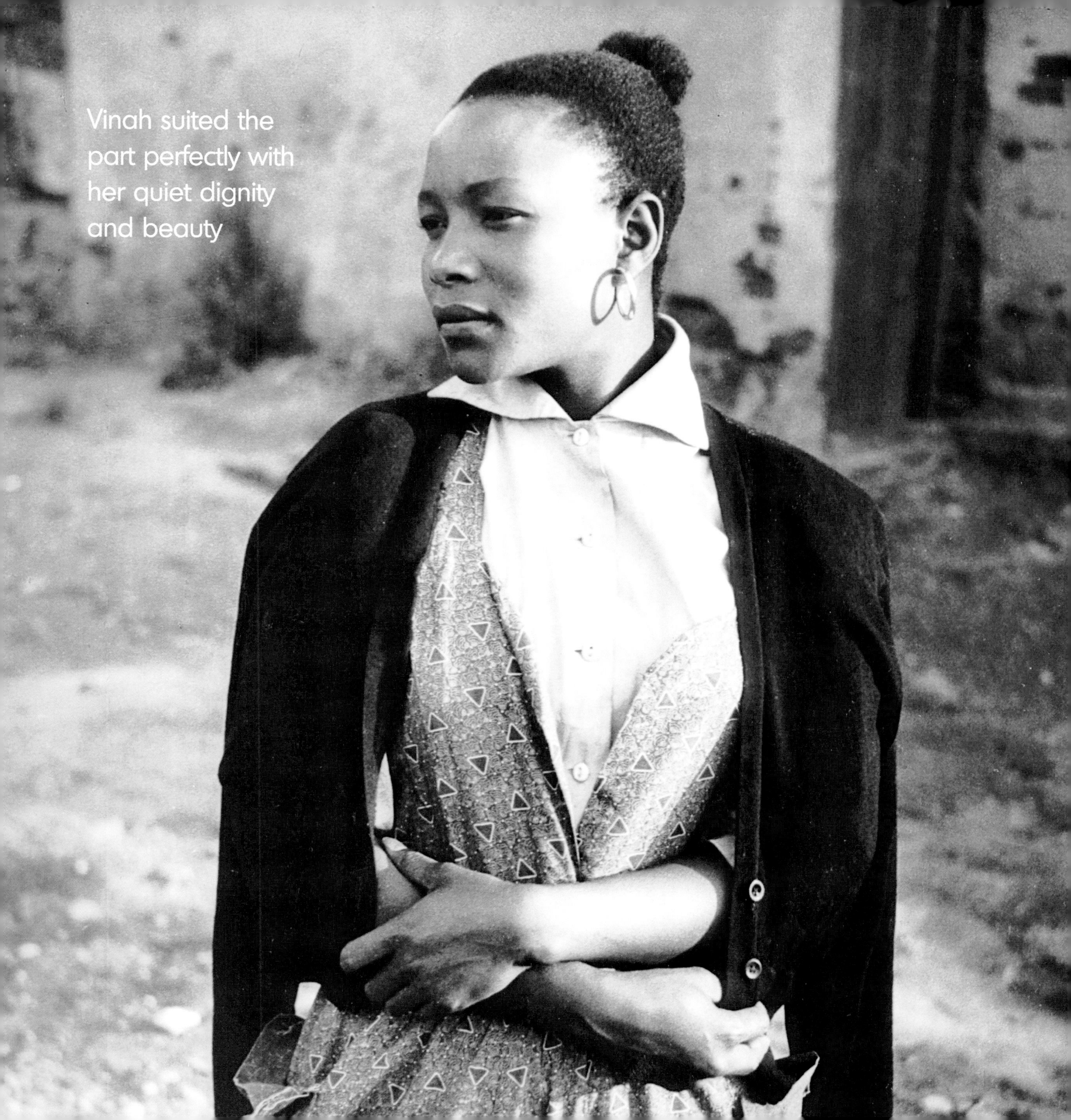

Vinah suited the part perfectly with her quiet dignity and beauty

wife of a Zulu tribesman to have a trained voice would have been a bit ludicrous. Vinah suited the part perfectly with her quiet dignity and beauty. I was delighted that she had a facility for acting and ad-libbing and the capacity to express emotion. Ellie, Bloke and Lewis agreed unanimously that Vinah was the best choice. I often tested my impressions against the experience of the Africans in order to maintain authenticity. In aesthetic judgements Ellie had the best sense, and I valued her opinion in these decisions.

Vinah worked as a domestic servant for a lower middle class family in Mayfair for five pounds per month. We needed her for about four weeks of shooting. She thought that she would be able to get this amount of time off without losing her job, because she had a sister who could substitute for her. Most of the men were hopeless in appearance and ability, except for Steven. I wished that he had never acted before, but I thought that with a little hard work and some judicious trimming in the editing room we might make him do.

It was impossible to find the perfect type for every part. However, one of the men, Solomon Rachilo, was rather good at acting and his face was almost right for the part, except that I knew at once that he was not a tribal African. He looked like a city boy. It was amazing how one could see this in the face of an African, yet I wondered if I wasn't being over-meticulous. Time was short and the quality I was looking for would never be missed, but it disturbed me. In retrospect I realise how vital that quality was, not only for his appearance to the audience, but for me as the director. With Zacharia, I had an excellent rapport. He was the man I had imagined. With Solomon there would have always been a conflict, whether overt or repressed. The artist must rely on his sensitivity in these matters, but commercial considerations usually don't allow it. I was uneasy about Solomon and I told the others that if I saw the right person I would know him at a glance. I had seen this face everywhere I had been in Africa. The audience would not know the difference, because most films are horribly miscast, on the theory that a star is "box office" even if not suitable for the role. I have been scrupulous to retain authenticity in my films because I am fascinated by this quality. Unfortunately, this fascination carries a huge penalty against financial success.

I was searching for some insight about Solomon's personality and I decided to have another tryout. After this rehearsal there was mild enthusiasm for Solomon, because he acted well. I was still disturbed, but I finally agreed to use him. Then John Bolon said something which brought me to a firm decision. He said, "I don't like him for the part, he looks too American." I knew what he meant. Solomon could have stepped right off Broadway. Bolon had verbalised what had been on my mind. I decided to continue the search, although I was running out of time.

As I had assumed, the casting session had failed to find the right man for the leading role. Everyone in Jo'burg that I knew was recommending someone who would be ideal. They must have been clairvoyant to know this without having my conception of the film. I evaded their help with the answer that I could only find the proper actor by his face. I had an image of the African I wanted. He had to serve the dual purpose of enacting the misery of living under apartheid and being a symbol of the ordinary African. I knew the face well. The warm and open face of many of the tribal Africans before they are disillusioned and embittered by life in the machine age set in the framework of white supremacy — a combination assured to destroy even the strongest human qualities.

The problem was to find someone in transition, who still retained some innocence and yet had enough experience to grasp the complexities of urban life. He had to express the corrosive effect of apartheid as well as the simplicity of the tribal African. He had to speak articulate but ungrammatical English. A conflict was inherent in such a choice. I feared that one quality would eliminate the other. If he were illiterate he wouldn't understand enough. If he were detribalised and educated he would be too sophisticated. He had to incorporate both qualities in one individual, since he would be an amateur and incapable of expressing a personality that was not his own. I felt I could only find a man of these qualities by seeing his face. It was a fragile and rare combination, and I knew that I had to see thousands of faces to find it. Everything else had failed.

CASTING AT THE BUS QUEUE

Bloke suggested the bus queue, and I asked him to accompany me in order to interpret and to avert suspicion, since the people might think that I was a member of the Criminal Investigation Department. Our appointment was for four o'clock at the Jo'burg queue for the bus to Sophiatown. After a long wait, Bloke did not show up, and I started searching slowly along the line. Behind me

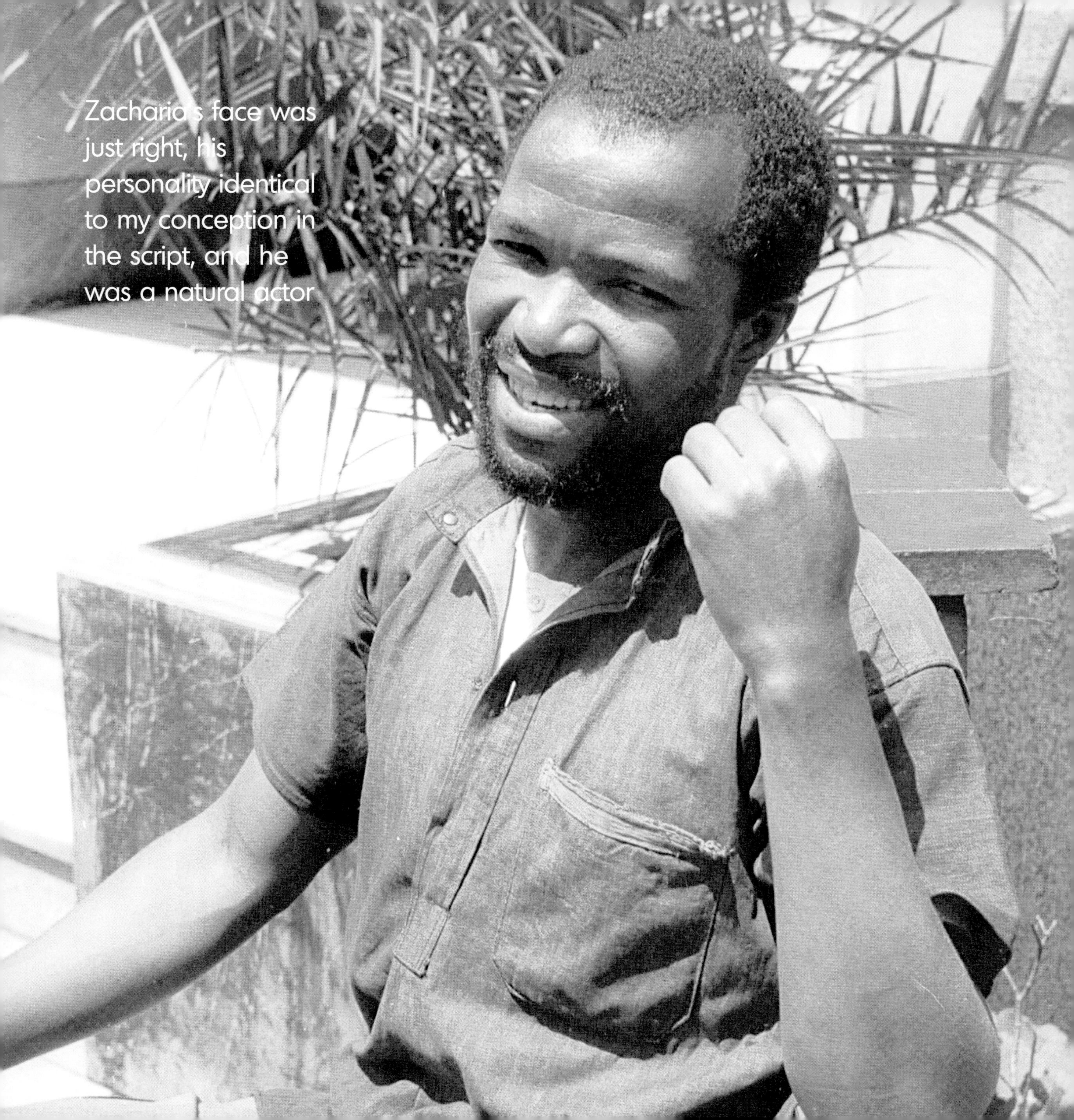

Zacharia's face was just right, his personality identical to my conception in the script, and he was a natural actor

was a group of white South Africans in mufti, who had the look of police. My strategy was to be as obvious as possible, in the hope that that would avert suspicion. I considered going over and talking to them. They kept eyeing me with what seemed to be suspicion, but so openly that I did not take it seriously, and continued with my search. Suddenly Bloke ran up breathlessly. The queue moved very slowly and we had a chance to interview those I had spotted previously. It was not rewarding. I then decided to try the railway station. Bloke was unable to accompany me so I prevailed upon Morris.

We arrived at four o'clock. Perfect. A sea of faces passing so fast that we did not have time to look closely at anyone. From amongst thousands I caught a glimpse of two men who I thought might do. On closer examination they both looked marvellous. One of these two finally played the leading role. His face was just right, his personality identical to my conception in the script, and he was a natural actor. It was uncanny how suitable he was, and it proved my theory that the ability to act is a personality trait to be found in all classes and all kinds of society, and that the director can intuitively find such an individual by his face. I must emphasise that this intuition must be verified by actual experience with the actor. This method is entirely different from the methods of film-directing which have evolved from the theatre. There the actor attempts to portray a personality usually not identical to his own. I was actually casting for an individual whose personality was identical to his role in the film. Here the primary task is selection.

Africans were frequently searched for passes and arrested at the railway station. Naturally the first man Morris approached was most apprehensive. He probably assumed that we were the police, since he had seen Morris together with me. An explanation of our purpose calmed him. He had a warm smile and natural charm. He was a dental technician, an exceptionally good position for an African, considering the policy of apartheid, which barred the sons of Ham from employment in skilled trades. We obtained his name, address and office telephone number, and said that we would call him the next day.

We returned to scan the crowd again, and I spotted Zacharia Mgabi, who was to become the lead in *Anno Domini 1957*, the working title for *Come Back, Africa*. When Morris tried to talk to him he started running, and Morris had to run quickly and call out to him to stop. From his startled expression he seemed even more frightened that the first man. In order to reassure him, Morris said, "Would you like to be in a film, a motion picture?"

I have often wondered what he thought at that moment, standing in the middle of the railway station, with the crowds rushing by, accosted by two strangers who were asking him to appear in a film. It must have seemed quite mad to him. Admittedly it seemed unreal to me.

He looked fine, but was extremely wary. We made every effort to assuage his fear, because we could not afford to lose him. Despite his hesitancy, in some way our proposal appealed to him. His reaction was ambiguous and when he told us that he was going on leave soon, I suspected a dodge. Nevertheless, the telephone number he gave us turned out to be the right one.

The following day I telephoned Nathaniel, the dental technician, who turned the call over to his employer. The dentist was an Austrian-Jewish refugee, who told me that Nathaniel was an excellent worker, extremely reliable and loyal. Later, when I spoke to Zacharia's immediate superior, a Scotsman named Ross, his recommendation was similar: Zacharia was the best man he had working for him, dependable, conscientious, intelligent and with the highest position of any African in the office. It was encouraging to find that my intuition had been so accurate. Both these men suited the role perfectly. I had looked for a man who would be universally liked and their faces had expressed this, although the first sight of them was a flash in the passing crowd. Ross questioned me thoroughly. I suppose he wanted to be sure that a fast-talking film producer would not victimise Zacharia. Considering the fact that this film would be very unpopular with the authorities, I did not take too kindly to this lengthy questioning. Ross was so meticulous that he was a downright nuisance, the white man's burden and all that rot, but he was unquestionably fond of Zacharia.

I made appointments with both Zacharia and Nathaniel for an audition. Nathaniel did not keep his appointment, but Zacharia's interest in the idea of acting in a film was growing and apparently he was not going on leave. Before he had agreed to participate, he kept repeating "Yes, make a good film like *Cry, the Beloved Country*, you must make it very good". This plea always unsettled me, because I had heard that *Cry, the Beloved Country* was not good, and the attitude of the book I found maudlin and patronising — an opinion emphatically shared by African and American Negro intellectuals.

Vinah was present at Zacharia's audition, and they looked very good together. I selected a scene for them to enact which would be a common experience in their society. It was an emotional situation, since I wanted to see if they could express a range of feelings. There were several people present, and as we watched the scene unfold I was astounded by Zacharia's ability to identify himself with the role. Again and again during the shooting he was to surprise all of us with this extraordinary ability. After this, there was no longer a shred of doubt — it was clear that he was perfect for the part; if only I had time to select the others as carefully!

NEO-REALISM

To see an individual on the screen against the background of his real environment has a new kind of poetry solely in that image. It does mean an infinitely smaller financial return, but it is art. I prefer to make this kind of film, since the pleasure is in the making, not the showing. The price is high. Films have been made this way sporadically throughout the history of the cinema. Only Robert Flaherty, the great American director of scripted documentary was able to maintain consistency by the worthwhile sacrifice of making relatively few films. The audience's sensitivity would not be offended if I had used a star, but a tribal African would give the film far more power. This was my experience at the age of ten, when I saw Flaherty's *Man of Aran* and years later when I saw *Shoeshine* and *Bicycle Thieves* (films by Italian director Vittorio De Sica, considered the master of neo-realist cinema). In making *On the Bowery*, this impression deepened, so that I came to believe that it would be impossible for me to work with professional actors. It was more than an aesthetic or moral principle for me. It was the only satisfaction that I was able to capture in the ordeal of making these films. I enjoy the involvement with the people that I am filming. It seems like sharing in a new life. The best period is before the shooting, when I am absorbing everything about the location and the people with my eyes and ears. Then I wish that my eyes were the lenses of a camera and could film everything I see and eliminate the grinding toil necessary to obtain three minutes of film per day. The editing room is an isolated, routine grind for me, despite its importance. Exhibiting the film becomes a sickening anti-climax, which diminishes the actual experience and drains away your enthusiasm. I resent the audience at the premiere, with their furs, jewellery and dinner jackets, as intruders who have no contact with this other life. There are small pleasures in the entire process. It is true that art is not a pleasure for the creator. There are always so many insurmountable obstacles that low-budget film-making becomes a head-splitting ordeal. Why choose such work? It is not entirely a matter of choice. Perhaps it is because the artist sees that life itself is an ordeal for most, if not for all, people. For complex reasons — sensitivity, a deficiency of that refuge of first resort, escapism — we are continually experiencing the rawness of life and have the imperative demand to express it. Our only weapon is to cry out against the barbarians, the enemies of life. This is hardly an enjoyable process, but there are grains of realisation. One feels intensely alive in rare moments, when not feeling overwhelmingly crushed by the odds. The reason this kind of film-making is an ordeal is that you must become completely immersed in the suffering and misery of your subjects. Secondly, you stick your neck out, and if you stick your neck out you can expect people to whack at it. You are not making films the way they are supposed to be made, which is not one battle but a battle every step of the way, from the first technician hired until you have ceased trying to distribute the film years later. For the preservation of society as it is, all defences are so interrelated that once you depart from the accepted way you are in a wilderness in which there are no rules. At one time I had thought that neo-realism and films without professional actors would catch on, but I feel now that it will take at least 20 years before we can break through the barrier unless by a miracle some society becomes enlightened enough to realise that the medium of mass communication must be financed and directed for the benefit of society. It is a function beyond any individual.

Besides my personal inclination, I had other reasons for wanting to use non-professional actors. I wanted the audience to have a direct personal contact with the individuals of another society. God knows what I will end up with. Some of those who saw *On the Bowery* said that at certain moments in the film they felt that they were in the room with the men. This was what I wanted for *Come Back, Africa* as well. No matter how true to South Africa our story was, by using a known actor it would have destroyed the unity of this truth.

Paradoxically, the script was deliberately written so that it would create a jarring effect. I didn't aim for perfect continuity. I didn't follow the first law of scriptwriting, using every sound, image and line of dialogue to advance the plot. I deliberately shattered the continuity to make the film more believable. Life never has the perfect flow. Therefore, I decided to photograph actual scenes of South African life. To give the audience the sense that they were witnessing the actual events, and not looking at fiction, I sandwiched between sequences of the drama these chunks of pure documentary material. This material was out of context to the plot, it jarred, but it was not out of context to the lives of these people. Certain important manifestations of African life would have had to be left out if one were to conform to conventional plot construction. In most films the ambience is missing because not one extraneous element is allowed. It was this quality that I had always missed in films, whether they were about Paris, New York or Nigeria; one could never grasp anything about the place or the people. We have to have films which move vertically away from the plot, just as we now accept this in novels.

Many critics praised the powerful realism of the film, but complained about the roughness of the construction. They did not realise that the power of realism was partially the result of this apparent roughness. It was often explained to them that there were certain flaws due to the conditions of work, but this was often misinterpreted to include those sections made to heighten the effect of realism. The insertion of this raw, uncooked documentary material is jarring and snaps the rapport between the viewer and the image, defeating my aim. Despite this, the overall conviction carried by the film is stronger, identification does come, and at the end of the film I believe the audience is deeply involved emotionally, because they have an inner awareness that the whole exercise is not fiction.

BUREAUCRACY III: BRINGING IN THE CREW

Choosing Vinah and Zacharia was an important step. Now I was anxious to obtain permission for the entry of the crew. I was becoming uneasy, because I had written to the members of the crew to apply at their local South African consulates for their visas on 1 March, 1958. It was now the middle of April and permission had not yet been granted. According to instructions extracted from Mitchell, I had also written to the Department of Immigration requesting permission for the members of the crew to enter South Africa for the purpose of producing a film.

One morning I received a telephone call from Oscar Knebel, Milek's brother, who had just arrived in Jo'burg from Tel-Aviv. He informed me that the British Consulate in Israel had cabled Pretoria requesting permission to grant the visa to Milek.

Oscar planned to call the authorities in Pretoria in the hope of expediting the formalities. Later that day, Oscar called me after speaking to Van den Berg, a minor official in the Department of Interior. Van den Berg (M1) had informed him they knew nothing about the cable and told him to call back on Thursday. That was Monday. It seemed odd to have to wait four days to find out if they had received a cable. I was a little inexperienced as to the functioning of bureaucracy. All these months of fear of being discovered had created a tension within me which flared up with the slightest sign of danger. Now, although there was no tangible danger, I anticipated trouble.

For the next two-and-a-half months the officials in Pretoria put me through the grandest run-around I had ever experienced in my life. By the time I was able to start filming, I had reached so high a pitch of nervous tension that I came to the conclusion that to be a good spy one had to be quite cold-blooded or one could never stand the pace. One never knew whether the devious and absurd demands of the officials were due to their suspicion or simply normal South African bureaucracy. This behaviour made the procedure particularly unnerving. I knew that the bureaucrats of South Africa were adept at obstructionism, because African friends of mine told me that it took a year or longer for any African or Indian to get a passport, not for any particular reason other than that it seemed to satisfy some infantile desire in these functionaries. I knew that unreasonableness was entirely compatible with normal bureaucratic procedure; I did not imagine the degree to which it was practised.

I was also aware that the Criminal Investigation Department (CID) kept a dossier on most foreigners, especially those who had any connection with the African cause. A hotel manager told me that he had been given orders to have the switchboard tap the phone calls of important clients. When I heard this, I was delighted that I had never made any revealing phone calls during our stay at the hotel. Friends had told me of the case of a rather meek South African, no revolutionary in any sense, who had had his passport denied to him for giving a lecture on jazz to a left-wing club, although he had never been politically active. Later, some foreigners had been censured and warned by the police for associating with him, and consequently dossiers were opened on them. This is the irritation which is South Africa. If you could ignore its nightmarish quality, South Africa did have its amusing facets.

The police took down the licence numbers of those attending controversial political meetings. A few days later the police would call at their homes with a stern warning to henceforth avoid such meetings, saying that their names had been entered in the records. This social call usually had the desired effect of discouraging any further political activity. By this classical technique of terror, the originally small white opposition movement was reduced to a minute one. The weaker members were bluffed by these threats, until the regime gained enough strength to crush the stubborn resistance. The prediction in South Africa was that the regime would become progressively more oppressive, a prophecy which has lamentably come true.

What stimulated my anxiety at the time was that I was uncertain of whether the Special Branch of the CID had started a dossier under the heading: "Rogosin, Lionel: film producer". I had tried to avoid this distinction, but it was impossible to make a film about Africans without constantly being in their company — a crime of momentous proportions. Having been stopped by the police at night in Sophiatown in the company of Morris and Lewis was enough to make the authorities suspicious. The police had not written down my licence number, but they might still have a record of this incident in Pretoria. With a little more insight into the nature of the South African police I would not have been concerned about this, since I would have realised that very few of them had enough intelligence to remember a number six digits long without writing it down.

Ignoring Van den Berg's advice, I did not wait until Thursday to call him, but I might as well have waited, for all the good it did me. I must have made hundreds of useless telephone calls in the process of persuading the South African authorities to grant permission for the entry of my crew. The high-pitched voice of Van den Berg informed me that there had been no cable. There suddenly

Ernst Artaria
Hochstrasse 101
Zurich 44
Switzerland

March 30th, 1958

Dear Lionel,

I thank you for your letter of March 22th.

Arnold u. Richter
From A.u.R. I have a letter concerning the confirmation of your payment and changed order, also a copy of the new proforma bill. The cost of airfreight charges are not definitif fixed. A.u.R. promesed me that we must pay only the price of shipment cost and that they will pay the difference to airfreights charges.* In the same letter A.u.R. fix the delivery date on the end of Avril. The May 1th in Europe is a sunday, also I think my trip to Munich will be on May 2th or 3th. By A.u.R. I will shot some tests with the blimps and an imediatly processing and printing is granted. I think 1 or 1½ day will be enough for all checking and testing works so that I can start from Zurich to Johannesburg around May 5th. Your New York-Bank will she send the rest of Money on my name to Bayerische-Hypothekar- u. Wechsel-Bank Munich ?

Visa:
I've spoken with the visa-department to the Swiss-legation in Berne. They have send the necessary paper for Wettler and me express and airmail to Johannesburg on March 14th. A normal delivery-time is 6 - 8 weeks. The visa people in Berne will do the best for make it faster. For speed it up sure they tink it will be the best, if you can make an arrangment with the department in Johannesburg. I have no copy of my visa-request and so I don't no the asked number and other details. In any case I will call every week to the legation in Berne.
Battery:
I will order the gadget for charching this week.

* With MAT-Transport Zurich I will find the cheapst way for airfreights-charges

For the next two-and-a-half months the officials in Pretoria put me through the grandest run-around I had ever experienced in my life

appeared to be some breakdown in radio communications with Switzerland and Israel. Hearing Van den Berg's soprano voice, I imagined him to be one of those tiny moustachioed Boers. There seemed to be two main physical types among the Boers: the majority were monsters with huge paws and enormous shoulders, probably due to a preponderance of Neanderthal man in their heritage; or little office clerks with faded blond moustaches and watery blue eyes, hardly the prototype of the super-race. The contrast between these two types was amusing and the comedy was burlesqued by the Boer women, who were enormous.

A scholar of South African history once commented to me, "They are not women, they are historic monuments." He had been analysing the sadism that exists to a high degree in Boer culture. As an example he described the extermination of the Bushmen. They were hunted down with dogs. The men were killed and the young boys castrated. This was done to tame them, so that they could be used as servants and would not run back to the wilderness. Their women, like the Malay slaves, Hottentots and Africans, produced offspring for their European masters whose descendants are classified today as coloureds. One can see a hint of this strain in the features of some of the most rabid white supremacists.

I called Van den Berg several times before he acknowledged receipt of the cable. Each time his voice seemed to get more and more grating. "Yes, Mr Rugazin, we have received the cable, but we cannot grant permission for the visas. You will have to get clearance from the State Information Office, and the Department of Immigration." These words came as the first of a series of shocks, which were to occur almost daily until the visas were granted at the end of June. I explained to Van den Berg that Mr Mitchell of the Department of Immigration had told me that a letter requesting permission for the crew to enter South Africa was all that was necessary. I had expected something like this to happen. Mitchell's advice had seemed to be too easy, too uncomplicated. Nevertheless, I was both extremely anxious and furious because Mitchell had misled me. On the basis of his information, I had made contracts with the crew to commence production on 15 May, 1958. I was now fearful that obtaining clearance would be a lengthy process and that we would never be ready by that date. I protested vehemently, but Van den Berg hid behind that refuge of the bureaucrat, the stock excuse: "Sorry, Misdah Rugazin, those are the regulations."

There is something diabolical about their procedure. The authorities hold up the regulations as if they were canon law, and even when you try to respect the regulations you are invariably given wrong information by the same officials, who later treat the error as a sacrilege on your part. Bureaucracy is taking increasing control over the functions of society everywhere, and has created a problem which deserves serious consideration. These functionaries must be made to serve the interest of the public. Presently the abuses are enormous. The civil service must attract the petty soul frustrated in all attempts to be something other than a nonentity, who revels in being nasty and arrogant for the sake of making others aware of his existence. They take a grim pleasure in harassing the public with the hope of extracting some graft to add to the enjoyment. If we survive nuclear warfare I envisage an uprising against the bureaucrats by the end of the century.

Dr Schneider of the United States Information Service had introduced me to Mr Hynes of the South African State Information Office, who was very cordial. Mr Mitchell of the Department of Immigration already knew of my case. After a few days I called Van den Berg again, who sadly informed me that no clearance was forthcoming from either department. I asked Ellie to call Mitchell. I didn't want to speak to him myself for fear that I might lose my temper. That evening Ellie had bad news to report. Mitchell, ignoring his original instructions, demanded a contract from Finches Travel Agency and a bank guarantee of one hundred pounds. I had suspected that they might want such a contract, but since Mitchell had not requested one originally, I had let months lapse without any further contact with Finches. There was a good possibility that they might have lost interest. I obtained the bank guarantee of one hundred pounds, which seems to be required for nearly everyone. (Miriam Makeba later had to deposit one hundred pounds to leave South Africa, a requirement for all "non-Europeans" seeking a passport.) I obtained the guarantee after two days' delay and rushed off to Pretoria hoping that Mitchell would overlook his demand for the contract.

This drive to Pretoria became an almost daily occurrence. Fortunately, it was only an hour from Johannesburg, yet it consumed an enormous amount of my time. Mitchell's office was in an old brick building of Victorian vintage, shabbily furnished, its mustiness suitable to the Kafkaesque world of the functionaries. I came to dread the sight of it. On arrival that day I had the usual long wait at reception. I desperately hoped to talk Mitchell out of the requirement for the contract, in case I couldn't obtain it. I reminded him that his original instructions were that the only requirement was a letter from me to his department requesting permission for the visas and stating the purpose of our project. His emaciated face stared at me out of his watery blue fish-eyes. He remained unmoved and politely adamant.

As usual, our interview was brief and impersonal, but during the conversation Mitchell stated that if the State Information Office was favourable to my project, their recommendation would carry a great deal of influence. Jumping at this straw I immediately called Van den Berg, who claimed that he had not received any information from Hynes of the State Information Office. Every time I spoke to one of these officials, I was filled with anxiety for fear that they might suspect my intentions. The more involved this investigation became, the greater the probability that they would uncover my intent. There was no alternative but to pursue the matter. Hynes was extremely congenial on the phone and said that he had already sent the letter to the Department of the Interior. His behaviour was opposite to that of the other officials who were dealing with my case. He amazed me by offering to read this letter to me. I was unprepared for the excellent recommendation he gave. I couldn't have written a better one myself. I pressed Hynes to send a copy to Mitchell as soon as possible, but for some reason he parried this with the suggestion that I have Mitchell call him. I was puzzled as to why he wouldn't send Mitchell the letter directly, but I suppose that he was adhering to good bureaucratic procedure. Since Mitchell hadn't requested the letter, he wouldn't send it. I knew that it was useless to ask Mitchell to telephone Hynes. When I informed him of Hynes's recommendation, he still demanded the contract, although he had told me that if State Information was interested in my project there would be no further obstacles. I cursed myself for ever having the idea of the contract. I was being trapped by my own device and began to consider seriously that I might be discovered.

About one week had passed since Mitchell had made his demand for the contract, and I was forced to try and obtain it. When I called Finches Travel Agency, I was told that Mr Lewis was in London and would return in one month. I then made an appointment with Finches' publicity man, Mr Hunter. I outlined the progress made since our last conversation. I described a

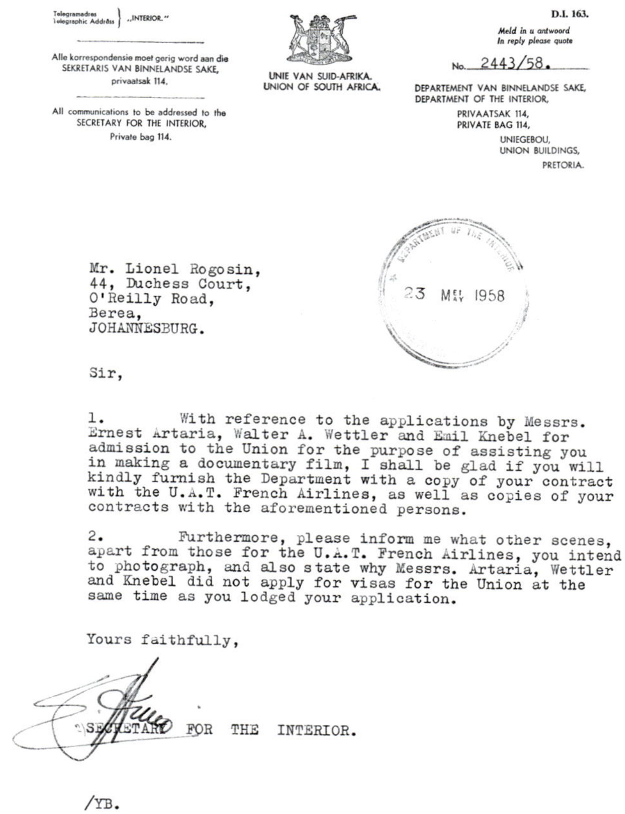

Telegramadres / Telegraphic Address } „INTERIOR."

Alle korrespondensie moet gerig word aan die SEKRETARIS VAN BINNELANDSE SAKE, privaatsak 114.

All communications to be addressed to the SECRETARY FOR THE INTERIOR, Private bag 114.

UNIE VAN SUID-AFRIKA.
UNION OF SOUTH AFRICA.

D.I. 163.

Meld in u antwoord
In reply please quote

No. 2443/58.

DEPARTEMENT VAN BINNELANDSE SAKE,
DEPARTMENT OF THE INTERIOR,
PRIVAATSAK 114,
PRIVATE BAG 114,
UNIEGEBOU,
UNION BUILDINGS,
PRETORIA.

DEPARTMENT OF THE INTERIOR
23 MAY 1958

Mr. Lionel Rogosin,
44, Duchess Court,
O'Reilly Road,
Berea,
JOHANNESBURG.

Sir,

1. With reference to the applications by Messrs. Ernest Artaria, Walter A. Wettler and Emil Knebel for admission to the Union for the purpose of assisting you in making a documentary film, I shall be glad if you will kindly furnish the Department with a copy of your contract with the U.A.T. French Airlines, as well as copies of your contracts with the aforementioned persons.

2. Furthermore, please inform me what other scenes, apart from those for the U.A.T. French Airlines, you intend to photograph, and also state why Messrs. Artaria, Wettler and Knebel did not apply for visas for the Union at the same time as you lodged your application.

Yours faithfully,

SECRETARY FOR THE INTERIOR.

/YB.

One never knew whether the devious and absurd demands of the officials were due to their suspicion or simply normal South African bureaucracy. This behaviour made the procedure particularly unnerving

magnificent motion picture with shots of lions, tigers and native dances filmed in 17 African countries. An extraordinary cinema, but quite impossible to accomplish. When I raved about these lion and tiger pictures, I often wondered when the public was going to get sick of them. In any case, I believe that there are no tigers on the African continent. I offered this film to him at no cost to his company except transportation and living expenses for the entire crew. In return we would arrange to have their name conspicuous throughout the film — not every 100 feet, but sufficiently to satisfy them. I was offering to produce a film of great value to them at a small portion of the cost — ideal from their point of view, but singularly disadvantageous from mine. In our last conversation Lewis hadn't realised this. He probably accounted for it by his cleverness at negotiating agreements entirely favourable to his firm, not at all considered bad form.

After this sales talk to Hunter, despite my glowing description and splendid offer, he asked me to come back in one week. I was thoroughly deflated. I would have offered him the moon in order to get the contract immediately, but I had to proceed with some caution so as not to frighten him off. After Hunter's unenthusiastic response, I felt that the chance of getting the contract was slight. It was almost hopeless to go back to Mitchell without the contract, but I hoped to prevail upon him to waive this requirement or to find some other loophole, since it was unthinkable to lose another week.

Mitchell remains a rock. He still demands the contract. The fact that the director of Finches has gone to London leaves him unmoved. Desperately I ask him why a contract was necessary, and he replies that it will guarantee that I have the necessary financing to produce the film. I offer to take the full responsibility myself, since any further delay will jeopardise the entire production. According to written agreements with the crew members, I would sustain a considerable loss for any delay beyond 1 May. I remind him that I had made these agreements subject to information received from him. Mitchell didn't even change his expression. As a last try, I ask him about the favourable letter from State Information. He says that he hasn't read it yet, but if they recommend the project everything will be all right. I wonder what kind of a euphemism that is. For some reason the letter can't find its way to Mitchell, although he continually tells me that it will solve all my problems. It is exasperating that Mitchell won't take the trouble to ask Hynes or Van den Berg to send him a copy. I am forced to call Hynes again. Hynes as usual is amiable. He informs me that the letter has been sent to Van den Berg, but he will call Mitchell and put in a good word for me.

Soon after that I was invited to a cocktail party at which Hynes was also present. I made it a point to have a long talk with him. I wondered what made him write such a favourable letter on my behalf — must be one of those curious manifestations of human nature. Whatever the motive, Hynes was extremely affable. His name, appearance and accent made me think that he was of English origin. As we talked I wondered if he could be one of those rare people who foresee that the government is leading the country into chaos. When I asked him if he was English he reacted with extreme sensitivity to the question. Emphatically he denied this with the statement, "No, I am a South African and proud of it. I love this country." As a continuation of this same reaction, he said, "I gave you a first class report and I will shoot you down in flames if you let me down." We both heartily laughed at this joke, while I desperately hoped that he didn't notice my flushed cheeks.

Hynes was the type that one meets in a society like South Africa, who makes one ponder at the behaviour of human beings. Friendly, outwardly decent people, who don't seem to harbour evil but who give no awareness of the great evil which they are indirectly abetting and benefiting from. The crude African-hating Boer, who overtly expresses his cruelty, is easier to understand. This is why many Africans say that they prefer the Boers to English South Africans. The Boer is not a hypocrite and you know where you stand with him. I prefer the former type, because I find cruelty repulsive and I think that there is more potential hope in such a person. He is not as blind and as rigid. It has often been observed how callous most human beings can be to the suffering of others, particularly when their own comfort is at stake. The rare individual who is not so is the salt of the earth. The vast majority of people are completely conditioned by society. It is a kind of brainwashing not artificially induced, but a natural sort that continues from infancy to adulthood. Everyone is a victim of his own culture, unable to comprehend the self-destructive forces inherent in every society. The individual is confused by an elaborate system of propaganda aimed at perpetuating the society. When a very small child in South Africa learns to call the African servant a "kaffir" and to order him to pick up a book that the child has been reading, the process begins which will continue right up to the grave. By the time they are adults, they have been thoroughly conditioned to accept the evils of their society, although if they are outwardly decent, like Hynes, it would prevent them from committing atrocities. They do not commit atrocities, but they accept the benefits of the system which is based upon these atrocities.

One of my reasons for making *Come Back, Africa* was to make such people realise the horror their system imposes. No one wishes to see the horror. To a degree, escapism is a natural protective device. If one were constantly aware of all mortal dangers, one would go mad or have too much anxiety to function properly. Unfortunately, this protective function, due to its pleasurable quality, causes the individual to shut out unpleasant reality rather than to take rational measures to remove the evils. This is the artist's role, and he is driven by his personality to continually probe deeper and deeper into the life of his culture. This is not a glorious task, but a painful one; not a natural process, but more in the nature of an obsession, absolutely vital for survival. The creative minority, because of this function, expose themselves to pain for the survival and elevation of the social structure. For this they usually earn the wrath of their community, which clings desperately to its illusions, and attacks furiously all attempts to face the pain of reality. I met individuals like Hynes several times in South Africa and I decided that it was important to include this type in the film. Men who are not essentially evil, but who, without being aware of it, contribute to it, or if they are vaguely aware of it, are either too weak or too helpless to do anything about it.

After that evening I was in the same spot as before, which seemed to be perpetual, since I hadn't made any further progress in weeks. Hynes has written the letter to the Department of Interior, but Mitchell won't read it. Extraordinary, but true. Mitchell and Van den Berg obviously have no intention to help me, so I try to recall all the contacts I have made in South Africa in the wild hope that someone can help. With reluctance I decide to call Dr Schneider of the United States Information Service. He says that there is very little that he can do, since he can't interfere with the authority of a sovereign government, but he will see how persuasive he can be. After that conversation I decided to try and obtain a lawyer who has good connections with government officials. A lawyer is recommended to me who claims he knows someone in the administration who may be able to help. To my knowledge he never did locate this so-called contact. One never

44 Duchess Court
O'Reilly Road
Berea, Johannesburg
May 26, 1958

Secretary For The Interior
Private Bag 114
Pretoria

Dear Sir,

In reference to your letter, #2443/58 of May 23, 1958 concerning the application by Mssrs. Ernest Artaria, Walter A. Wettler and Emil Knebel, for admission to the Union, much of the information you have requested in this letter, I have previously given to the Department of Immigration in Pretoria.

In February of t is year I made inquiries at the Immigration Department as to the necessary procedure for bringing in these people to the Union. I was told that if I produced a letter to each of the respective parties indicating that I was requesting their services, and if I would purchase a round trip ticket for each person insuring their transportation to and from the Union, this would facilitate the matter. On the basis of this information, I entered into an agreement with these technicians. I then complied with the information given to me by the Immigration Department and about March 1, 1958, the technicians had applied for visas to the Union from their respective countries. About five weeks later, around April 9, 1958 I was requested by the Department of Immigration to supply other information similar to that now requested by you and with which I complied.

On the basis of the original information given to me, I selected May 1, 1958 as the commencing date for these contracts and therefore the delay is involving me in considerable expense. I would therefore, appreciate it if you could give this matter your immediate attention.

I had complied explicitly with their instructions and they added new demands at the last moment

knows whether one is in more danger from one's lawyer or from one's opponent. I wait for a few days impatiently for him to reach his contact.

CID: COLONEL SPENGLER

One afternoon I returned home and found Ellie rather upset. A man from the CID had called. She tried to reassure me by prefacing this news with the qualifying phrase that everything was all right.

"What did he say?" I enquired.

"Nothing, he was extremely polite and asked if you would call their office and make an appointment with Colonel Spengler."

This request gave both of us quite a jolt, since Spengler's name was infamous among Africans. He was head of the Special Branch of the CID, whose particular function it was to investigate and thwart all political opposition.

I was quite shaken, and immediately called Mr Cole, my lawyer, to find out how serious it really was. He reassured me in the manner one always does when he himself has nothing at stake, "It is probably a routine check, and you have nothing to worry about." As with nearly everyone else I dealt with in South Africa, I had given Cole only the minimum amount of information necessary to perform his function. During the entire shooting there were only a few people who knew what kind of a film I intended to make. I agreed with Cole's diagnosis, but I asked his opinion about the time I had been stopped in Sophiatown by the police and searched for liquor. Mr Cole was absolutely positive that there would be a record of this with Spengler. This was not reassuring to me. If the CID knew that I had been to Sophiatown at night, they might consider it very suspicious behaviour. Such a report might make Mitchell wonder about the kind of travelogue I would film in Sophiatown.

I prepared thoroughly for all the questions Spengler might possibly ask. I was particularly anxious to have a good alibi for the incident in Sophiatown. At the suggestion of friends, I decided to say that they were my servants and I was taking them home from work. This might not sound like a valid excuse, but in South Africa it was a common occurrence. There is a curfew for Africans after 10 pm, and to avoid having their servants arrested their employers sometimes took them home from work. When I had gathered my nerve sufficiently, I called Spengler's office and made an appointment. On the selected day I arrived at his office at about 11 o'clock. I received meticulously polite treatment and after a short wait was ushered into his office. My pulse seemed to be going at an alarming rate. I made a great effort to calm myself so that I wouldn't give myself away. I was afraid that my nervousness would be obvious to everyone, but the instant I stepped over the threshold of Spengler's office, I saw something which calmed me instantly — I saw that Spengler himself was nervous. If he wasn't, then I was suffering from the illusion that he was, and it gave me confidence. Once I sensed that he was uneasy, it gave me the upper hand. His appearance certainly did not express any quality of shrewdness. A typical Boer face, pug-like, almost devoid of intelligence or sensitivity, sat on his bull neck. He motioned me to sit down and opened the conversation with the explanation that he had been requested to conduct an investigation of my activities by the Department of the Interior.

"Yes, I've been trying to obtain visas for my crew to enter South Africa," I answered.

"What kind of film do you want to make, Mr Rogosin?"

"I am planning to make a documentary of South African wildlife, native customs, music, etc. South Africa has marvellous potentialities. I could have made the film in Kenya or any other place in Africa, but I decided to work in Jo'burg because it is the only place in Africa that has labs, studios and equipment, which are necessary for the film I want to make."

"Who is it that you propose to make this film for?" (The idea that one could make a film for oneself never seemed to occur to these people.)

"Well, I have been discussing this project with Finches Travel Agency, and they are interested in my making the film for them to promote travel in South Africa and to publicise themselves."

"Do you have a contract from them?"

"No, not at the moment, because I don't have my final script written and the director is now in London, but it was definitely set before he left."

"What will happen if they fall through."

"I am not completely dependent on them. I was planning to make a film similar to this one anyway, and they heard of my previous work and became interested in this project. This kind of travelogue has a large market and if they don't come through I will be able to finance the film myself."

The fact that this was all nonsense didn't make it any easier to say. I think that one of the major reasons I was not discovered is that films are such a mystery to the average person. Often when someone asked what kind of film I was making, I would answer "a documentary" in a rather brusque and slightly annoyed way that implied, "If you don't know what that is, you are very uninformed." I was surprised that nine times out of ten that answer finished the discussion. They would say, "Ah, yes," and give a wise nod to indicate that they understood. During the shooting I took special care that no unauthorised people saw the rushes. Actually, it wouldn't have made any difference, since there was no sound on the film and amateurs can't understand the raw film at this stage. Near the completion of shooting we had trouble with the cameras and it was necessary to have the laboratory screen some of the film with us. We were amazed that they didn't seem to have the slightest suspicion. The lab personnel were completely absorbed in their technical problems and concerned about keeping us as customers. When they look at a print they don't look at the subject matter of the images, they are only concerned about the quality and the gamma of the developing bath; the point of view regarding apartheid is not of interest to them. By understanding their mentality we were able to work safely with them.

Suddenly Spengler's tone changed, and he said ominously, "What were you doing last week at the bus queue during the stay-at-home?" At last the fencing was over, and Spengler was onto something serious. When I heard this question I was relieved, since my presence at the bus queue was easily proven innocent. Spengler had said that as if he were playing his trump card and that indicated to me that it was all that he knew. If this was the extent of his information about me, then I was safe for the moment. (So they hadn't taken down my licence number that night in Sophiatown!) I took his question quite lightly and laughed, to convey my innocence. I told him that I had been casting for actors at the bus queue, since I like the use of ordinary people rather than actors. "You can verify this by asking the people I interviewed. Would you like their names?" (I thought this would satisfy him, but he jolted me at the end of the interrogation when he in fact asked for the names).

"I am a film producer and my profession is to entertain people, not to get involved in political activity."

He leaned forward very melodramatically, and said, "Aha, yes, yes, that's how all the spies get in, either as journalists or film producers." With that statement I almost laughed in his face. I found it amusing that in his absurdity he was almost clairvoyant. I left Spengler's office feeling elated. Apparently, the only suspicious evidence in my dossier was my visit to the bus queue. Barring an accident, I was sure he would clear me, unless, as with Mitchell and the letter from Hynes, Spengler felt like being an obstructionist. Anything could happen.

By this time I had become quite adept at imitating the conversation of the white supremacists. I rambled glibly on about the happy natives, their folk music and dancing, the marvellous wildlife and the natural splendour of South Africa. It was this technique more than anything else that enabled me to get the film through — that and luck. Their mentality and propaganda are extremely unrealistic, and this leads them into self-defeating positions. It was this that led them into believing me. They believed me because they desperately wanted to believe me. As they deluded themselves about their behaviour towards Africans, they deluded themselves about my intentions. My experience may be a pattern of how their blindness will in the long run defeat and possibly destroy them. If there were only some way to make them see what they were doing, for their own sake as well as for the innocent, who will suffer terribly. There is no way other than to impose it upon them. If it is done from outside of South Africa, it will be more merciful than from within.

Because of their mentality it is difficult for them to comprehend how a white person can attack their policy. They always seem so shocked and horrified when it happens, which it does continuously. Some people in South Africa guessed my intentions, even though they had less evidence. They guessed because they were not obsessed with hatred for the Africans. Once Boris gave me a fright when he warned me that his cousin, whom I never remembered meeting, had found me out. We had met at a party where I was asked the usual questions about my film. I gave them the standard tale that I was making a musical travelogue. His cousin reported to him, "He's not making any musical travelogue!" I knew exactly what he meant by that. Boris's information gave me an anxious moment, but he told me I was quite safe. Those who guessed didn't give me away, but it was a bit like walking a tightrope.

Keeping up this subterfuge was draining, and sapped my energy. Even though my line became quite habitual, and I would reel it off automatically at private gatherings, I still had to be on my guard constantly. In conversation I had to be particularly careful about my phraseology, because each group in South Africa had its separate terminology and the wrong usage could make me suspect. Amongst the Boers it was dangerous to say "African" instead of "kaffir". Africans were referred to officially as "natives" or "Bantus", privately as "kaffirs", "boys" and occasionally as "niggers". The film-maker Jamie Uys used to take a special delight in using this word. I don't know if it was because I was an American and this word was more hateful to me than "kaffir", with which I had no previous association. The degrading quality of names depends almost entirely on association. No Englishman would be offended to be called a "native", but around the globe, in Asia and Africa, where they have ruled, this term is offensive because it has been used for centuries in its derogatory sense.

Africans and progressive and liberal whites call the Africans, of all things, "Africans". The Boers consider this a monstrous idea, and are ready to fight over it, because African is "Afrikaner" in the Boer language, which is the name they have given to themselves. The name has political significance, since the Boers claim to be the only valid inhabitants of South Africa. The Boers hate the name "African" because its usage would be an admission that Africans are the valid inhabitants of South Africa. In conversations with the white supremacists, this word had to be avoided, for it would make a ruinous impression. Such an expression was used only by reds, agitators, radicals and kaffirboetjies (brother to the kaffir — the equivalent of nigger-lover).

It has always struck me as ironic that the white supremacists, who are rabidly religious Christians, seem to consider it despicable and worse than criminal to like or love an African. There were endless discussions of this controversy in the press. Each paper had a definite policy about it. The Johannesburg *Star* used the word "native" exclusively, and the *Rand Daily Mail* only the name "African". There were debates in Parliament about it. One plaintive voice once wrote in Letters to the Editor, "Why not call the Africans what they would like to be called?" No one in Parliament ever answered this.

I reported the Spengler interrogation to my lawyer and he felt certain that they would clear me. I then called Dr Schneider and told him that I had no news. He informed me that he had called Mitchell, but there was very little that he could say because he couldn't interfere with their regulations. Yet he told Mitchell that this was a bad way for a country to behave, that they shouldn't be so restrictive; in the United States a film producer could come in and take pictures of whatever he wanted. He told Mitchell that he was being an obstructionist. I was amazed that he had gone that far for me.

BUREAUCRACY IV

I doubted whether Schneider's comments had helped, but I was anxious to find out if there was any news regarding the CID. Mitchell claimed he hadn't received the report from the CID, but mentioned that I would still have to obtain the contract. What an endearing chap! Time was running out and I was getting more desperate. I called the lawyer, Cole, and he offered to go to Pretoria with me to see Mitchell. On the way he told me that his contact had gone out of town. During the entire process of obtaining the visas, this contact never once appeared. At Mitchell's office I began reacting like Pavlov's dog. Instead of salivating, I had palpitations, with visions of an intrigue against me, in which Mitchell's death's head comes to the reception desk. Looking at me with his watery blue eyes, he speaks ominously. "I'm sorry, Mr Rogosin, we have discovered your plot, we are confiscating your equipment and film and will deport you in the next 24 hours." The lawyer spoke to the receptionist in Afrikaans, which sounded like two files rasping together, and snapped me back to reality.

After the appropriate wait we were ushered into Mitchell's cavernous office. He was offended by Schneider's criticism. I was amazed at such a human reaction from him. I expected him to say that such questionable procedure is frowned upon, or not to mention it at all, but to put a black mark against my name. Cole and I are told that he is not being an obstructionist, but that these are the demands made upon him by the head of the Department of Immigration. This is another trick of the functionaries. When they decide to change their instructions, they throw the blame on a higher authority, whom you have never had contact with. I had complied explicitly with their instructions and they added new demands at the last moment. Subtly I reminded Mitchell of this and explained to him that I made binding contracts subject to his advice. I don't remember whether Mitchell nodded his head ambiguously or forced a faint smile. During the conversation he stated, or perhaps intimated, that if the CID cleared me, he would also. I don't understand why I didn't hate the man, but it was not because of charity. Although Mitchell was acting in a most unreasonable manner, he was unwittingly proceeding in a way that could have ruined my plot, and I found this ironic. I began to imagine that their procedure was diabolical, that it was designed to make me panic and expose my real intentions. If so, they were quite adept. I was becoming thoroughly demoralised; yet their behaviour was causing me to become more determined to complete this film.

Back at Finches, Hunter tells me that Lewis has agreed to give me a letter stating that they are interested in the film that I intend to make in South Africa. So is my landlady! This is hardly a contract. I tell Hunter that such a letter will not be acceptable to Mitchell. I mention the commitments that I have made on their behalf and the losses that I will thereby incur. He says that he is sorry, but that this was all that Lewis has authorised him to do. Further argument was useless, and I decided to take the letter since it was better than nothing. I had let my relationship with Finches lapse because of Mitchell's instructions, and now they seemed to have lost interest. I could try and obtain another contract from some other company, but that would take valuable time and might create suspicion. I had the sinking feeling that I was trapped.

Yet I had to go ahead with the preparations. I called Hysveld to order the magnetic tape. 100 000 feet of Kodak film waited patiently in my closet. Hysveld asked me how everything was going regarding the visas. His lab needed work and he was anxious for me to start filming. He offered to help me with the government. One of the members of the board of directors of his company was an ex-Nationalist Member of Parliament, who had a great many contacts in government ministries. Good Lord, this seems like sticking your head into the lion's mouth! Certainly a temptation, but I was frankly terrified to talk to a rabid racist, fearing that he might ask too many questions. I thanked Hysveld, and told him that I would let him know if I needed his help.

Letters arrived from Ernie Artaria and Milek saying that their local South African consulates had sent cables to Pretoria and were awaiting answers. After a week of constant prodding by Cole,

June 2th, 1958

Dear Lionel,

We got your letter of may 28th. The fact tath the visas are still not granted is very disconcerting. For the last for weeks Wettler and I have prepared ourselves for this venture: I was"on call" to leave end of april, Wettler begining of june. Thus we were both unable to accept any work for the summer, not even for on short notice. I had at least 5 offers for documentary and commercial films which I turned down under the assumption that I would be working on your project. With Wettler the case is similar: the summer months being his main recording season he sufferred considerable loss from this insecure situation.

We understand of course that the visa difficulties are not your fault but we hope that you will understand our difficulties likewise.

In our opinion on immediate decision must be taken. We are both not in a financial position to wait indefinitely for your "green light". You must understand that we are professionally crippled and totally unable to pursue our normal interests and income channels. Our position is getting critical. We would therefore appreciate immensely if you could think of any way to bridge this critical waiting period financially. Naturally we will both procure ourselves the necessary visa endorsement for the British Commonwealth.

Hoping that this plea will reach your understanding we wish you both good luck and -au revoir.

Regards

I had made contracts with the crew to commence production on 15 May, 1958. I was now fearful that obtaining clearance would be a lengthy process and that we would never be ready by that date

Mitchell acknowledged the receipt of clearance from the CID. A week seems to be the smallest unit of time on the functionary's calendar. A week to receive a cable, a week to read a letter, a week to receive a report from Johannesburg. I had already brought the letter from Finches to Mitchell, fearful that it would not be satisfactory. Mitchell had accepted it without comment. Cole claimed that Mitchell would clear me and would send his recommendation to the Department of the Interior. At the usual rate that should take several months. I then discovered that Van den Berg was on leave. This was the proper sequence of events, according to Parkinson's Law. In the middle of a case someone goes on leave; usually the petty official who is the only one who has the keys to the official stamp.

Periodically during this process I felt that I was going mad. Although we called every day for a week, the letter did not reach Interior. It was now the middle of May. I was frantic — there is no other description — my production was being completely destroyed. Ernie Artaria should have already arrived to help to set up the production. I should have already begun rehearsing, script-rewriting, and planning the camera angles together with Ernie, and actually I had no idea of when I would get the entry visas, if ever. I was feeling more desperate every day, making frantic telephone calls to every possible source of help. After ten days Cole was able to get Mitchell to send the letter to Interior. Dr Schneider of USIS suggested that I see the ambassador. At the same time through all my friends I frantically tried to find a lead to someone who could get me through the net. The ambassador was out of Pretoria for ten days. Ellie remarked that everyone was terrible, and wondered how we would ever get through, but I insisted I would find a way; there seemed to be a demon driving me, I had to make this film.

What I had witnessed in South Africa increased my determination to expose the horror. The callous way in which I was being treated added to this determination. Almost every day in the press and on the streets of Jo'burg one saw and read of incidents that made one seethe with indignation and frustration. They made me vow to do everything in my power to get the film out: any sacrifice was worth it. I was determined to show what the regime was doing. We had witnessed too much of this sort of thing, it was time to put an end to it. I must have believed that the film could help stop them. It was fortunate that at that time my passion blinded me to how tiny an effort it was, what little effect it would have on the forces of history, which will inevitably resolve themselves in tragedy. It is indicative of the indifference and callousness of the world that only the African, at great cost to himself, and the white population, will finally smash this yoke.

I had a theory that eventually I would find someone, perhaps within the system, who for a purely subjective reason would help me. This was a matter of chance and might take a long time and I was already weeks late. Whenever Ellie said, "I don't see how you will ever get through," my answer was, "I'll meet someone yet, I don't know who or where, but there is someone in Jo'burg who will help me. If only I had more time."

I saw the American Ambassador Byroade on his return to Pretoria, a tall athletic-looking man, pleasant and friendly. He quickly made me feel at ease. He described his recent hunting trip in South West Africa and he talked as if these expeditions were frequent. Witnessing the hardships of the Africans and knowing that this agony-torn country would soon be in a state of crisis seriously involving the United States, I was not impressed by his prowess as a hunter. I felt that he could make better use of his time, but those were the Eisenhower golfing days. I had heard that our ambassadors were of the Ivy League, Wall Street broker and fox-hunting sets. Byroade, I believe, was from all three, and he certainly looked and talked the part.

We were chatting pleasantly, and he was beginning to impress me as a decent sort. Off-handedly, as an introduction to my subject vis-à-vis the South African authorities, he said that he had been touring the country and they had serious problems. I agreed heartily. He continued: "No matter how one feels about apartheid, it is the South African way of life, and one has to respect that. Apartheid is the system in South Africa and outsiders shouldn't interfere. It is their problem and they should solve it in their own way." I was stunned, although I might have expected this point of view. I had heard one US official say that South Africa was in our orbit, which I suppose meant that any kind of inhumanity was excusable in order not to antagonise them. Byroade was a congenial man who obviously believed in "live and let live", the equivalent of believing in nothing. "Live and let live"— the fact that the Africans weren't being allowed to live didn't disturb his congeniality. Whether this opinion was motivated by self-interest or the normal indifference to human suffering, I don't know. American diplomats are picked for their charm and personal wealth. I've heard that a few are short on charm, but I suppose inherited wealth often develops a certain charm of its own.

APARTHEID AND GEO-POLITICS

Returning from Africa later in 1958, I encountered the same mentality among many people. "It is a pity about the treatment of the Africans and one would like to see them free, but after all, the people in power are anti-Russian. Political leaders have to be practical. How they treat those people is secondary in the struggle against Communism. We can't take the chance of a pro-Russian government coming in." The other consideration, that there are heavy investments of US capital in the gold mines, is not mentioned in this polemic. This is a worn-out polemic and many intelligent people have argued against it. They have said that it is against the long-term interests of the US and that it is antagonising the mass of colonial people. The interests of a few large corporations are not identical with the interests of the American people. By supporting the exploitation of Africans we identify ourselves with their enemies.

The real source of this policy, which appears to be Cold War tactics, is irrational. It is not a precise and logical conclusion worked out on the basis of survival, on the contrary it is a defensive psychological bias of an emotional nature. Its source is largely fear and has elements of a destructive and self-destructive quality. It is this that leads us to support the reactionary governments of South Africa, Spain and Nationalist China. It is this that allowed Hitler at the head of the Nazis to crush Europe and nearly annihilate civilization. It is this that has made the US consistently take the wrong course in world politics since World War II. Unfortunately this is the way that policies are motivated and the affairs of men are run. Logically it becomes clear that allowing ourselves to be associated with such regimes will cause us irreparable damage and is absolutely inconsistent with and contrary to the interests of the American people.

A member of the South African United Front, posted in Ghana, laughingly told me that it wasn't healthy to be seen with Americans in Accra. I'm certain that the American public is not aware of this attitude. Our policy in the Congo has succeeded in fooling the

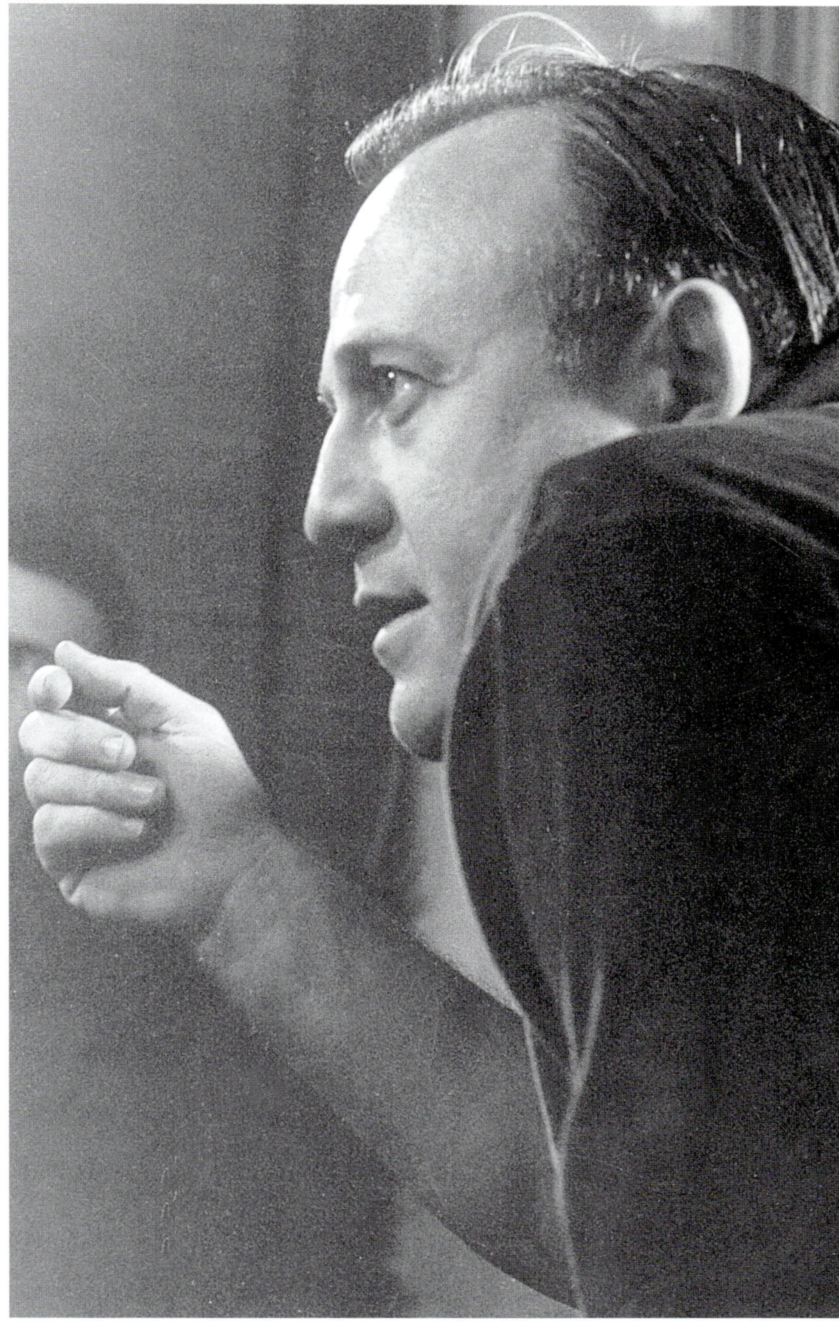

There seemed to be a demon driving me, I had to make this film

American public, but it has not fooled the Africans. The policy of the United States, France, Great Britain and Belgium in the Congo follows the same pattern as the policy of the Western powers regarding Ethiopia and Spain in the Thirties. They thought they were being practical and protecting their self-interest, but this policy in a short time led to the conquest and the subjugation of France, the destruction of Europe and the harrowing bombardment of British cities. Our foreign policy today is an extension of this same mentality and every year it becomes increasingly clear that we are obtaining similar results. Our policy will eventually isolate us from the largest segment of the world's population, and our media of mass communications keep the public completely ignorant of this trend. In 1958 I asked a European journalist why so little information regarding the situation in South Africa was reaching the public. I was told succinctly that since World War II there was a conspiracy of silence in the West. Only when there is an explosion, as there was in Algeria, does the press explore the underlying tensions which can no longer be suppressed. If our policy is entirely a reaction against Russian policy then we will ignore the aspirations of Africans and Asians and treat them as pawns.

When I returned to New York, I heard many radio and TV interviews with visiting African nationalists. They were questioned as if they were on trial: "How do you stand on Russia?" "If you become independent, will you be friendly to Russia?" "Are there many communists in your movement?" Africans have told me that this attitude gives them the impression that the US is not concerned about them, but only about their value as a political weapon against Russia. It is infuriating to be treated so cynically when appealing for help. Africa nationalists are primarily concerned with their overwhelming problems in Africa. Very few are pure Marxists. It would be a wise policy, consistent with our best ideals, to extend our support. Supporting their oppressors will be remembered.

Regarding my difficulties with the South African authorities, Byroade told me that he could not pressure them. I hadn't expected him to. I had come mainly on the suggestion of Dr Schneider that he might be of some help. I certainly didn't expect him to act against American policy, but it was sad that this was American policy. We talk about "freedom" and our "free world" when we associate ourselves with the actions of such a government. South Africa is a country economically dependent on the US and Great Britain, yet we exert no pressure on it. Now that so many areas of Africa have become independent we are taking a sterner attitude towards apartheid, but it should have commenced long ago. Africans who once had great faith in the US were embittered by our policy. They complained, "How can the US let us down like this; you don't invite Africans to official gatherings. You respect all the discriminatory laws of South Africa, and then on Lincoln's Birthday you show us films about the great emancipator, the American Way of Life and the Free World. We know that it is actually the gold mines which are your primary interest." The area of the "free world" includes South Africa and countries similar to it. It would be more meaningful for us to realise how galling it must be to people under the yoke to hear this meaningless cliché. I was not going to hedge with my African friends. I said, "You are right, we must take firm action against it. We must disassociate ourselves from exploitation, and not essentially as an anti-Russian action. That will defeat the purpose, since those we support with this attitude will be justifiably cynical. They will be aware that our reason for helping them is so that they will become our pawns. We should aid those historical forces which will strengthen the stability and progress of the world without the increase of dangerous tensions."

Byroade advised me to see Tom Karis on the embassy staff, whom he claims has a good relationship with the South African officials. Karis is amiable, but can accomplish nothing. He is told that we must go through channels. I know what that means. I feel as exhausted as you do after completing a film and I haven't yet commenced shooting. I then receive a letter from the Ministry of the Interior, demanding information I have already supplied to Mitchell, plus the contract from Finches. How long is this going to go on?

The next time I speak to Karis he tells me that they are perturbed because I originally entered on a tourist visa, before applying for a working visa. My explanation that I wanted to tour Africa first before making my decision didn't satisfy their doubts. In certain countries they want you to submit a script before your arrival. A proper film cannot be written before you see the country, but only a few independent producers work this way and they are unimportant. No respectable motion picture corporation would waste time by having a script written after long observation of the location. Everyone knows that you cannot make money that way.

In the letter from Interior they ask for the reason why the crew didn't apply for their visas when I had applied for mine. If they had applied when I had, then the officials would have asked why they didn't apply after I did. The letter was so official that it made me very apprehensive. They were absolutely determined that I bring them the contract. I was afraid that the slightest suspicion now would cause a long delay. If it should come to their attention that I frequented Sophiatown, or that Africans often visit us, they would investigate more thoroughly. From the time that I landed in South Africa the possibility existed that I might have the film confiscated. Abroad, I imagined that I had a 50% chance of succeeding. As I became acquainted with Jo'burg, I realised that my chances were greater. I told Ellie repeatedly that if I had five months in the country, no one could stop me; even if I didn't have a script written, I would have seen enough of the system to reproduce an accurate film somewhere else if necessary. Nevertheless, it would have been heartbreaking not to film it on location in South Africa and thereby lose so much of its unique quality. Is it a mistake to be so completely uncompromising? If one has the vision that a particular course of action is disastrous, that it will cause infinite suffering, one has to give the warning. Those who are blind to it are sometimes lucky, and sometimes annihilated. I know that I can't make many such films.

I had an alternative scheme in case I was discovered, which I designated "Plan B". Africans occasionally escaped over the borders and this gave me the idea for "Plan B". It was likely that after the first suspicion it would take the authorities some days to clearly establish what we were actually doing. I would plead our innocence, and during this diversion Ellie, the crew and actors would slip out of Johannesburg and cross the border. Undoubtedly I would eventually be deported. Then I would rejoin them as soon as possible and complete the film with the original cast. After I received the letter from Interior, I immediately made enquiries about the requirements for visas to Swaziland.

I was certain that somewhere in Jo'burg there was one person who could and would help me. I believed I must keep on trying every possibility and had to make as many contacts as possible and eventually that person would turn up, but it was maddening how I was running out of time; this was what really made me feel trapped. With enough time I would find the right man. Time, time, time was desperately needed.

I had barely two weeks left when I received a letter from a Mr Bemel who had recently met my father in New York. From the tone of the letter and the letterhead, I sensed that this was the man who would help me. I ran to Ellie waving the letter: "This may do the trick." I telephoned Mr Bemel immediately, he was extremely cordial and we made an appointment to meet the next morning.

At Bemel's office I was given a grand welcome. After all these weeks of being harassed by officials, it was a relief to be treated with some respect, whatever the motives. If Bemel knew what I was up to, he would have shuddered with terror, because he talked with great affection for South Africa. He was not a man whose conscience was troubled by the racism there. On the contrary. South Africa had given him great opportunities, and he said that he was indebted to the country. He did not include the Africans when he spoke of his gratitude. He was excessively effusive and hospitable to me. He insisted that I come to dinner with my wife as soon as possible. Bemel seemed an interesting character, although not exactly trustworthy. Obviously he was an opportunist. He couldn't believe that rot about South Africa, his love for the country etc., unless he was thinking about the gold mines. He was a financier, but he dabbled in many things. He had even been involved in the film business. At dinner the most amusing individual was his youngest son, who was quite unusual, especially for a South African. He was a type you would find more commonly in America, impudent, wild but very bright. For all of his bad manners, I rather liked him. He was only about 13, but he saw through the shallowness of his environment and was not particularly impressed or cowed by his father's newly acquired wealth. Some of his remarks were hair-raising.

Bemel gave me the impression that he was anxious for me to produce a film with him. It's a pity to have such opportunities when you are making a film secretly. I should have persuaded Bemel to invest in my anti-apartheid film under the guise that it was a heroic epic of the Boer War.

He met my father again about a year later. When he saw him he rushed over in a state of animation to tell him that he had met me in South Africa. My father was rather chagrined to tell him that he wouldn't be so happy when he found out what I had been doing. Bemel was staggered when he heard the story.

After the pleasant interlude with Bemel, back to the ordeal at Pretoria. I was still getting nowhere and becoming more and more desperate about the time that I was losing. Soon my visa would expire and I might have to leave the country. This created the possibility that I might have to work with a South African crew, if I couldn't obtain the visas. This alternative was dangerous, because there were no trained African technicians and it would be difficult to find an all-white crew that wasn't pro-apartheid. A colour bar designed to protect white technicians operated in the South African film industry, consequently Africans could not get training. There were some English and Australian cameramen working in Jo'burg, but it was difficult to judge their attitudes regarding Africans. Besides, I couldn't use just anyone, they had to be rather special. They had to believe in the film and be willing to work with unusual methods and conditions.

There was an even more desperate choice. Since Commonwealth citizens didn't need visas and could enter immediately, I could hire an English crew. Unfortunately, I didn't know any soundmen or cameramen who were willing to come. Therefore, I would have had to fly immediately to London and select a crew in just two or three days. The immediate reaction of my advisors, Boris Wilson and Jack Bolon, was that I shouldn't dare leave, because if the authorities had the slightest suspicion they would have the discretion of denying me re-entry into the country. There was still the telephone. I could call some of my friends in Britain and have them choose a crew for me, but directing a film unit is essentially a matter of personal rapport which cannot be left to someone else.

However, I could hire a local production manager to help me with the preparations before the crew arrived. If he seemed sympathetic, I could use him later during the filming, and if not, then I could easily hide my intentions from him before the shooting started. In answer to my inquiries I was told that McPherson was one of the best unit managers. At our interview I found him quite genial. He didn't give the impression of being a bigot. He seemed to have some experience and to be efficient. I decided to try him. The important consideration was how far could I trust him? In a few days I would have a good idea about his attitude towards Africans. Until he saw the script he wouldn't know what my purpose was. Nevertheless, I felt strange to have to work so closely with a unit manager who didn't know what the film was about. Since the locations were the gold mines and Sophiatown, my standard explanation that I was producing a musical travelogue would be bizarre. After long deliberation, I decided to tell McPherson that I was making a TV series of 13 films on South Africa and I would need varied locations. He asked me why I wanted to use Zacharia in all of the series. I explained this by saying that I didn't quite want to make a conventional documentary film, which was completely impersonal; I wanted a personal link between each one of the series.

By this time I had changed my description of the film several times, and I began to worry that two sources would check stories. I had to modify my explanation to fit the situation. If I was discovered by the police in a shebeen in the slums of Sophiatown, I couldn't very well escape with the excuse that I was filming, or doing research for a musical travelogue. There were many things that might puzzle McPherson, therefore I had to mislead and confuse him. To discourage him from asking questions, I patiently explained to him that my methods were very unconventional, indicating a great deal of contempt for film-making that had no originality. He was cautioned not to expect me to work in the normal way. After that he didn't ask too many questions, for fear of showing his ignorance. Some of the things I told him sounded quite wild to Ellie, but he accepted them gravely. My previous film, *On the Bowery* had won many international awards and was known in South Africa.

For several days I outlined what was needed for the filming. Through these discussions I began to get a clear idea of McPherson's mentality. After he learned that one of our locations was Alexandra Township, he took a .38 revolver out of his briefcase and said, "You'll need this, if you go in there." I said to myself, "So that is the story with you." He insisted that it would be impossible to go into Alexandra Township without weapons. I said, "Really?" and feigned wide-eyed innocence. He then went into a long harangue about the dangers of the African locations and townships. He had been to Alexandra Township once or twice, but I couldn't tell him that I had been in the African townships for months without incurring the slightest harm. The only protection I used was three or four African friends to accompany me during the night, but then McPherson had no African friends. In the daytime I wandered around Sophiatown quite freely. I realised how little most whites knew about Africans. Of the hundreds I knew, hardly a dozen had ever been to an African's home or to an African party; they didn't know what they were missing. For that matter, how many people know others of their own race across the "class" barrier — one of the reasons why I started making films.

McPherson shocked me when he pulled the revolver out, particularly since he wasn't the type. He was a decent person, not given to extreme and violent opinions. You would not imagine him to carry a dangerous weapon with which he might kill someone. This is how fear corrupts the Whites. Seven out of every eight white South Africans carry some kind of lethal weapon. They give the Africans plenty of reason to be hostile towards them. I never carried a weapon and I never felt that I had to either. I had no hatred for the African and therefore assumed he had none towards me. It is said that one expects harm from one whom one wishes to harm. This is the psychological basis of the white South African mentality. Equality for the African terrifies them because they are sure they will be exploited as they have exploited and oppressed Africans. I don't believe this is inevitable, but white South Africans are making it inevitable.

An Austrian who had lived many years in South Africa, while chatting to me casually, pulled out a concealed knife blade attached to the handle of his cane. It made me shudder. There seemed to be no conscience or restraint about violence in these people. They considered Africans inferior beings, animals. They were a threat and they could be killed. The idea that Whites caused Africans to become their enemies, and that the responsibility for such a killing would be theirs, in short, murder, never seemed to penetrate. But of course we accept war, legalised murder, in our predatory civilization. If we can kill Germans, Frenchman, Jews, then of course, why not Africans?

In describing the cast to McPherson, I said that Vinah was beautiful. He stopped me dead, in his earnest, kindly way, and cautioned me. "Look, I don't care myself, but this is South Africa; don't ever say that an African is beautiful, don't ever be seen shaking hands with an African and don't ever go into a location without a machine-gun. In this country, you have to be careful, the Whites won't stand for such behaviour." For the accumulation I had made of these felonies, I could have earned a life sentence. I knew that what he said was true, but it was so insane, it made me feel sick.

After I had thoroughly disguised my intentions, McPherson was given a list of locations to scout — gold mines, hotels, garages, etc. I wanted to shoot everything on location. I didn't want to build sets. For the introduction of the film I planned a series of images of Jo'burg, most of which I had already photographed myself. I was anxious to finish these quickly and requested McPherson to recommend a local cameraman. The images themselves would give very little indication of the plot of the film, except that I wanted them photographed in such a way as to create a weird, gloomy mood. A local photographer might resent such adjectives in describing his city, therefore I had to invent synonyms for these words which would not indicate my attitude. Our working relationship was getting more and more bizarre; hiring a unit manager who was not told what the film was all about, and having to direct the cameraman in synonyms in order to obtain the proper mood. McPherson hired a first-rate photographer who unfortunately could only work on Sundays. He did some work for me before the crew arrived that was quite satisfactory.

LOCATION SCOUTING: THE MINES

For months I had been worrying about how I was going to get into the mines. It seemed so hopeless that I couldn't overcome my inertia to begin. I had approached someone in the publicity department of the Chamber of Mines with the idea of producing a film for them. He had not shown any interest in the plan and I let the matter drop. Looking over the list of locations, McPherson amazed me by saying that it would be simple for him to arrange for us to get into the mines. This is just what I had hoped for, but I never imagined it would be so easy. McPherson claimed to have an excellent contact in the publicity department of one of the mining companies, whom he had made films for. I decided to remain out of the discussions completely, because McPherson could talk to him alone with complete conviction. It is easier to be convincing when you believe in what you are saying. He spoke to his friend and told him that I was a famous American film producer who was planning to do a sensational film on South Africa for television. We wanted to include a section about the mines, which were of great importance to South Africa. He did an excellent job of promotion. His friend suggested that as a first step I visit the mines. McPherson arranged for me to visit the East Geduld mine. It is eerie to be 5 000 feet underground, thinking of all the tons of earth above you — a dark, grey world. Visually tremendously exciting. A great sequence can be made here. A film could be made about the gold mines alone, but my purpose is to reveal the entire society.

After the tour McPherson called up his friend at the Chamber of Mines and told him that I was thrilled by what I saw. He applied the flattery generously, and permission was shortly granted for us to shoot in the mines. I never imagined that it would be so easy, but I suppose those in control in South Africa feel invulnerable. They are so conditioned to their society that it is difficult for them to imagine that anyone would want to expose their "benevolent system". Many of them do not consider the disastrous effect this has on the African. This rationalisation is made easier because the colour of their skin is different. In this conflict everyone wears a permanent uniform. The only place where there could be any equality in South Africa was on the telephone. I was determined to make them a little more aware of the horror they were part of. I wasn't optimistic that they would like it, and I was anxious that their awakening didn't take place until I had the negatives out of South Africa.

BUREAUCRACY V

Everyone had failed me, my lawyer, Ambassador Byroade and Finches Travel Agency. I disregarded caution and called on Hysveld, from the lab, for the help he had offered. He arranged a meeting with the ex-Nationalist MP Du Plessis at a government office in Pretoria. They arrived together, and as they approached me I could see that he was a kindly, grey-haired old man. This appearance was disconcerting. I must say this constant subterfuge was distasteful. He was very congenial in manner as well as appearance, and suggested that we have a talk before going to see any of the officials. They led me to a coffee-shop in the cellar of the administration buildings. I still remember it clearly, lined with Delft china tiles which they proudly brought to my attention. What a pity there has to be so much unnecessary conflict! There was no real reason for these men to hate and exploit the African. Yes, they benefit by it temporarily, but in the future it would create problems and perhaps a hell for them. As Du Plessis talked to me in a fatherly way, I could see that he was a real Santa Claus type. I liked both of these men.

Hysveld explained to him what my difficulties were and what they could do to help. I gave him the lions, tigers and happy dancing natives routine. Then he quietly and patiently explained to me that the authorities were afraid of outsiders, that they had had a lot of bad experiences with the foreign press. He said Alan Paton's book *Cry, the Beloved Country*, gave the wrong impression of South Africa to millions of people abroad. By then I was so quiet that I wonder if they noticed how unnerved his conversation was making me. I sat there speechless as he described the exact thing I intended to do. In conclusion he said that he knew that I was all right and did not have such intentions, but I must understand why the authorities were so sensitive. I replied that I understood, but as I said it I wondered if he noticed that the words stuck in my throat. I was almost inarticulate, but I must have nodded my head in the right way because they didn't become at all suspicious. I couldn't understand why they couldn't hear my heart pounding.

When he finished his explanation I desperately gathered my wits together and repeated the story I had worked out and memorised. I told him that I had travelled to many places in Africa, looking for opportunities for producing films. After this survey I decided to work in the Union because it was the only country that had all the facilities that I needed; labs, equipment and also the varied range of subjects, wildlife, tribal life, dancing, etc. One could find practically all the magnificence that was Africa right here in the Union. The government officials had delayed me for so long that I had lost a lot of money. My crew was waiting in Zurich and I had to pay them for every day lost. If I didn't get the clearance soon, I would be forced to change my plans and go to Kenya. As a businessman and member of the board of directors of Irene Laboratory he was considerably more sympathetic than the officials in this same building. The studio was having financial troubles and if I used their facilities it would mean an income of eight thousand dollars. After listening quietly he suggested that we would emphasise that I had made a mistake in obtaining a tourist visa first; that I didn't realise that this was not the proper procedure, and that I should have originally applied for an entry visa for the purpose of producing a film.

We agreed on this strategy and proceeded to meet with a Mr Hugo. Hugo, after paying proper respect to Du Plessis, mentioned

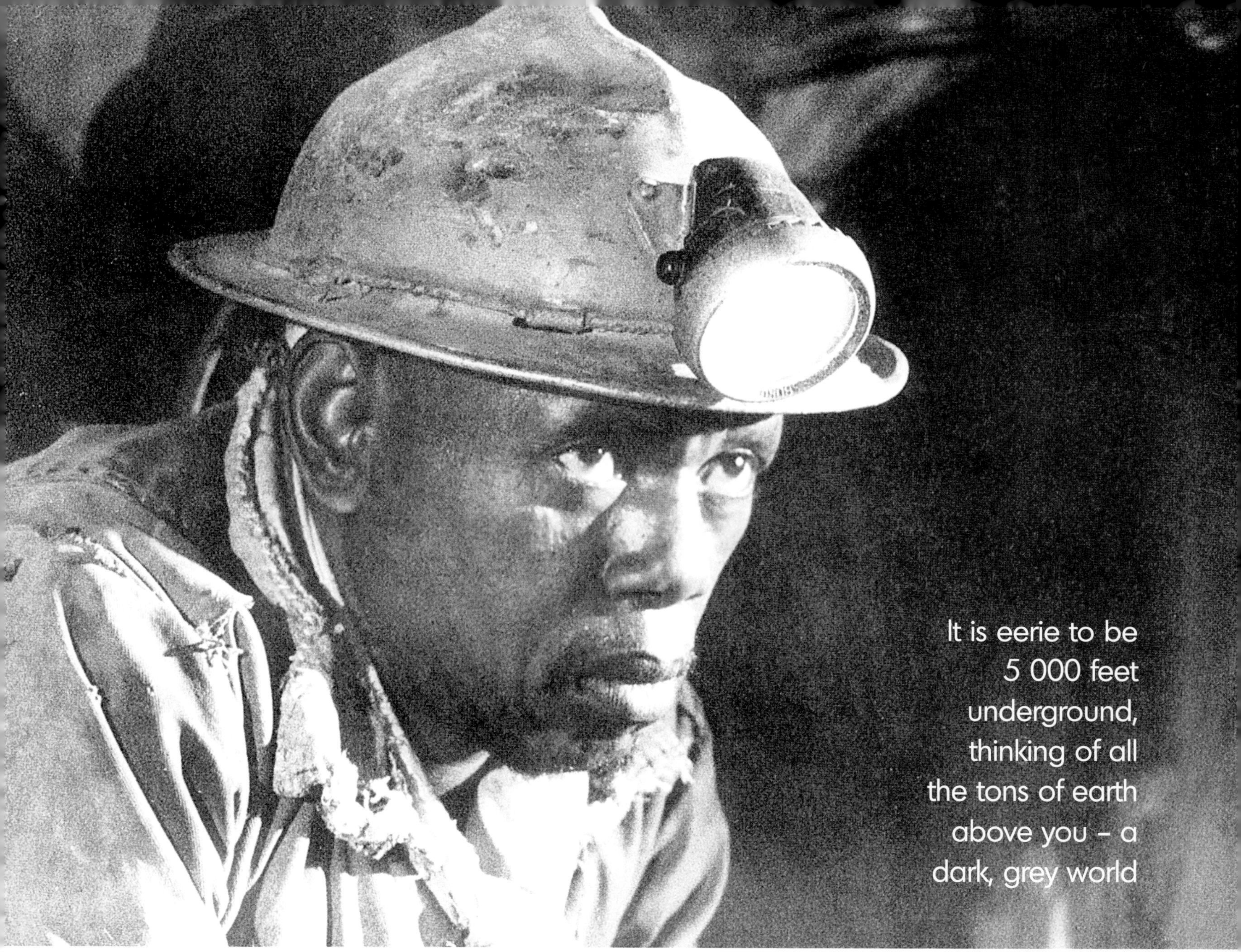

the tourist visa and lectured us about my failures to follow regulations. He informed us that the case was now before Mr Potgieter. In turn, Potgieter informed us that the visas were clearing through channels, which is another way of saying, they are now on a clerk's desk and he is on leave for a month. This is the standard procedure. Du Plessis keeps on trying. We proceed to the secretary of the Minister of the Interior, who tells us that my papers are on the minister's desk. I exclaimed "Whose desk?" although I had understood him perfectly, but the shock of his words was too much and the words just came out. I said to myself, I'm cooked; they must consider the matter serious to have brought it to a cabinet minister's attention. They will now really investigate and I will be discovered.

There was no particular need for such alarm, but it does indicate the suspicion with which all outsiders are viewed. Usually visa applications for journalists and film producers are thoroughly checked before entry, and since I hadn't done this, they were checking me extremely thoroughly. The fact is that up to that time they had no reason to be suspicious. Du Plessis had still another friend in officialdom who promised to expedite the matter. Several days passed, and there was no expedition. Hysveld telephoned them several times and finally decided that we should pay another visit to Pretoria with Du Plessis. We see Hugo again, who announces to us in the grand manner that the minister went to Cape Town. At the time of our previous meeting with Hugo, the minister was in the Kalahari Desert where he had had a hunting accident. (It was the only time that I was anxious about the health of a minister of the government). Hugo said the Minister left implicit instructions that unless I produced the contract, the visa was not to be granted, and there was no one else to talk to.

Every day lost was a terrible hardship. One would have thought that such pressing matters could be turned over to someone else during his absence, but it was my inconvenience, not theirs. It made one wonder at the kind of treatment Africans and Indians received. We withdrew for consultation, and I told Hysveld and Du Plessis that it was an impossible situation. I could not wait until I received the contract, since Lewis was in London and wouldn't return for a few weeks. It would be disastrous for me to wait for him. Both of them were very understanding. I had told them before that the contract was not essential for me to proceed. I would have no trouble finding a distributor for the film. Hysveld, who also knew Bemel, suggested that I try to get a contract from Bemel as a favour, and he also suggested that Du Plessis telegraph the minister, asking him to grant the visas on the basis of another contract. I was hesitant, because it might cause more difficulties, but I had no choice. There was no question between Hysveld and me that Bemel was our best hope. We decided to try to get the contract from him and then telegraph the minister.

The next morning I was in Bemel's office asking him to give me a letter agreeing to distribute my film upon its completion. The fact that Bemel wasn't a distributor was of no significance and didn't seem to bother him either, because after all he was a big shot and could arrange everything. As his secretary typed the letter, I related to him the story of my difficulties with the officials and with Finches. At the mention of Finches' name he jumped with recognition and said, "Why didn't you tell me they were the cause of your trouble? Your problem is solved; one of the top executives over there is a good friend of mine. He once worked for me and I helped him through a difficult period. He will do anything I ask him." This was unbelievable. How can it be that the one person in Johannesburg who was willing to help me happened to be friendly with the one person in Finches who can give me the contract? Bemel was the individual I knew I would eventually contact, but the suddenness of it was unexpected. What a relief! Now I didn't have to risk trying to get a new contract. With a short telephone call, Bemel reaches the manager of Finches, Mr Mauser, who agrees to give me a firm commitment for the film. An appointment is set for that afternoon. I danced with delight outside Bemel's office — perhaps it seemed a bit mad to the African sweeping the hallway, but for me it was being saved from weeks of agonising waiting. Previously when I had been told that I would soon have the visas, I always sensed that I was getting the run-around. This time I was sure the visas would finally be cleared.

At two o'clock that afternoon I cautiously entered Finches. I wanted to avoid Hunter. He would probably warn Mauser that Lewis had refused to give me a contract. Unfortunately, I met Hunter at the entrance. It was too late, but I realised that I should have met Mauser somewhere else. Before I could prepare myself, Hunter asked me if I had come to see him. I had no way of knowing whether Mauser had spoken to him about the contract. Instantly I decided that it was safer to assume that he knew everything, therefore I said, "Yes, I'd like to talk to you." As we walked down the corridor to his office, I tried to gather my thoughts. I had to find out what he knew. I told him that I hadn't yet obtained the visas and that the government wouldn't grant them without a firm commitment from his company. This was ruining me. He learned that I intended to see Mauser and said that perhaps Mauser would consent. He himself could not believe Lewis hadn't authorised it. I repeated all my former enticements to Hunter, this time offering him free publicity in the film at no charge to their company. At that moment our conversation was interrupted with the announcement that Mr Mauser was ready to see me.

Mauser was a burly, easygoing man, who didn't look as if he would be much trouble. In order to avoid delay, I had typed up the letter of agreement exactly as I wanted it. Before we had a chance to begin talking, the telephone rang and Mauser became involved in a long conversation. I sat on the edge of my chair praying that he would finish quickly because I was terrified that Hunter would enter and warn him not to give me the contract. I desperately wanted to get the letter that afternoon at all costs. Finally Mauser finished the conversation, and after a pleasant chat agreed to my request. He asked me exactly what it was that I wanted. I took the letter out of my briefcase and thrust it onto his desk. "Here it is; I've already written it exactly as it should be." It struck me that I was acting a bit desperately, but apparently he wasn't aware of it. He agreed, and said he would send it to me on Monday. With this my temperature shot up three degrees and I blurted out that that would be very inconvenient, since I had an appointment the next morning at the Ministry of the Interior. He then suggested that I come in tomorrow and pick it up. I felt I could not leave his office without that contract. Using my most casual tone I replied that I would prefer to wait and get it that same afternoon. It would only take his secretary ten minutes to type it up and I had time to wait. Mauser again agreed; my first impression of him was right.

Out in the ticket office I waited for what seemed an eternity. I was nearly faint with anxiety, but yet was able to see the comic aspect of my situation. I felt as if I was acting out a part in a Hollywood spy thriller. As the clock ticked away, my entire project, all the months of effort and expense, hung by a thread. Will Mauser give me the contract before Hunter speaks to him? I was praying for the secretary to hurry. Hunter comes down the corridor, and nods to me like the silent reaper and strides into Mauser's office. My stomach plummets. "Now I will have a lot of explaining to do. Mauser will be angry when he finds out, he might even refuse to give me the contract; even worse he might question the entire project." Suddenly Hunter walks out again, smiles benignly and says, "Well, he's going to give it to you." I was absolutely bewildered and delighted. Probably I will never know what took place in Mauser's office or in Hunter's mind. Did Hunter take pity and decide not to mention anything, or did Mauser himself consider it an unimportant matter and decide to help me as an obligation to Bemel? Actually, the contract didn't commit them to pay for the film, so that it would appear to Mauser that there was no risk involved. It would be very strange if Hunter had decided not to say anything. Human behaviour can be quite unpredictable. Thank God.

The next morning Hysveld, the letter and I travelled to Pretoria. I had complied with all of their requirements and was almost sure that my difficulties would soon be over. A slight apprehension would exist until I had the clearance in hand. This day we are honoured to talk to the secretary to the Minister of the Interior. Good Lord, some Boers are huge. This one was red-faced, gross and insensitive as well. I was amazed; now where else would you find such an individual as a secretary to a cabinet minister? I wanted to cast him for my film as a roadgang foreman; he would have been perfect. His manner, harsh and belligerent, suited his appearance. After reading the letter he proceeded to give me an unexpected tongue-lashing, as if I were a schoolboy. Really, it was quite absurd, his rudeness. "Why did you try to pull a fast one," he fired at me. "What do you mean, applying for a tourist visa when you wanted to make a film?"

"I hadn't decided where I wanted to make the film when I left New York. I wanted to look around first." I would have thought this a plausible reason.

He charged back, "Don't lie to me." This man was persistent. "Don't think that you can get away with ignoring our laws and regulations." Ah, so that was it — the small-nation inferiority complex. Here again we meet the paranoiac mentality. These officials had to prove to me that this small country was as important as any other country. It was common knowledge that South African officials were touchy about this subject and their defensiveness was reinforced by the constant external criticism of apartheid. It is not inevitable for small nations to have an inferiority complex nor is it inevitable for people to hate those of other races, but it so happens that people behave this way almost everywhere on our globe. I believe that the Danes, Norwegians and Dutch are not possessed by extreme chauvinism, so I suppose there is hope. With the Boers, one was in greater danger, since their paranoia excites a rage against criticism. An error on the part of a foreigner could easily be mistaken as an affront to the dignity of South Africa. When I objected vehemently to his accusation, he smiled as if he might grant the permission, but said, "Come on now, don't deny it." His final words to us were that he would consider the matter.

I returned home and waited anxiously. Early the next week I received a letter from the ministry granting the visas for the crew. Hallelujah! It was then the third week in June. I cabled the crew to come immediately. The following Saturday, 28 June, 1958, they all arrived at Jan Smuts Airport, amidst great jubilation on both sides and an enormous sense of relief on mine.

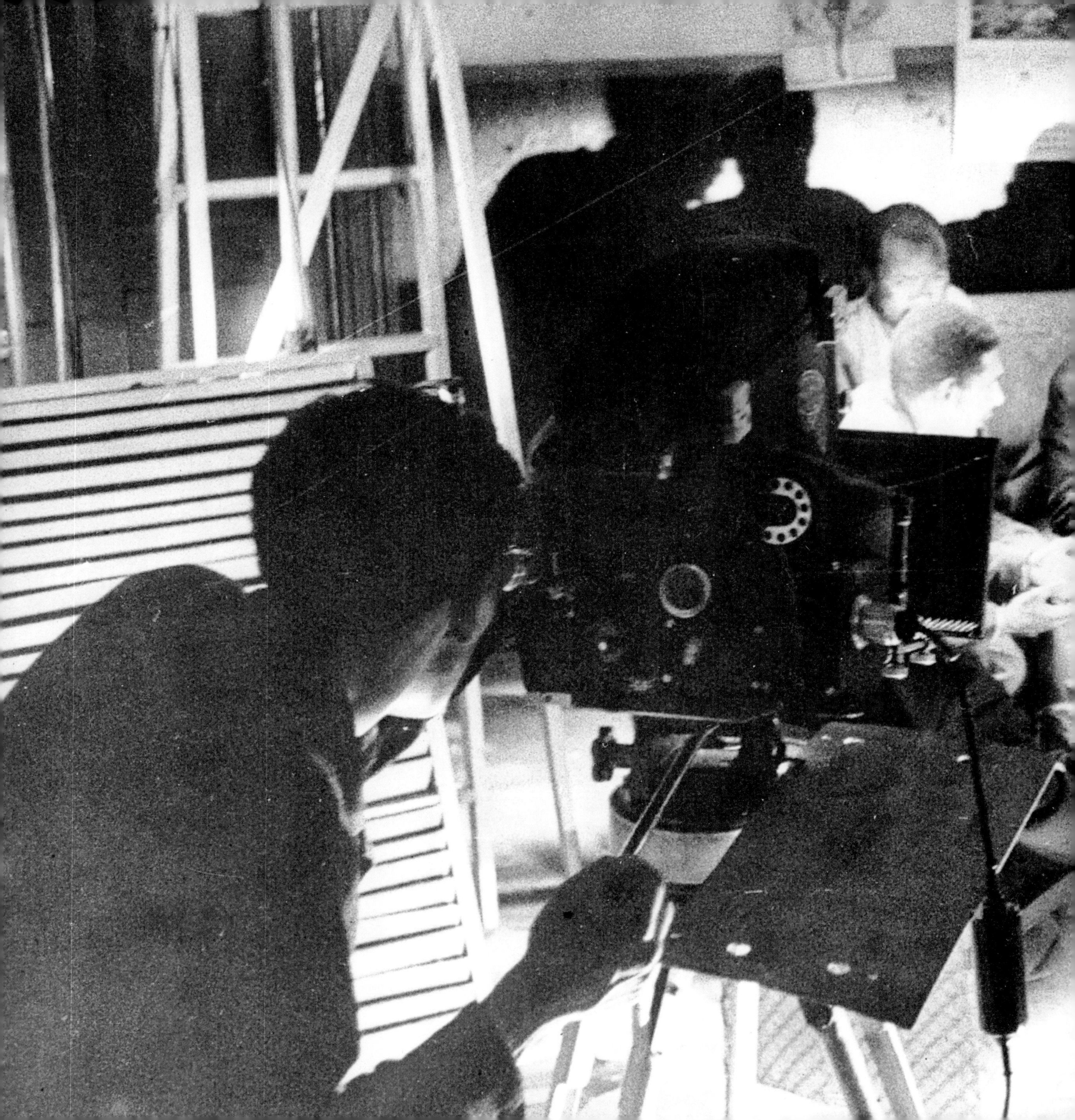

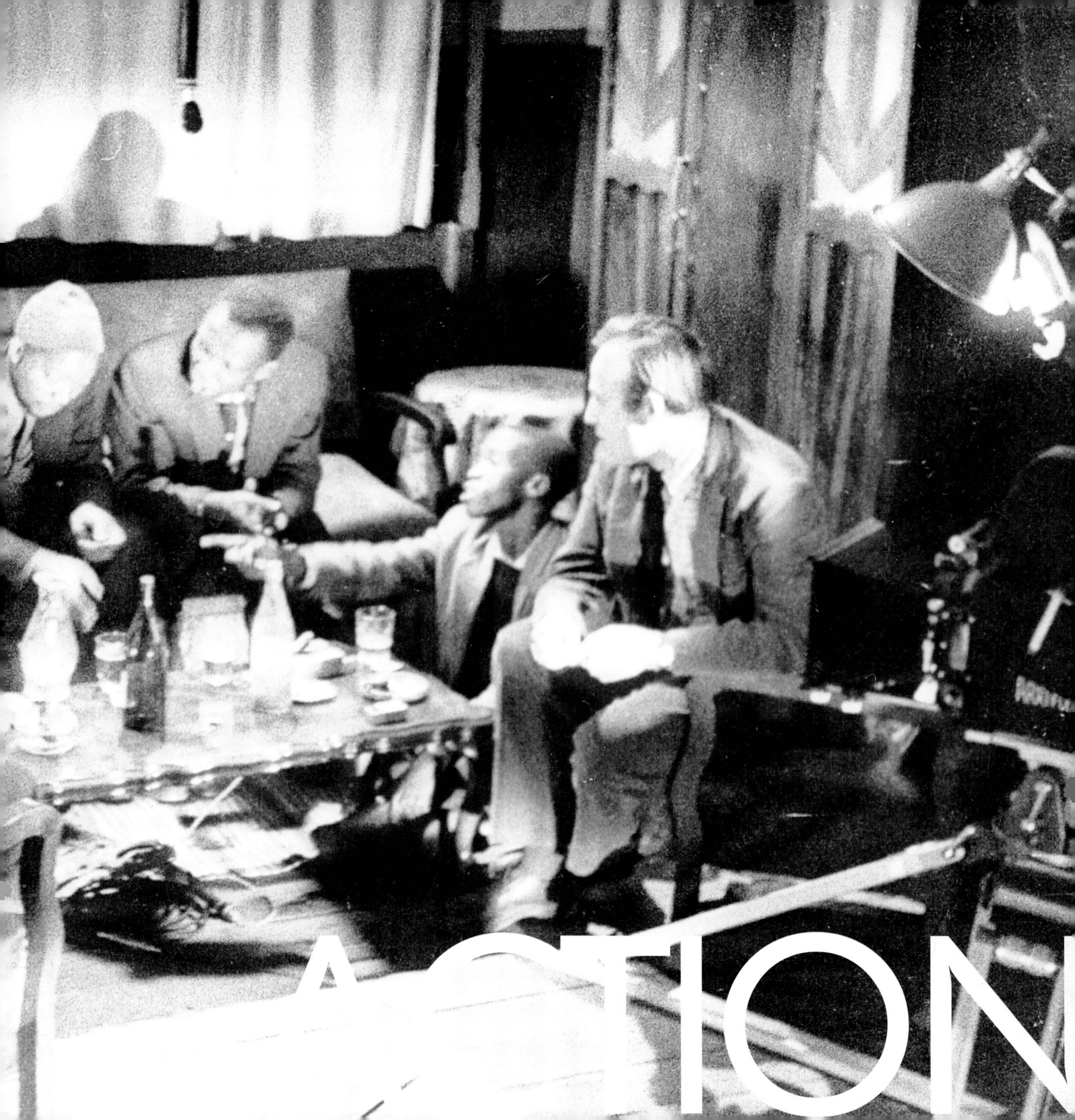
ACTION

THE CREW ARRIVES!

It was now six months after our scheduled starting date. Our visas allowed us only three months. Ernst Artaria was to have come before the rest of the crew to prepare the production in advance. We had now lost that advantage, and it was an enormous undertaking for our tiny crew. That evening, although everyone was tired, we talked for hours. I had never sent the script to Fred and Ernie. When I told them what the film was really about, everyone laughed. They said that they had guessed my intentions. I proposed that the next day we make a tour of Jo'burg, so that they could get a general idea of the appearance of the city. Particularly I wanted them to see the African sections; and we decided that the next evening I would read the script to them. They were anxious to hear it. This was a wonderful moment. There was an air of excitement and anticipation from the whole group.

The next morning everyone was up early. We drove to Bloke's house in Sophiatown. As we sat there drinking coffee in the cramped quarters, Bloke described the life and conditions of the African. This was an entirely new experience for these Europeans who had never known violent racism. I realised that as an American I had an advantage. South Africa never seemed foreign to me. On the contrary, it was amazing how it always seemed so familiar.

They were absorbed and fascinated. That afternoon we drove around Sophiatown. Luckily we found the Bapedi dancers who make the most extraordinary music with old pipes, rubber tubing, toy horns from the bazaar, and all sorts of bits and pieces that most whites would throw away as worthless. The sound to my ears was striking in its modernity, like an African baroque. I had decided long before that I must use the music and show the dance in the film. Besides its cinematic quality, it had a symbolic importance. These Bapedis worked all over Jo'burg. They were partially detribalised, wearing western dress and living an urban existence. For ritual observance they would gather together on certain Sundays and the men, with the women watching, would perform tribal dances in their western dress and with their improvised instruments. They, like the majority of Africans in the cities, were in transition to the machine age. It was wonderful to see this marvellous exuberance and sad to think of the destruction of this potentiality.

We then drove to the African locations. Meadowlands, Orlando, Moroka — what an unbelievable wasteland they are. It is hard to believe that I was criticised later for not having shown these locations in the film as an example of the government's benevolent policy.

That evening the crew was in the proper mood to hear the script. As I read it I felt that they were intensely drawn into the drama. At the end, Milek shouted, "Great!". Ernie was hesitant. He said that the script was exciting, but it would be impossible to realise. It was not a simple documentary as he had thought, it was a full-length feature film. Amateurs could not portray such roles. With a crew of only four it would be impossible to complete a two-hour film in three months. Fred agreed that it would take much longer. On this point I did not agree. I wanted more time, but three months was all we had, and we had to try and finish within that time. We might be able to get an extension from the government, but they might discover our purpose before that time. Looking back at that moment, I didn't realise how close to the impossible it was. I said, "I can't prove that Zacharia can perform this role, but I have absolute faith that he can, and some way or another we will finish it — if not in South Africa, then in Swaziland, Nigeria, Haiti or Harlem."

It was good that we did not know the ordeal we faced, or we might not have had the determination to carry it through. Feature films are usually made with a crew of 20 to 50 people with a schedule of 60 shooting days. We were four professionals, an African driver, a South African coloured (Morris) with no film experience acting as a semi-production manager under Fred's and my guidance, and Ellie, who did a multitude of jobs, and was then seven months pregnant, which didn't prevent her from accomplishing an enormous amount of work for us. After the baby was born and she left us, no one took over her work and our progress became chaotic. We exerted ourselves close to the limit of our endurance, and the aesthetic quality of the film suffered. I did not ignore this; it worried me constantly, but I had to take the risk as well. I felt and hoped that the film would be strong enough to withstand these flaws. When the film was completed, I hated the screenings. It was nearly too much to have to listen to people who felt like Columbus when they discovered a flaw. Film-making is either art or entertainment, it is not supposed to be an endurance test.

Despite the objections of Ernie and Fred, there was no question of turning back now. Our *esprit de corps* was excellent, the theme of the film and the location were exciting to everyone, and we were elated at having fooled the authorities and gotten through the barriers. Fred and Ernie had guessed the purpose, and for this reason Ernie had brought many extra magazines for the camera. In case we were discovered while shooting, we could hide the exposed magazine and give the police one that contained innocent material of music or dancing. Referring to Plan B, they told me that when they received a cable saying that they should obtain visas for Swaziland they nearly flipped. Milek went to the British Consul in Jerusalem, but even the consul didn't know where it was. They had to look all over the map of Africa to find it. We reached quite a pitch of excitement that night and were anxious to plunge into the task, confident that we could accomplish it.

SCREENING ON THE BOWERY

The film society asked me if I would bring in *On the Bowery* to be shown to their members. After some consideration I decided to let them have a 16 mm print, but I suggested that in addition we have a special showing open to the public, since no distributor in South Africa was willing to handle the film. We scheduled our screening for July, 1958. Since my original starting date for the filming was 1 May, I figured that by July I would be finished with the film, but the delays that we incurred caused us the loss of so many weeks that we were only beginning the film by 1 July, a few days before the opening of *On the Bowery* at the auditorium of Witwatersrand University.

When Fred and Ernie heard this they said, "Oh boy, now you'll have trouble. If the authorities see *On the Bowery* they'll become very suspicious." They laughed rather nervously about the whole situation, but I said, "That's all right, don't worry, it will be all right." A few months earlier I would not have taken this attitude because I was very concerned myself at that time that the authorities should not discover that I had made *On the Bowery*, which was a film with a very strong social point of view about the people who were down and out on Skid Row in New York, but I began to understand the mentality of white South Africans and I realised that they would never make the connection between doing a social film in New York and something similar in South Africa. I think it is very significant, this attitude. It shows how blinded people can be to the reality of their own society. Anyone who was a foreigner in South Africa who had heard about *On the Bowery* immediately suspected what I was doing in South Africa, but neither the public nor the authorities ever tied the two things together. Why is this? Well, after being in South Africa and having situations like this happen to me I have come to the conclusion that it is this obsession which creates a blind spot. An obsession is such that it so focuses one's complete mentality that it blanks out thinking in certain areas, and becomes a danger to the person who possesses it.

To the South African mentality one could make a film about homeless men, drunks, derelicts. They could have compassion about people in another society, but there was no earthly reason why there should be any connection between this and a feeling towards Africans, who after all don't count, to their way of thinking. Partly they think of them as animals and partly they don't think of them at all, in a certain context. Sometimes I wondered why white South Africans, who seemed to be very kind in many ways, could be so inhuman to Africans and so disregard their human feelings, such as the way they herded them in the mines, treating them like cattle. After a while I came to the conclusion that the mental trick is to consider them like animals, and once you do this then it is quite possible to treat them like that, so that you can believe that you are being kind when you are actually being inhuman towards your fellow man. Despite the fact that I felt fairly sure that the people would not catch on to my intentions from seeing *On the Bowery*, I was still not certain, and I would never have okayed the screening before our film was completed. But it was done, and I had to go through with it, figuring that there was at least an 80% chance to get away with it.

Fred and Ernie were half amused and half apprehensive about it. I told them, "Don't think of South Africa as you would other places. It's a bit crazy here. You can never tell what reaction you will get. You won't get the normal reaction. Things you think you can't get away with you can, and things that you think you can get away with you can't." About a week before the film opened articles started to appear in the press, and they were extraordinary. They could not have been better reviews, and one of the big papers, the

Sunday Times, gave us practically a full-page spread. It assured a good sale of the tickets, and by the middle of the week we were pretty nearly sold out. The auditorium was quite large and we were sold out for three nights in a row, and on the last night people were turned away. Over 2 000 admissions in all, and the distributors had said that this film would be unsuccessful.

SHOOTING COMMENCES

We started feverishly preparing for the first shoot — the political discussion in the shebeen, which was to be the climax of the film. It was one of the most difficult scenes to shoot of the entire film, considering that I had never worked with these people before, and I was trying something rather new in the form of dialogue. I was very disturbed to have to do this scene first, but I was forced to do so because Miriam Makeba was leaving for the Cape on a tour with *African Jazz* at the end of the week, and would not return before September, 1958.

When I showed Fred and Ernie our locations for the various scenes, we discovered that we would have to build sets, since shebeens and houses in Sophiatown would be too small to do any proper shooting in, because the cameras would be too close to the actors. I found this disturbing, not only because it meant an enormous amount of work before the first day of shooting, which had to be Thursday of that week at the latest, but I also had never shot on a set before. I had always used the natural location, since it was my principle to make it as real as possible simply for the sake of non-professional actors who needed a natural setting. We thought that we might perhaps find a place on somebody's private estate that had lots of land on which we could build a set and be undisturbed. Of course, we did not know anybody like this at the time whom we could trust.

During rehearsals at Martha's shebeen, I discussed with the crew where we were going to build our sets. We couldn't find a solution, until finally Martha suggested using the Community of the Resurrection's empty schoolrooms that the priests had closed down when Father Huddleston refused to comply with the Bantu Education Act. I immediately said, "Marvellous, that's exactly the place, that's it! They will let us do it! It's great, it's wonderful!" This was ironic, because the government's Act had caused the school to shut down, but had given us a studio set.

I set out to contact Father Singleton, whom I had met earlier, to find out if it would be all right for us to use this school as a studio. Permission was granted the next day and we were ready to begin shooting there. In addition to building the sets, all the equipment had to be put in order, cables attached, and a lot of work done before the first day of shooting. Besides that, I had to try to rehearse the group. It was an extremely difficult scene, involving many people, a scene with intellectual and perhaps philosophical concepts — a great number of factors to control, in a directorial situation which I had never handled before, with an entirely new crew who had never worked together.

I brought the portable tape-recorder to one of the shebeens and Bloke Modisane, Can Themba, Lewis Nkosi and Morris were all there for a rehearsal. I had them discuss their ideas about the political situation in South Africa and their attitude towards the whites, and the social situation under apartheid. The rehearsal didn't go too badly.

It was my idea that in order to maintain spontaneity, I would have them discuss the same things that I heard them discuss many times in the shebeen. These were things that they were familiar with and believed in. I had found in my shooting of *On the Bowery* that when one uses non-professional actors who are actually part of the scene, they can speak about their own lives with great ease, without written dialogue, and spontaneously. However, an enormous amount of time and film footage is used up in shooting this way. I hoped that by having them discuss their ideas only on tape beforehand, I would have a record of their conversation as a guide for shooting.

By Thursday we were ready for the shoot. We started on the set early in the morning, and it took us quite a long time to set it up, so that we didn't start shooting until the afternoon. Most people came late, which is not untypical of Africans. Miriam came in the afternoon and stayed for two hours, and then said that she had to leave, but would return at eight o'clock.

In the meantime we were ready to shoot the scene, and we started the conversation rolling. There seemed to be some personal conflict with one or two of the people, and we got off to a very bad start. We had a few good takes, but then suddenly the thing bogged down. Can was quite good, but the others were flat. I kept trying

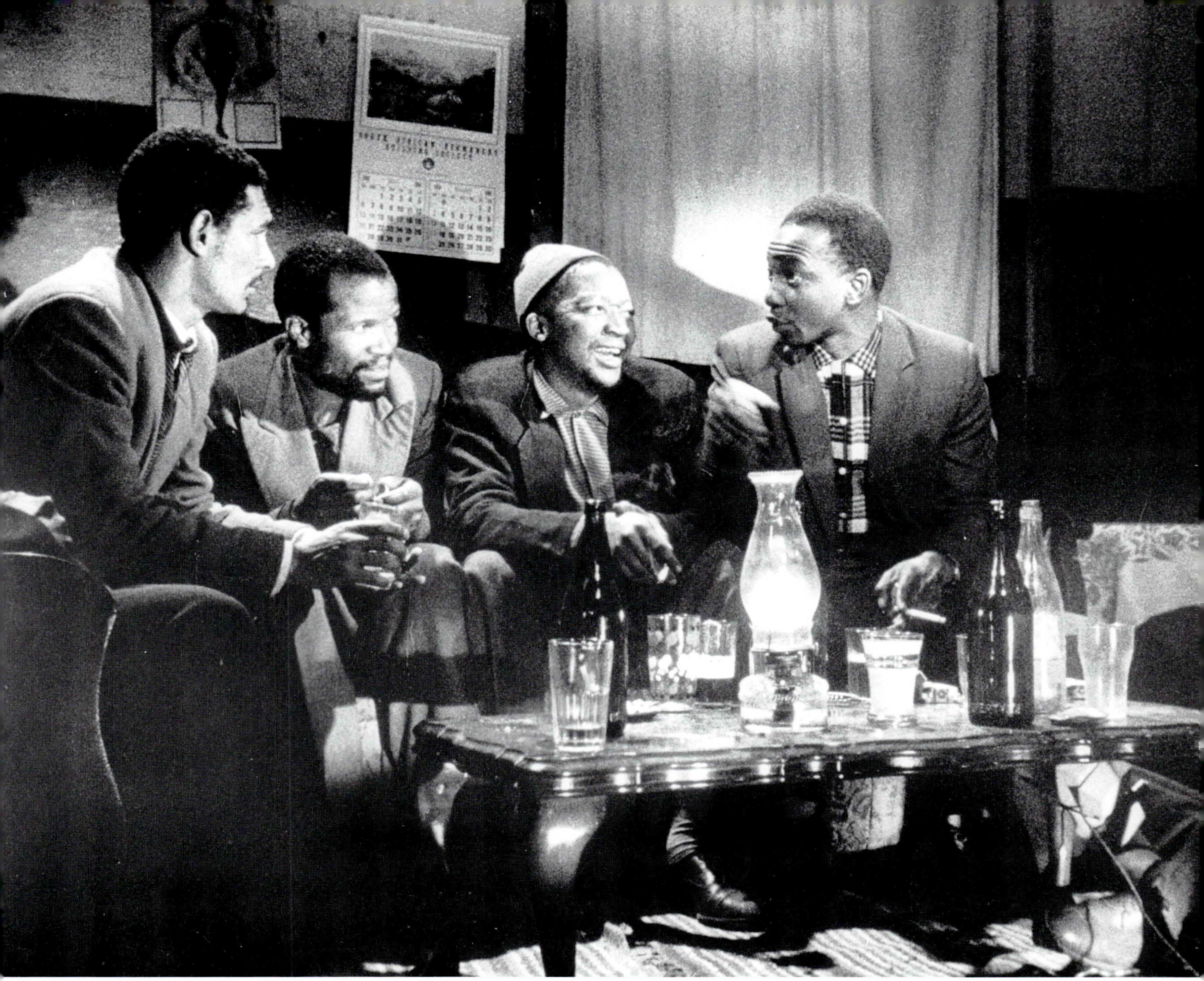

"It was one of the most difficult scenes to shoot of the entire film, considering that I had never worked with these people before, and I was trying something new in the form of dialogue"

rehearsal after rehearsal, and take after take, but we just could not seem to get started. Finally I said, "All right, there's no point in continuing. All of you go home, and we'll try again tomorrow." By this time Miriam had returned, but instead of eight o'clock it was 12, and too late to do anything further with her.

Miriam had now decided that the amount of money we had agreed to pay her was not enough, and was holding out for more. We agreed to her terms since it was imperative that we finish the scene, and she agreed to come back again later on during the week. She had engagements every evening, so we had to arrange our shooting schedule to shoot her songs at midnight.

The next day some of the cast were extremely late, and we didn't get started until several hours after the scheduled time. We went back to the group discussion again, and this time they were excellent. I think that Bloke, Lewis and Morris were a bit upset by the fact that I had said that they were no good the day before, and had been thinking over what they were supposed to say, so that by the time we came to the scene, it went along handsomely. I always found this to be true, that when we were able to do a scene over again it always went much more smoothly than on the initial try. It seems that people had a chance to absorb the ideas, so that when they tried it again it came out freely. Late that night, Miriam came by for her songs, and we worked quickly and finished with her in the one night.

We finished shooting the discussion group in the shebeen after a few days of very heavy shooting. We then started shooting some of the other scenes, which were a little easier. On Sunday we were up at five am to shoot some of the dawn scenes of Johannesburg. The filming was very difficult, considering all our problems and the small crew. We also had to ferry our heavy equipment back and forth between sets and our flat. I can remember many nights arriving back between 11 and two in the morning, and hauling the stuff up the stairs, and getting up the next day at seven o'clock.

We now had been shooting about a week and I was determined to ship everything that we had shot out of the country as soon as possible. We made arrangements to ship by Pan American Airways. There were two flights a week, one on Tuesday and one on Saturday, and I wanted all the material out, as much as we had shot, on each of these days. After the first week's shooting we did not meet the shipping date because of difficulties with packing the film. We were not able to find anyone to do it for us, so in addition

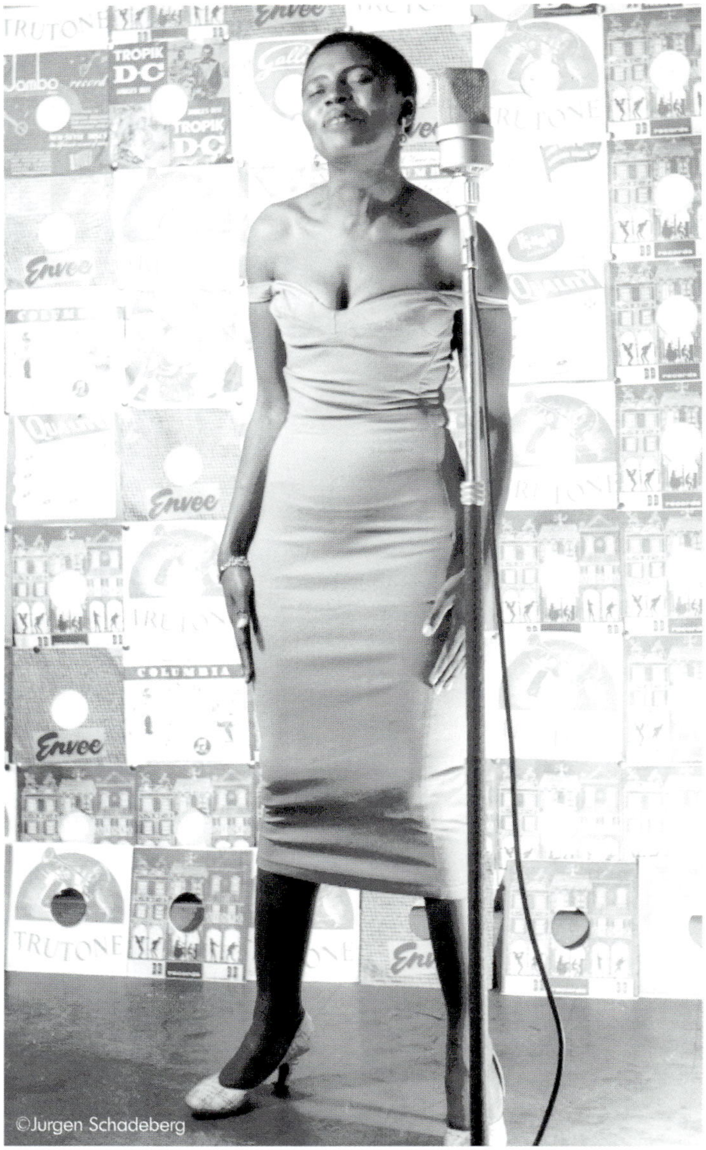

©Jurgen Schadeberg

"Late that night Miriam came by for her songs and we worked quickly and finished with her in one night"

to all our other work, we had to do this too. It was time-consuming for the already heavily overworked crew.

We were beginning to feel fatigued.

A MAN POSSESSED

After four weeks I was affected by a numbness, and I found myself directing in a kind of forced stupor. The constant fear and the chaos resulting from the lack of a proper production manager became agony — I had to drop McPherson because I wasn't sure I could trust him. Fred and Ernie's estimation that we would need much more time was more valid than mine, but they were being driven by a man possessed. I don't believe I can do another film against such odds. I will never forget Ernie saying one evening at dinner a few weeks after we had begun that if I continued to make films in such a way, in a very few years I would be dead. Fred and Ernie were right according to logic and usual procedure, but it is the irrational and the emotional which often makes things possible.

Odd that during that time I was never discouraged. After the film was finished, when I was submerged in the sordid and depressing effort to get it distributed, I often had a profound sense of discouragement. Selling the film was more discouraging than making it, but with such a film every step is agony. Yet in those days, at moments I felt a kind of joy in our attack, a release to be able to fight back at these monsters — so like the Nazis who had killed millions of defenceless people. I kept my head at some fairly dangerous moments because of this.

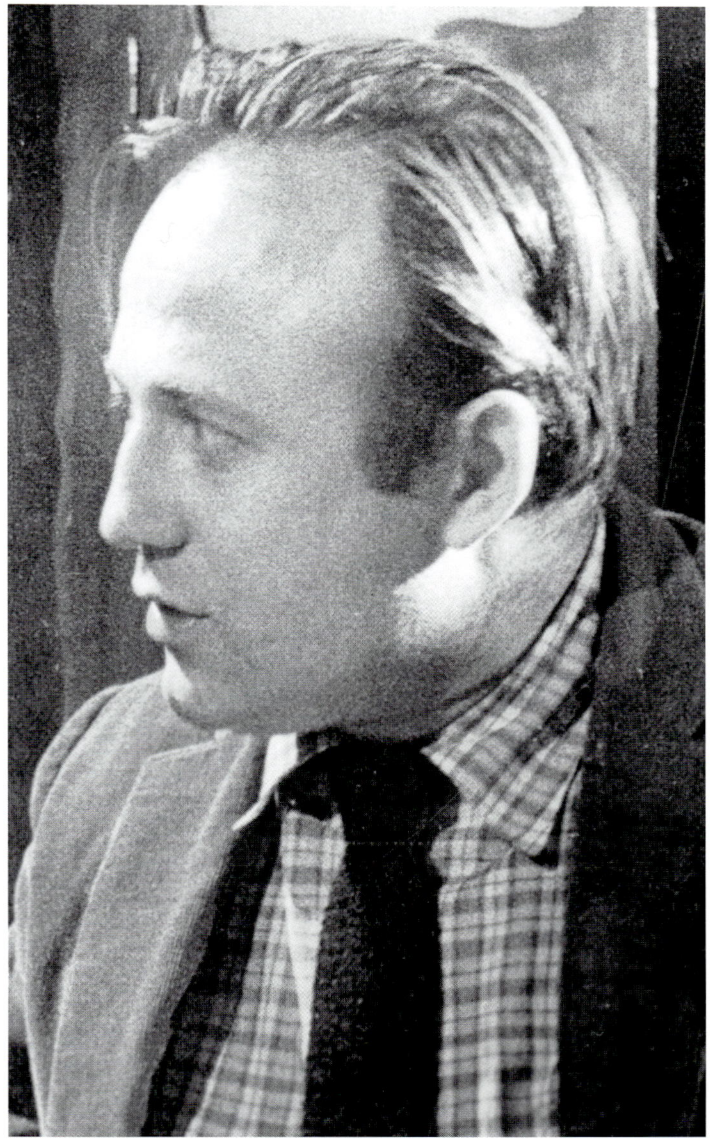

"After four weeks I was affected by a numbness, and I found myself directing in a kind of forced stupor"

MINE SHOOT

We had been going nearly a month, with only one day off. This was largely because Fred and Ernie wanted to get back to Switzerland as soon as possible, and of course I was agreeable since I was anxious to finish the film before we were discovered, but I felt now that Fred and Ernie were pushing us to the breaking-point, and I insisted that we take a weekend off. We decided to go to Rustenburg in the mountains west of Johannesburg. While visiting some caves, Ernie felt faint, and we felt sure that he was going to pass out before we got him to the surface. Apparently he had some problem with closed spaces, and once nearly fainted in a cinema in Zurich. He would be no good for shooting in the mines, and I would have to use one cameraman for this work. I was a little concerned because I wasn't sure that Milek had enough experience to light the mine sequence alone without Ernie's help.

I sent Milek and Fred out to the gold mines of Marievale. Then we all went to see the mines and make arrangements with the general manager, a Mr Stoddard. He was a Canadian rather affected by his position in South Africa, and he took on the air of an admiral or a general. He was quite cordial, but one had the feeling of an undertone of temperament.

I told him that we would like to shoot the entrance to the mine in the early morning, and the elevator itself, the trains below and the underground work. I felt very uneasy discussing this with him, since there was a fear of being discovered, and here we were going right into dangerous ground. But he said that this would be quite all right, and asked us to discuss it with the supervisor who would set up anything we would need.

The supervisor was extremely helpful. We went around with him all over the mine and down to below about 6 000 feet. We also looked at the school where the recruits were trained. Milek went to another official to discuss shooting in the mine compounds, and it was very amusing because the man he spoke to kept saying, "It's a pity you've come at the wrong time of the year, there's no green." Later I went to talk to the same man, and he reiterated the same thing. After we left them we looked at each other and laughed, thinking about the pity that it wasn't so green, and how it would affect our film.

Actually, the school here was pretty much the same thing as I was going to get at East Geduld, and I wondered if we couldn't shoot all of it here to save time. I asked the supervisor, and he said "Okay".

We were back early to film the training school. It was about 11 o'clock, and we were shooting the scenes of the Africans learning to shovel, when suddenly I saw Stoddard coming over in very rapid strides. He motioned to me peremptorily. I felt a sudden surge of nervous tension; I sensed trouble. As I went to him, he started to shout in an extraordinary manner that shocked me. At the top of his lungs he was yelling that I had duped him.

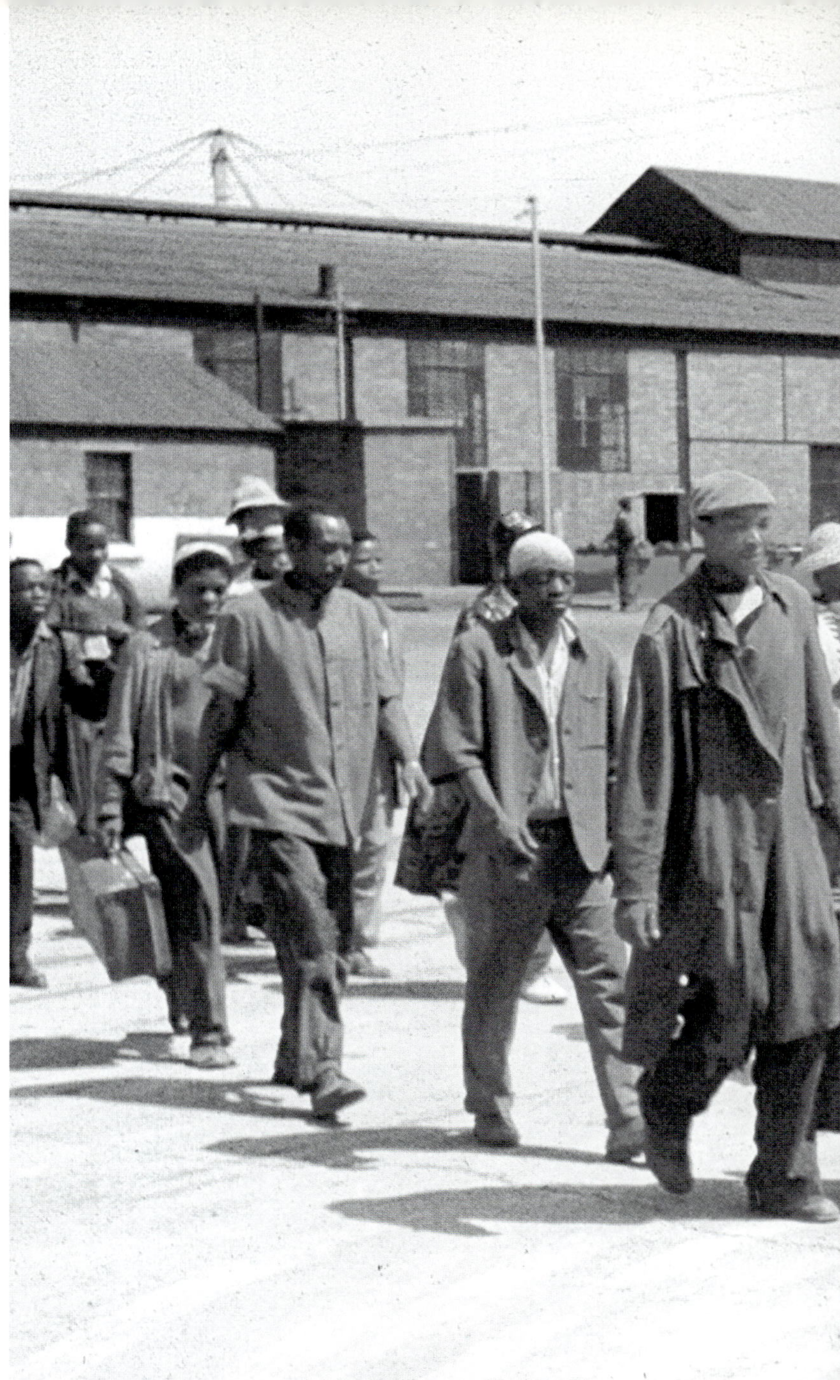

He was angry because we had started to shoot scenes on the surface instead of below, in the mine, as we had originally told him

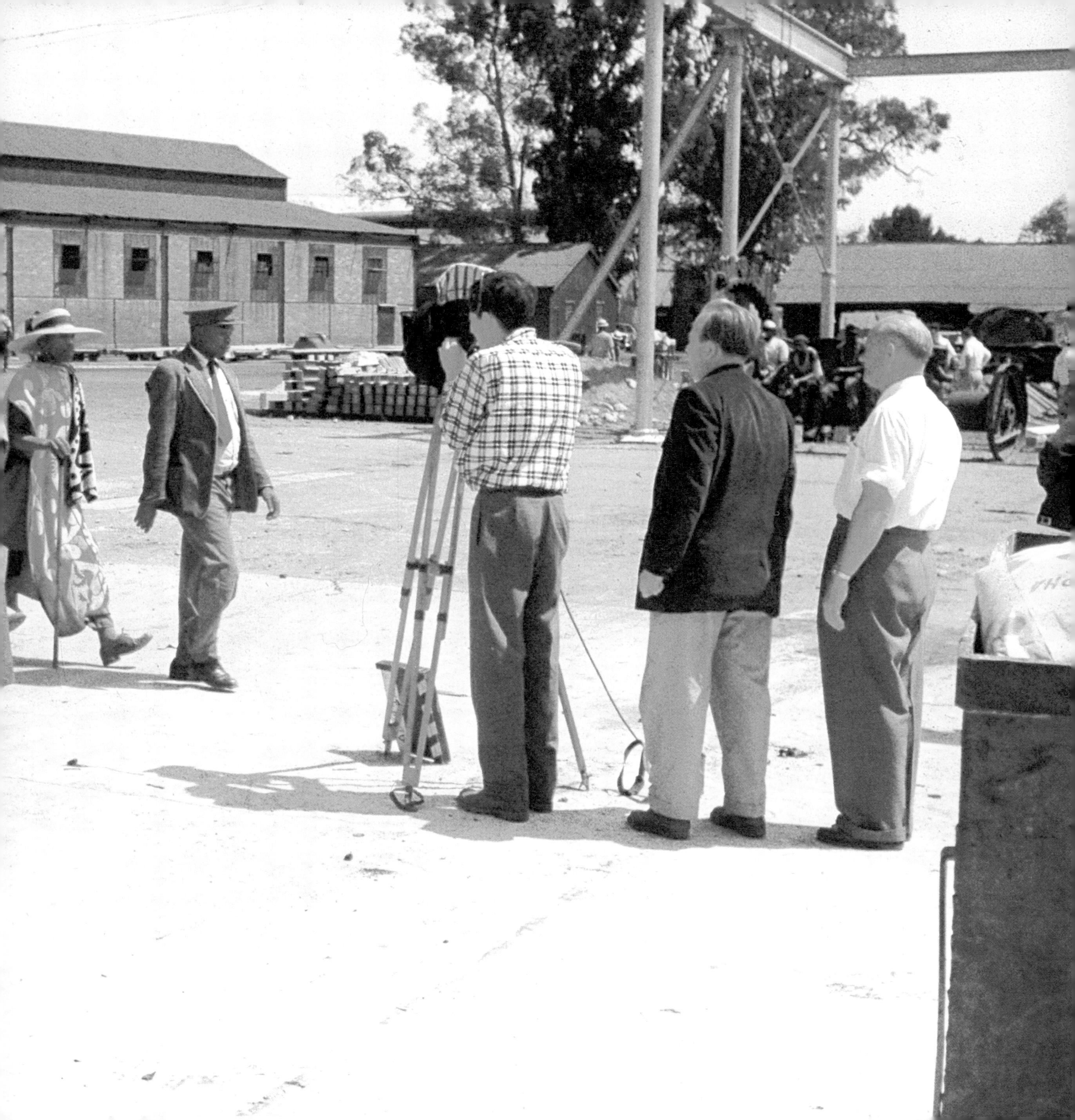

At first I was terrified, because I was sure that he had discovered what we were doing, but I soon realised that he was talking about the most amazing thing — he was angry because we had started to shoot scenes on the surface instead of below, in the mine, as we had originally told him. I was perfectly innocent in this; I felt that with the supervisor's okay it was quite all right.

I was amazed at Stoddard's fury and began to wonder what kind of fear lurked beneath the exterior of this man. I am sure that if one were to probe, a lot of guilty feelings would be found in these people, who certainly know that they are exploiting the Africans, and that what they are doing is not proper according to their own conscience. There must have been fear on his part that we would discover something somewhere that wasn't quite right, and of course our doing something that wasn't strictly according to instructions brought out this fear.

Certainly he gave me a terrible fright: in his anger he might investigate us more thoroughly and find out what our game really was. He was so hysterical that I realised that arguing would be to no purpose, and that I must keep calm myself. This was a very dangerous moment, and any loss of control on my part would cause us to be discovered. So I used all of my energy to calm him down. I apologised profusely, told him that it was not my intention to go against his orders, and that I wasn't aware of breaking the regulations. He still continued to be very abusive, but he calmed down considerably. He told us to stop shooting immediately and not to do another thing.

I said, "All right, if that's what you want, we'll do it," and we immediately started packing up to leave. He said, "As soon as you have your equipment packed up please come to my office." I did so, and told him that the supervisor had given us permission to shoot. He called over the supervisor and questioned him, and the supervisor agreed that he had given us permission, but Stoddard said that that didn't matter, because I had asked him to shoot below and then I started shooting the mine school; I asked permission for one thing and then did another. I told him that I thought the supervisor had the authority to let us shoot in the mine school, and he said that this didn't make any difference. He said, "You must stop working, and I'll check with head office." By this time he was somewhat mollified and a little more congenial. He said I should call him later.

Now I was extremely concerned. I was afraid that his questioning might cause suspicion at head office, and that there might be further investigations with Pretoria before we were allowed to go any further. Since my permission to bring film into the country was based on a travelogue and there was no mention of shooting the gold mines, this might cause suspicion there and sabotage our entire project. I was filled with apprehension from this moment on.

As I was getting into the car someone from Stoddard's office called me, and I slammed the door and caught my fingers. It was the very heavy door of a Buick and it was quite painful, and I was sure that I was going to lose the fingernail. We went over to the surgery and tried to get medical attention. I must say that I was quite annoyed with myself, because this was no time to have such a problem occur. I had two extremely painful nights, and the finger was quite swollen for a couple of days. But my fear of not getting into the mines overshadowed the pain.

In the meantime we did not want to stop, so we went to East Geduld and did our filming of the surface there, and the mine school, the compounds, etc. Then after a suitable amount of time I called back at Marievale and spoke to Stoddard, and he told me that he had spoken to head office and had gotten the okay for us to go ahead.

It certainly was a relief. I sent Milek over to make arrangements for the shooting. We planned to leave at four o'clock in the morning and drive over to Marievale. George Malebye, our driver, was supposed to bring our lead, Zacharia Mgabi, at this time. They didn't arrive until 4.30, which delayed us. We started off in a hurry, and suddenly after ten minutes of travel Milek discovered that he didn't have his light-meter, so we drove back to get that. Then began the long haunting drive through the night, the lights coming the other way giving me nightmares. We finally arrived quite late, around 5.45 or six am.

We went immediately underground. Down below, we loaded all the equipment onto a large cart, and trudged a mile underground. Milek set up the shooting, and as we were filming the men working, the lights started to burn out. After a few minutes, all were extinguished except three. I didn't say anything, but I felt desperate that we could lose the entire day's shooting.

Now we were going along quite well when suddenly the foreman smelled gas from an explosion. This is one of the dangers of the mine, in that cyanamid gas is given off from an explosion, and five minutes of inhalation burns the lungs so badly that the victim will die within 24 hours. There was only a slight smell, so we had to stop for only about half an hour.

After we finished our day's work and came to the top I received word that the general manager wanted to see me. I wondered what rage he was in this time. Apparently his hysteria was quite accepted by his subordinates; they were rather amused by his tantrums. By this time I was beginning to realise that this was his personality and nothing particularly to do with us.

He was furious because we'd arrived late. He said that we had caused him a tremendous amount of trouble and enormous cost because thousands of miners had to stand around. We had been a bit late, but I didn't have any idea that it would cause so much trouble. I don't think that it really had; he was just a man that needed to make a fuss. He was quite abusive, and his language was pretty obscene, and I was getting a bit annoyed with his behaviour. He was talking to me as if I was one of his servants. Under ordinary circumstances, I would have certainly told him that he had no right to speak to me in such a way. However, in this case I had to hold my tongue. It was an effort.

But he was right about being late; it was my responsibility, even though it was not my fault. I was quite annoyed at my crew, at George, our driver, and Zacharia, for having caused us this difficulty.

Stoddard claimed that we were supposed to be there earlier than I had thought. I told him that this was not my understanding. After much discussion, we finally mollified Stoddard again, and made sure that we agreed upon the time for the next day's shooting. In order to avoid any further problems, we decided to get up at three am the next day.

By this time it was becoming almost agony. We were already fatigued from our days of hard work, and these hours were very wearing. But we arrived at five am the next day and were well prepared for the shooting. Ernie took shots up on top, and we went down below for the long walk to the working gallery.

Zacharia seemed quite apprehensive and frightened. During the morning, as we were working, the side wall started to burst. At first there were little explosions, as if a bullet had hit the wall and splattered, only they were coming the other way, from the wall out. I was the first to notice it, and called the attention of the foreman. They told us that this was the way a cave-in usually began.

The foreman walked over to the wall and pounded it with a hammer. He stood back and said, "We had better get out of here. This doesn't look too safe."

We went out, and came back a few minutes later when the wall had settled a bit. We finished all of the underground shooting that day, which was a good thing because we had about reached our limit for the moment, particularly with all the tension Stoddard had added. We went to the surface and decided to take a long shot. By about four in the afternoon I began to feel rather numb, as if my feet were stepping about a foot off the ground — that strange feeling one gets on rising at an unusually early hour.

EXHAUSTION

Shooting in the mines seemed to have completely exhausted us, and the next day Milek came down with a fever, which was diagnosed as the flu. I decided to continue shooting, and I said to the rest of the crew that even without one cameraman we could still shoot with two cameras. I suggested that Ernie set up both cameras, and Morris would switch on when the dialogue began. Even though he had no experience, it would be a simple matter for him. It was a pretty drastic procedure, but I couldn't afford to lose a single day.

The pace seemed to be telling on all of us; Fred came down with an infection which put him out of commission for a day or two. Later I got a cold, but luckily it wasn't too severe and I was over it after one day in bed during our day off. We were under such physical strain at this point that I prayed that we wouldn't all get sick.

In the meantime we were having great difficulty directing the actors. I found that Zacharia and Vinah Bendele, who played his wife, were not as good as I had hoped with ad-libbing. I found it particularly difficult with Zacharia, who had trouble understanding and speaking English. Contrary to my expectation, I was not able to just give the theme to Zacharia and Vinah and have them ad-lib, but I actually had to make up dialogue for them as we went along. It was like writing a dialogue script on the set. I found that this, in addition to the normal functions of directing, was very tough.

I was also having trouble getting the actors to the set on time. It was George's job to pick up Zacharia and Vinah and all the other actors appearing in the scene for that day, and to arrive on the set promptly at eight. For several days Vinah, Zacharia and George appeared a bit late, and one morning they kept us waiting for quite a while, holding up shooting. The situation was becoming difficult; we were losing time and it was crucial that I finish according to schedule. I spoke firmly to Zacharia and Vinah, telling them that this would have to stop. Vinah's answer was that she was late because she had to have her breakfast after arriving in Sophiatown; she couldn't have her breakfast earlier because she couldn't eat that early.

This angered me considerably, considering all the problems that we had to face. She really had me over a barrel. I couldn't afford to lose her by then and would have had to give in to most of her demands, but I decided to take the risk of being strong with her in the hope that she wouldn't call my bluff. I took an on-the-spot decision: I replied that if they couldn't be on time, and this included Zacharia, who I knew was quite reliable, then I could get lots of other people who would be anxious to work in the film.They both backed down from their position and from that day on I had very little lateness from either Vinah or Zacharia.

The next Sunday we were up early again to shoot the views of Johannesburg. It was now getting on towards the middle of winter, July and August, and becoming very cold in the early morning. We were not prepared for this, since the days were warm and we had summer clothing, but it was really freezing some of those mornings.

We still had two unsolved difficulties regarding security. One, we couldn't shoot efficiently from a production point of view because we had to leave the most dangerous scenes (i.e. those involving whites) until the end, rather than shooting in the most desirable order. And two, we could not use local facilities for looking at the rushes, because then the technicians would have seen what we were doing. Finally, I located by accident an old 35 mm portable projector, so we were able to screen the rushes in my flat every night after our work on the set.

Before we started shooting in Alexandra Township, I was again concerned about what would happen if the police saw us. I met a film director at the same time who said that he had been shooting in Alexandra and had been stopped by the police, and that he

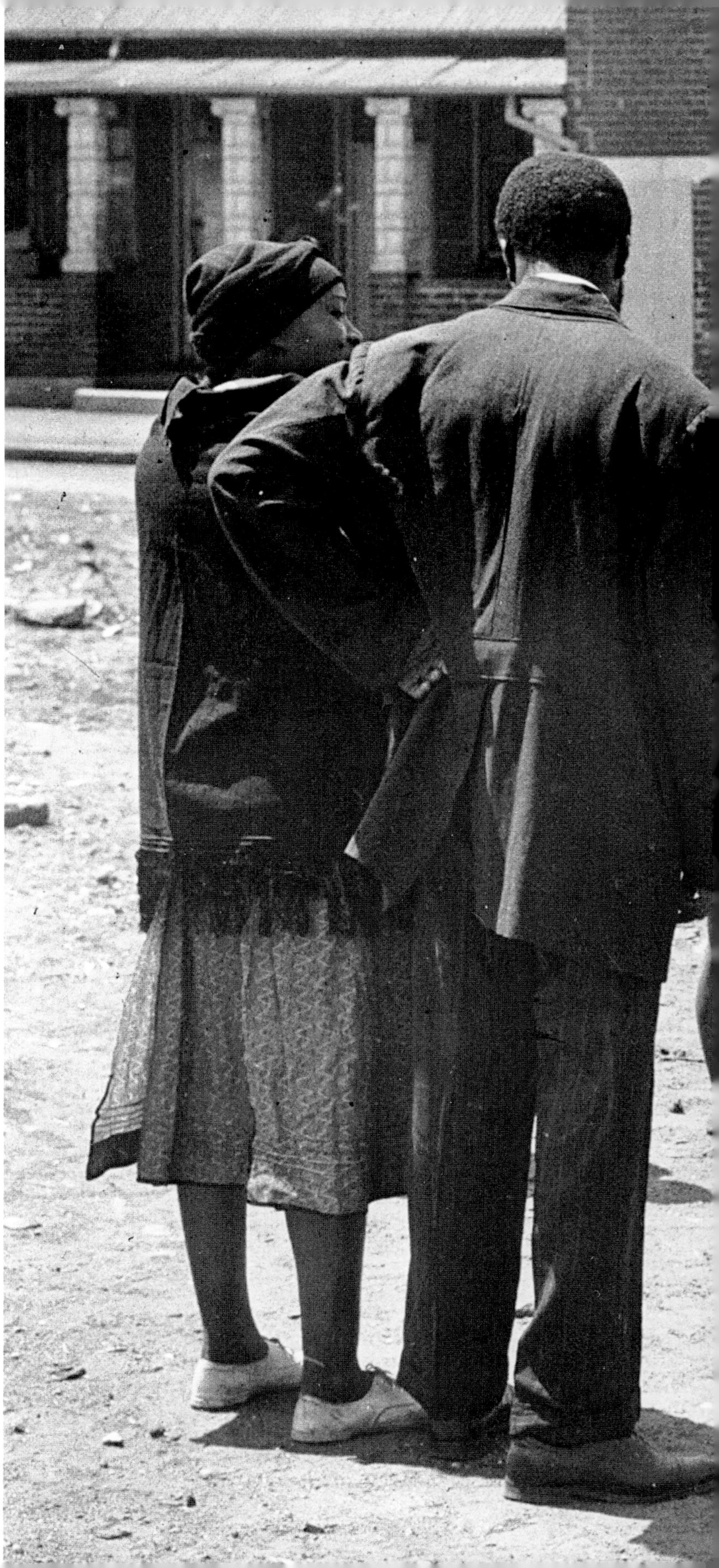

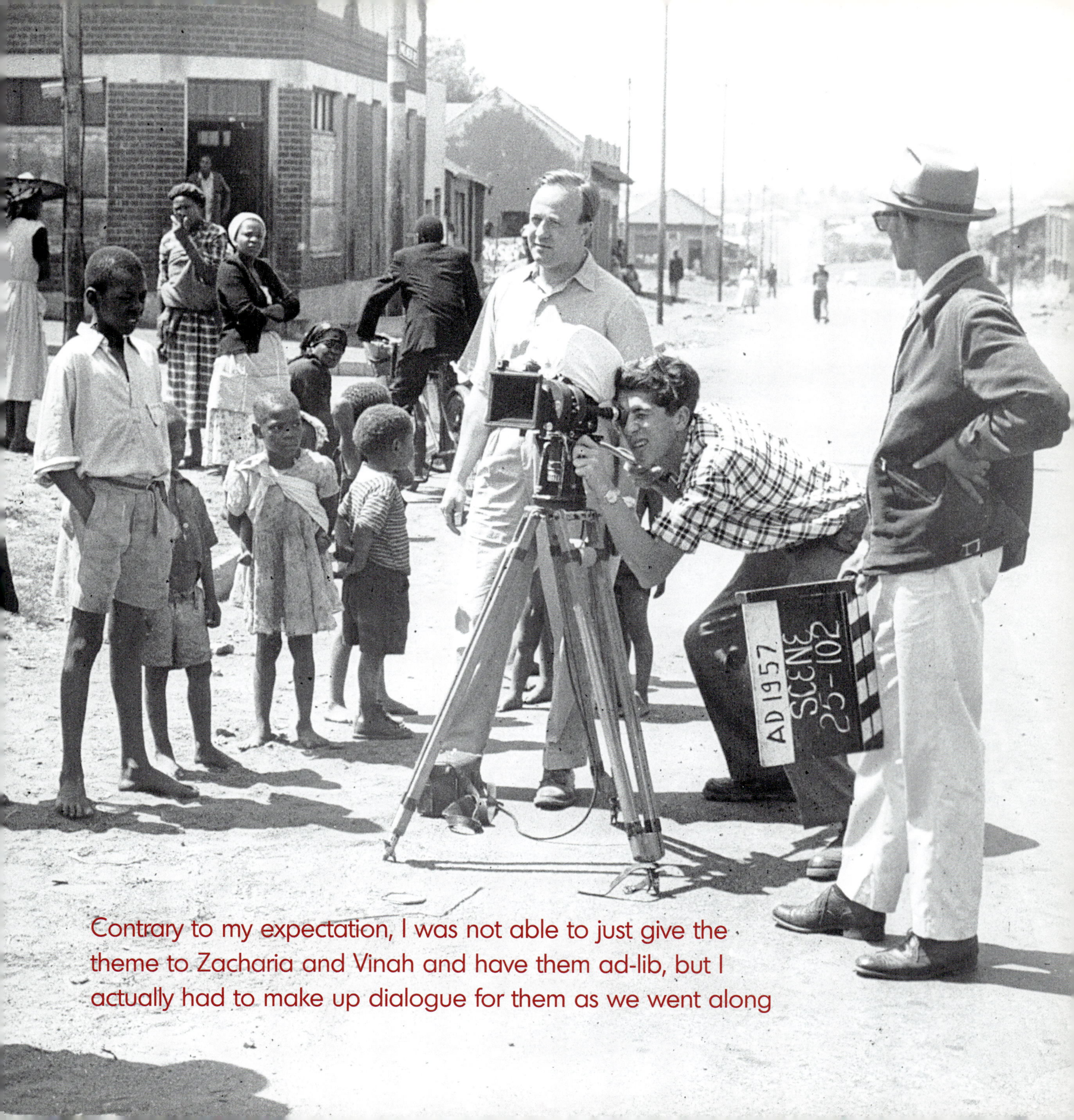

Contrary to my expectation, I was not able to just give the theme to Zacharia and Vinah and have them ad-lib, but I actually had to make up dialogue for them as we went along

merely showed them another permit and had been able to fool them into thinking that he had permission. Since such a mistake, if discovered, would jeopardise the entire production, I was unwilling to risk it.

I got advice from several sources, including my lawyer, who advised me to tell the police that I was going to film there, since there would be nothing wrong with this, and it might be better to have them know about it. This sounded like good advice. However, knowing bureaucrats, I was against it.

It was Bloke's opinion not to say a word to anybody. Bloke felt that there was too much danger, and if I told the police they might feel it incumbent to check with Pretoria.

So in the end I decided it was better to risk being caught, and to try to talk our way out of it if we were questioned. With my knowledge of bureaucracy from this experience and others, I think that our method was sound, because the problem is that if one asks a bureaucrat what has to be done to obtain permission, the usual reaction is terror of making a mistake. Since they usually don't know the proper procedure, this means great soul-searching, and in order to protect themselves they take every possible precaution. Whereas if one just does something and it is discovered and one acts perfectly innocent about it, the question does not take on such monumental proportions.

This was the decision I took; I decided to brazen it out. It worked out for us and seemed to be a good manoeuvre, but it was certainly quite nerve-racking and caused a lot of tension for the crew and for myself, particularly during the shooting.

PENNY-WHISTLERS

I found a group of penny-whistlers that lived and practised in Alexandra Township. I explained to the crew what I wanted and Ernie insisted that we use reflectors. I thought that would be impossible, since we had to do this shooting very quickly, and extra equipment would only get in the way. However, I decided not to fight this issue too strongly but to allow the difficulties we would encounter to win the argument.

We went out to the location and started to shoot, but we found that the children were rather sullen and unco-operative. The use of reflectors made me very impatient because I could see that this was making the children even more difficult. They became impossible to control, what with waiting so long while we set up the shot. I shot several scenes and the action was very artificial — I couldn't get the kids to co-operate with me. Of course, one could hardly blame them for their sullenness, considering the social conditions under which they lived. However, this was something that I couldn't tolerate because of my time schedule, and I didn't have the patience to wait for them to come around.

Finally Ernie, now realising the reflectors were making the job much more difficult, agreed to shoot without them. But when we came back a second day, I found the kids just as difficult as before. I started to get a little rougher with them, hoping that this would bring them round. There was a momentary burst of energy, but after that they settled back into their old lethargy. Finally, after half a day's shooting I decided that there was no use, and told everyone that we would quit for the day and that we would not use them in the film.

Since the boys from Alex hadn't worked out, we ended up with another group we found. Even though their music was not really first class, I felt that perhaps this might be more authentic, because I wanted the feeling of what most of them were, and that is amateur groups.

I quite liked this group. They were young, ranging from about eight or nine to 11 or so, and their dress was very colourful. One of the boys was wearing tails and earrings and the others had all kinds of assorted caps and jackets.

The scenes with the penny-whistlers had to be shot on the street and I was still quite anxious about the police. We were filming a scene of them fighting another gang when I saw the police pass us in the distance. They turned around a corner and started coming down our street. I immediately stopped the fight and had them start playing their musical instruments.

The police hadn't seen the fighting. They went up the street and turned around again, circling around us, and seeing that we were filming the music, did not stop to question us.

I felt that shooting openly this way we were bound to be questioned, but there was no alternative. It had to be done in order to finish the film, but the nervous tension of the constant worry was draining me. There were so many extraneous factors to contend with — directing nine actors for whom I had to make up

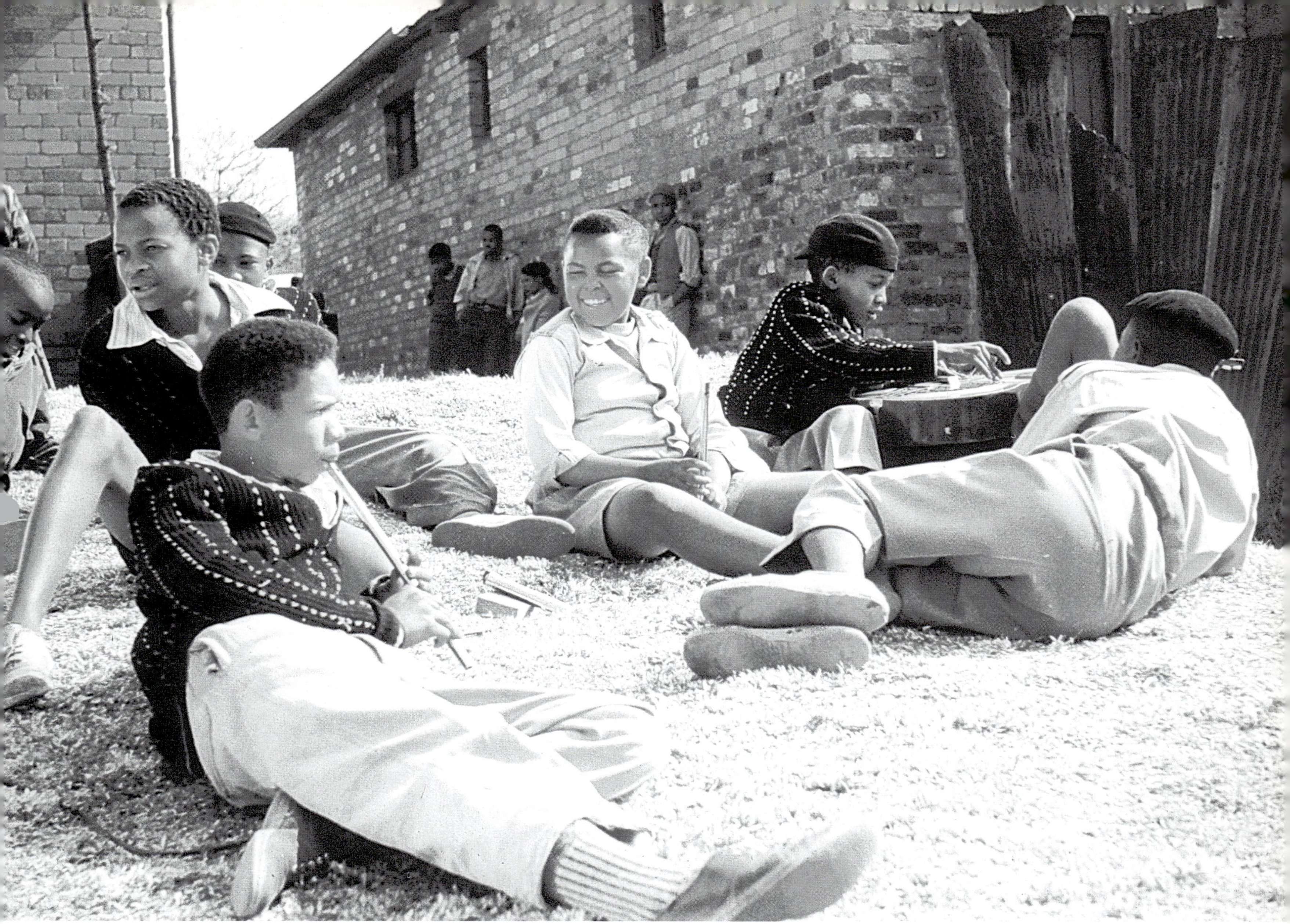

"I couldn't seem to get the kids to co-operate with me. Of course, one could hardly blame them for their sullenness, considering the social conditions under which they lived "

dialogue, and the fact that Fred and Ernie were anxious to get back to Switzerland, the frequent incidents such as the problems at the mine, and the constant fear of the government and the police. After all this I had some energy left over for directing the film — but not much relaxation.

A VIOLENT SOCIETY

It was a society that seemed to be seething with violence. I saw frightening things myself happening on the streets, not only whites against Africans but African against African as well. Once, walking on the main street in Hillbrow, a suburb near the city centre, I saw an extraordinary sight. An African walked up to a woman — either a coloured woman or a light-skinned African — and suddenly lashed out and hit her in the nose with his fist. She started to scream and everybody stopped and turned around. The man did not run off but stood there defiantly.

For some strange reason she ran directly to me. I felt a little apprehensive because I had heard of stabbings on the streets of Johannesburg and I was not anxious to get into a personal battle. She was bleeding quite profusely. She said that she didn't even know who the man was, and from the way the action took place I could believe it, it seemed so absolutely unprovoked. By this time a few more people had gathered and the man went off, luckily.

One night Milek and I were walking down this same street when we suddenly heard a terrible commotion on the next street-corner. People were yelling, and they seemed to be hysterical. One woman was saying, "Catch him!" and we could see up the street two white men running off after a coloured man at top speed. They caught him and brought him back. He was terrified and it was rather frightening. I didn't know what they were going to do to him.

Meanwhile the woman kept yelling hysterically, "Catch him, get him, I saw him over there, I heard something!" Then she turned to us and said, "I don't know what happened, I don't know what happened, but I heard something."

It seemed that nobody knew exactly what was going on and why this man was being treated in this manner — least of all this stupid woman. She could have caused his death and she did not even know what he was supposed to have done, but was just yelling hysterically. She had just gotten caught up in her own imagination.

I turned to her with as much contempt as I could summon and said that I was glad to see that the white race was so well protected. She looked at me bewildered. She realised, I think, that I hardly approved of her behaviour.

By this time it had been decided that the man had done nothing wrong, so apparently he wasn't harmed, but one could see how a crowd could be worked up into hysteria by some idiotic woman.

MORRIS PROBLEM

One Sunday afternoon I received a telephone call from Milek, who was very agitated. He told me that Morris had been beaten up while he and George were preparing the set for the following day's shooting. Morris was half-drunk, in a terrible state, and threatening to go to the police. Milek was desperately afraid because he thought that this might lead to our discovery. Milek felt that I should come as soon as possible to see what I could do to calm Morris down. I abandoned my much-needed rest and rushed off to Sophiatown. When I arrived it was getting dark and I found Morris standing on a street-corner, raving. He was shouting, cursing, and in tears, saying that nobody was helping him, that he was going to the police. I couldn't make head or tail of it, but apparently Morris had antagonised some Africans who didn't like him anyway, and there was also his brother-in-law who had a grudge against him.

Apparently they had beaten him up quite severely, and his face was in bad shape. Milek was shocked at the violence, and he said that no one had tried to stop it. Morris seems to be the kind of person who deliberately provokes people to attack him, as if he wanted to be beaten. I suppose that this is the kind of personality Morris's background produces.

There was something very unusual about Morris. He was extremely intelligent, remarkably capable. He acted as our production manager although he had never worked on films before. He did a wonderful job of building sets and was excellent in helping me to direct actors whose proper customs or behaviour I didn't know. He had an extraordinary grasp of things. Yet at the same time he seemed to be a person who almost had to undo

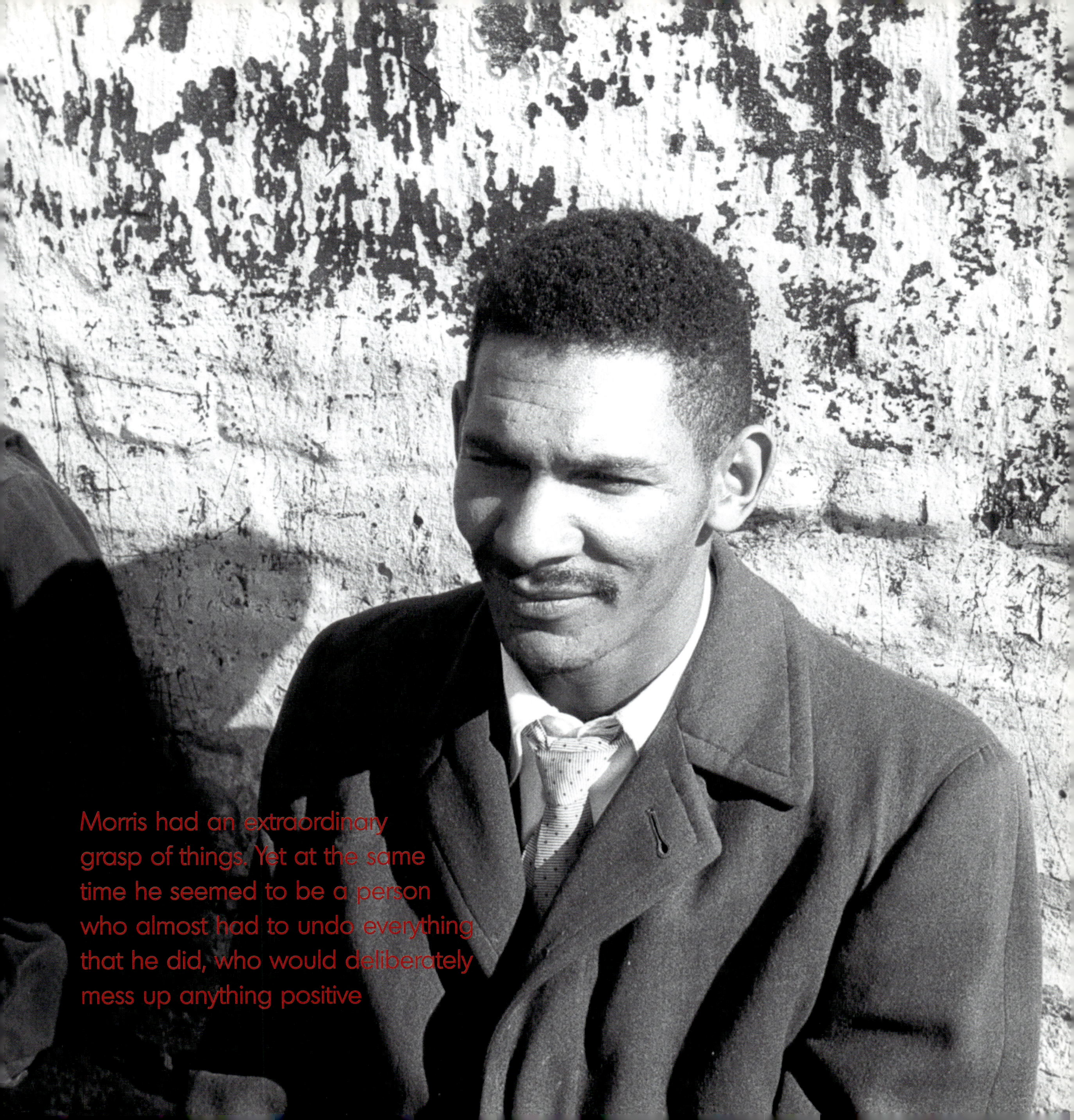

Morris had an extraordinary grasp of things. Yet at the same time he seemed to be a person who almost had to undo everything that he did, who would deliberately mess up anything positive

everything that he did, who would deliberately mess up anything positive. He could be a nuisance and a pest to everyone. He drank a great deal and could talk complete nonsense.

We tried to calm Morris down and persuade him not to go to the police, knowing he would get no help from that quarter, and that rather than helping him they might even throw him in jail. But he was too drunk to realise this, and was feeling very sorry for himself and accusing all of us of letting him down and not fighting for him and not helping him. I realised that if I told him the police might even lock him up for being drunk, he might not pay any attention to me, feeling I was only saying this for my own self-interest. So I decided to get Bloke to talk to Morris. We found Bloke, but rather than helping, this seemed to make matters worse, and I realised that there was some antagonism between the two of them. We tried to talk him out of going to the police and finally gave up. I decided that perhaps if we took him to a hospital instead and had him fixed up, this would satisfy him. Morris was complaining bitterly and behaving like a child. His pride had been hurt as well as his feelings, and I realised that we had to make some gesture of support.

Bloke warned us that they would take our licence number at the hospital. I tried to avoid it, but it was taken anyway. We took Morris inside. One of the nurses looked at him and told him that there was nothing serious, but she pampered him, babied him, patched him up and jollied him along and soon he was smiling and feeling quite delighted from all the attention he was being given. And so we have gotten through another minor crisis.

CASTING WHITES

So far, we were shooting only scenes that included Africans. These were the safest for us, since we could shoot them in a completely protected area with only the Africans involved, and without bringing in whites, whom we had not yet cast, and with whom there was a problem of political security. Fred and I and the others had constant discussions as to how we would time the shooting. We kept going over and over the same things, because essentially there was no easy solution. We wondered whether we should shoot the outdoor scenes first and then the scenes with the whites, or whether the whites first and then the outdoor scenes; whether the police would stop and question us on the street, or whether some white that we picked might inform the authorities about us.

I had started filming without having cast a single one of the white actors, and since there were many more whites this was quite a problem and would probably delay us during the shooting, causing a loss of time and money. But there was no easy way to get around it. I felt that I wanted to leave it until the last minute, because the more people who knew about the film, and the longer they knew about it, the greater our chances were of being discovered. Perhaps this caution did save us, since rumours started to go around after we did pick our white actors, and we were actually uncovered two weeks after leaving, when our cameraman Milek was still in the country.

During this time Fred was constantly asking me about picking the white actors, and I kept telling him, "Don't worry, somehow or other I will pick them without losing a day. We will find our actors for the next scene during the night, and next morning we'll have them ready on the set." I knew this would be a killing pace, but there was no choice.

I was continually looking for white people wherever I went; on the streets, at parties, everywhere, I kept looking for the proper faces. The only problem was that the people who had the right faces were usually people who would have the wrong attitudes, and whom I could not risk to let in on the secret.

We knew that shooting with the whites would be our greatest danger. Shooting on the streets would also be risky, and so would the scene in the servants' quarters, since we would probably use real servants' quarters in a residential area, and the noise might attract attention.

There was no way of avoiding these things. We just had to go as cautiously as possible, and then forget all risks. As a matter of fact, too much caution was a mistake, it would slow us down.

I was obsessed with using real people as much as possible, not actors. I actually wanted to use real police as I had done in *On the Bowery*.

My original plan had been to shoot everything, leaving the scene where Zacharia is arrested until last. Even if we were caught, the film would be completed. This scene involved using whites as police. I wanted to shoot the scene twice, first with actors to make sure I didn't miss it, and then later with real police. But after a lot of consideration, I gave up the idea of using real police. I was sure that it could be done, since I have found out there is always a way to reach almost everyone, particularly if you are able to understand their mentality and make them feel that you are on their side. However, it was an added risk and our time was running out. It was becoming very clear to me that I was going to have trouble finishing the film within the three-month deadline.

After the favourable publicity I had received from my screenings and the article about my intentions to make the Boer epic *Commando*, I received a lot of requests for auditions. I had the names and addresses of all these people, and I decided to have a trial casting session. Also other people had been making their recommendations. We set appointments for try-outs at the Rep Theatre, but they were all too much like actors — either they were too affected, or their voices were too cultured and their faces and features were not right for the parts that I wanted. In addition to the natural quality of the South African personality, I also wanted people who spoke with a strong South African accent, either English or Boer.

Neither the casting session nor the personal recommendations yielded us any results, except for one whose name was Smull, quite a pleasant man with a strong Boer accent, who was dying to be in the film and who kept on calling me for weeks, saying, "Gee, I would love to be in the film." He didn't seem to be bright enough to catch on to what we were doing, so I decided to use him as one of the more innocuous policemen.

The rains began early that year, at the end of August instead of the middle of September. We started getting heavy rains every day, particularly in the afternoons, and this was causing us to lose time. Black rain-clouds would roll in. So we had to shoot our outdoor scenes in the morning.

Fred had suggested several times that Myrtle Berman might be good for the shrewish housewife. I resisted this for a long time, mostly because I knew Myrtle as a friend and thought of her as a wonderful person that I could never think of as a racist housewife. Fred continued to insist that she would be good for the part until finally I convinced myself that she might possibly be able to do a good job since she knew racist types so well.

I discovered from among our acquaintances a man who was suitable as her husband, Jan Hoogendyk. These people were amateurs who had never acted before, and we just took them on

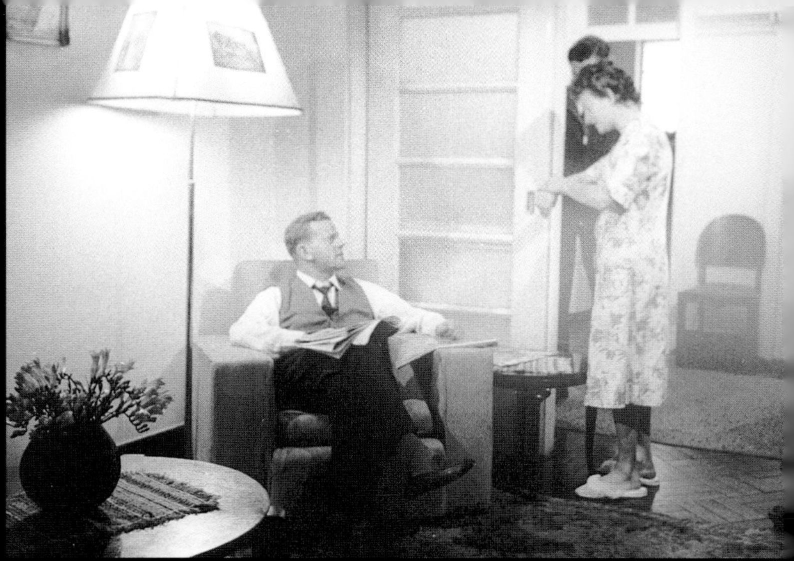

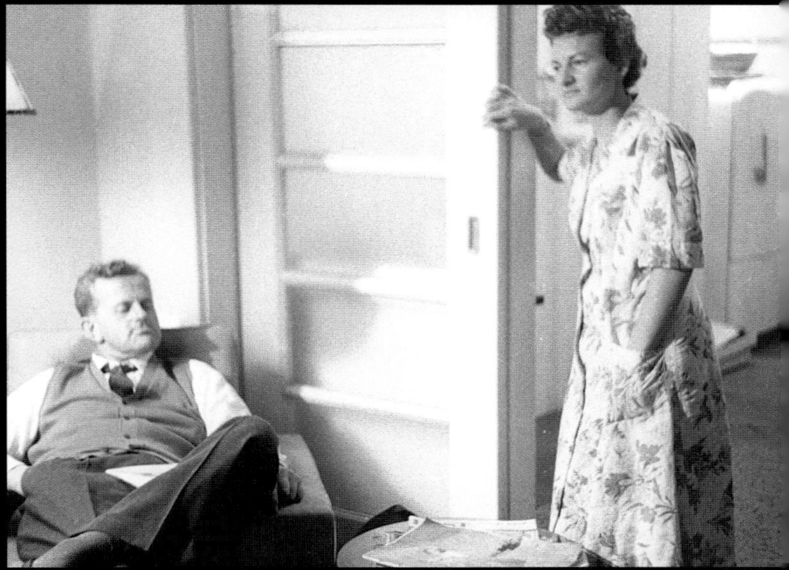

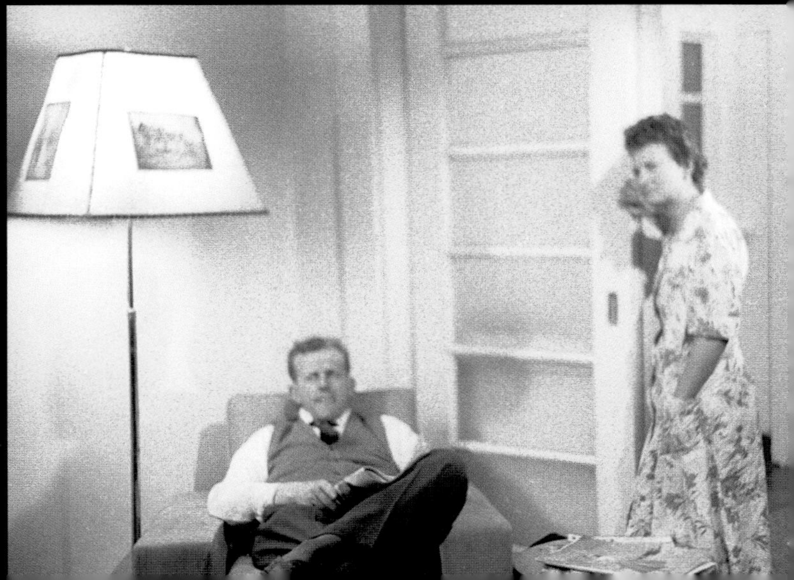

without a rehearsal, bringing them on to the set and demanding that they start acting.

Well, Myrtle was fine. She knew exactly what to do and what to say. She knew the type of shrewish South African housewife, always complaining about the servants, whom she treated miserably. She had the pet phrases, the language and attitudes down pat.

But for some reason Jan was not able to contribute. He was the right type; he had a good face and looked the part of the kindly, more understanding husband. The only difficulty was that he had trouble ad-libbing. We kept shooting and shooting without getting the proper results, until finally before lunch Jan started to warm up and get better. This is always the case.

After we stopped for lunch he had an appointment and could only come back later in the afternoon. This is the problem when working with volunteers, that such an unprofessional thing can happen, but it can't be helped. In the afternoon, Jan finally came back and we started shooting again — but this time, for some unknown reason, it was worse than the morning. I simply couldn't get the proper response from him. But we kept on shooting, hoping that with all the material we would have enough to cover the scene.

The problem was that this made Myrtle's job much more difficult. It made her overact and overdo her part without having enough of a counter-action from Jan. I later found out what the trouble was. Jan told me that he had gone out after lunch and had a few cocktails, and when he came back he simply could not get over his inertia. He became absolutely inarticulate.

Milek as usual told me when the scene wasn't good, and I said I knew this but that there was nothing that could be done; if we had time at the end we could go back and re-shoot it. Even a scene shot badly with professionals would have a certain standard, but with amateurs one can get a complete non-performance. When I had the time to rehearse and re-do scenes until the actors grasped the method, I got excellent results. In the cases where I had grabbed people in the middle of the night, telling them to be on set the next day, having them act something without any preparation, unless they were exceptionally good, I got poor results.

The parents of one of my friends seemed right for the couple who ran the hotel, and I asked him if he could get them for the film, and we had two more people. Later, at a party, I suddenly saw a woman who I thought would be perfect for the spinster. I asked

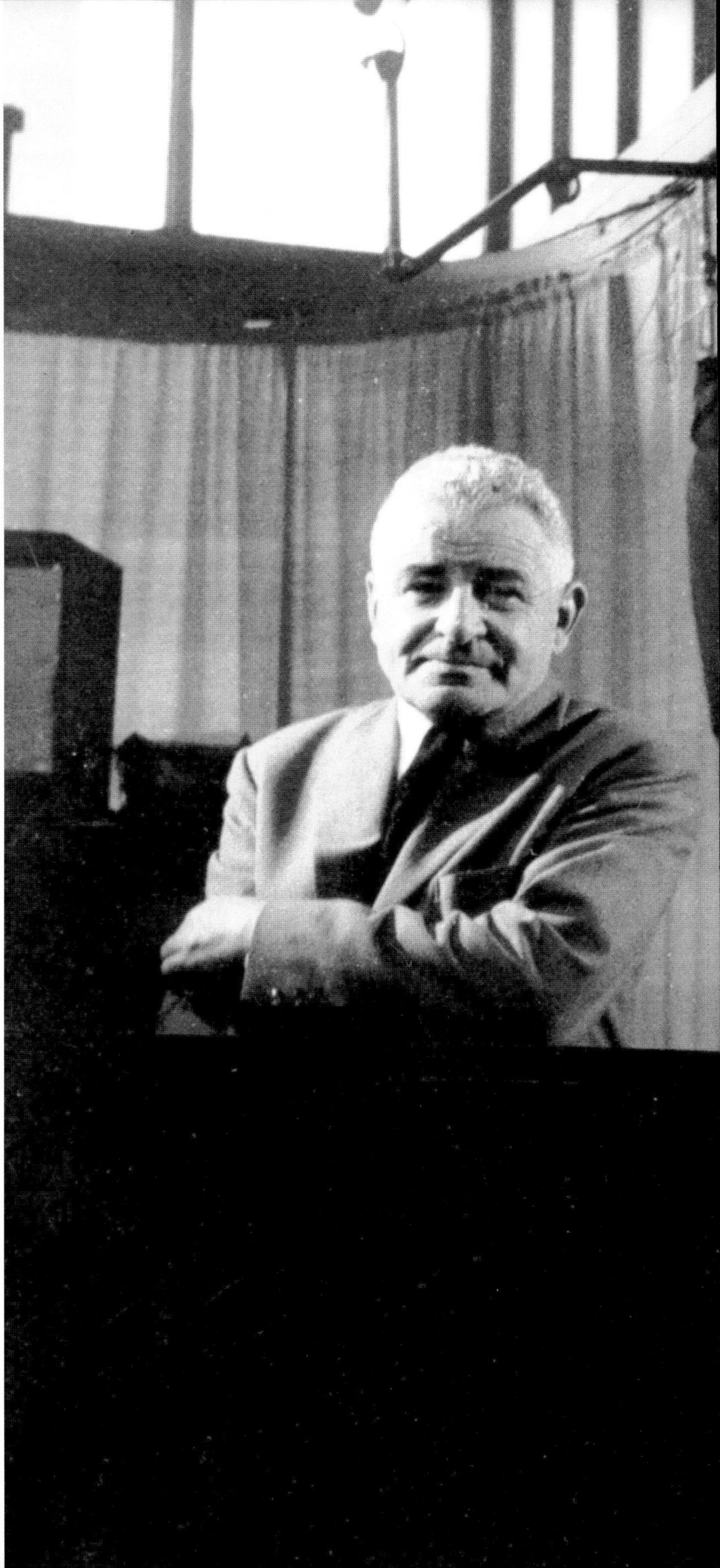

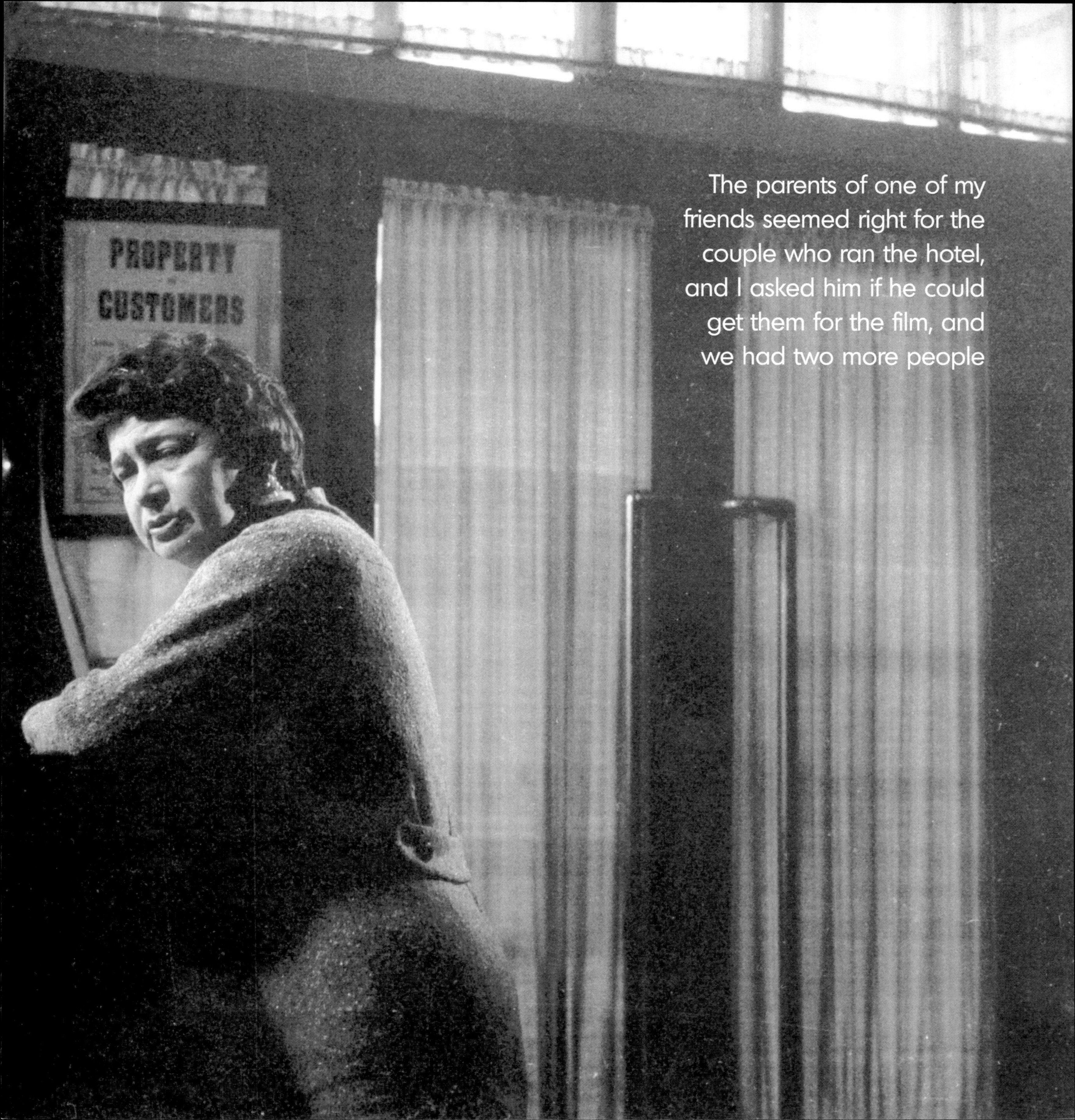

The parents of one of my friends seemed right for the couple who ran the hotel, and I asked him if he could get them for the film, and we had two more people

the host to speak to her. She agreed. She turned out to be very nice and helpful.

The scene she had to act in the hotel was to scream when she sees Zacharia in the hallway, as she is passing from her room to the bathroom in her nightgown. We did not have time to build a set and we were using a real hotel. I was quite worried that her screaming would attract attention. At this stage we were rushing madly and we shot the scene so badly that we had to drop it in the editing.

Scenes were shot in the lobby of the hotel and I was quite worried because there were people coming in and out. The manager of the hotel seemed very pleasant and co-operative, but I was afraid that his wife might react against the film. She was a rather unpleasant Boer woman, a bully to the African employees of the hotel. While we were there she got into quite a row with the African clerk. But on the other hand she was extremely pleasant to us, to the point of civility.

I was shooting these scenes and at the same time looking for the cast for the next scene, and in order to not lose shooting days we were going out at night, after dinner, and searching Johannesburg, looking for actors. Milek and I would get into the car and drive through the suburbs from one house to the other, getting leads from one person whom we knew to another that we didn't, but always making sure that the leads were to people who were sympathetic to Africans.

We would arrive at someone's house after perhaps telephoning them or not, at about eight or nine in the evening, saying we were making a film about African life which they may have heard about. We would tell them what the film was. We would say that we were looking for a garage owner, a hotel manager, a spinster, etc. and then after a few minutes of conversation we'd say, "Oh no, you won't do — you're not quite the right type. Can you give us the name of somebody else?"

We were never turned down, and off we would go into the night, arriving at some other house until finally we had found the man we felt was right for the part. Whether he could act was only a guess. And so in this way we got all the actors together for the white parts. From one or two people we contacted all the others who acted in the film.

GARAGE SCENE

We decided to shoot the garage scene on a Saturday afternoon. The garage owner left the foreman with us, and as we were setting up I noticed that he was a bit drunk, but he was quite helpful.

I had to go away for some reason and when I came back there was quite a commotion. The foreman had become even more drunk and was quite angry. Obviously something had happened. He was shouting, "Why do you make a travelogue in a garage? You can't use Africans to work in cars. Don't you know that's not allowed in this country? I am a shop-steward in the motor mechanics' union. You must stop at once!"

I tried to calm him, but it didn't work. He seemed determined to keep shouting. I was a bit concerned but at the same time amused by him, because after all the difficulties that we had encountered and all the people who had heard about the film, this drunk was the only one who had actually discovered what we were doing.

I couldn't quite understand how it had happened. Was it because of the way we were working with the Africans or did Morris say something? There was something about the whole situation which made me suspect Morris, particularly since I had heard snatches of remarks mentioning him. It later came out that Morris might have told the man that he was stupid, or made some other rude remark, which had started him off.

I couldn't stop his ranting, so I decided to walk away, because I had to direct the scene and supervise what was happening on the set. The foreman seemed to become obsessed by this and became even more abusive. He shouted, "Why don't you go back to Little Rock?" — referring to the attempt in 1957 to integrate nine black students into hitherto segregated schools in Little Rock, Arkansas, in the US, which led to riots by local whites. "You left plenty of trouble there. You don't have to come here as a foreigner and take pictures of us."

It was funny. He wasn't an Afrikaner and he didn't seem like an English-speaking South African. I couldn't really tell, but he sounded like he might have been an Englishman.

He continued to shout: "You don't belong in this country!"

Finally Piet Beyleveld told him to be quiet.

The foreman's answer was, "Shut up, we don't have to take that from you, you foreigners."

At this point Piet lost his patience. He is a fairly large man, and he raised his hand in a fist and said, "*Ek is 'n ware Boer*" — I am a real Boer. The tiny foreman said not another word, but suddenly this little runt ran like a terrier and jumped into his car and off he went. It was a marvellous scene. I certainly didn't have the nerve to do it myself, but Piet took the situation into his own hands and saved the day for us.

I was almost sure we would be reported. But for some reason or other nothing ever happened. Perhaps he woke up the next morning sober and had forgotten all about it.

Smull acted the part of the policeman in the garage scene and did it very nicely, except for the fact that he was much too pleasant, but I couldn't risk pushing him into being too harsh without the danger of his discovering what we were up to. However, all the police in South Africa are not monsters. I have seen one or two cases where they have behaved quite decently, and I think that it gave the film a certain balance to have a policeman just carrying out his normal duty. But even so, his normal duty is to enforce laws which in themselves are unjust.

The shooting was extremely difficult. We were shooting at the back of the garage and had to stop every time a car came in for gasoline because of the noise and also because I did not want people hearing what was being said. Everyone of course tried to watch and stay there as long as they could. I had chosen to shoot on location, and this was one of the problems that one encounters, and it really is a great difficulty. I think that in such situations it is better to build sets using natural actors, as you get pretty much the same results. The stopping and starting that goes on when you are shooting publicly on location is very unnerving under ordinary circumstances. In our case it was doubly so.

NIGHT SCENE

The police scenes, Marumu's fight, the Sophiatown streets and the Indian store were all scenes that I was leaving until later. By this time we had almost finished shooting the township scenes and we decided to try to shoot the scene at the entrance to the shebeen. It was fairly harmless but it was on the street and we would be exposed to the police. This was a night scene, and we had to use a few large lights. The only place that we could draw the electricity from in the vicinity was a Chinese store next to the house that we had picked for our shebeen exterior. There wasn't enough current, and shortly after we started the fuse blew and the lights went out. By this time quite a large crowd had gathered, and I was getting more and more nervous. The Chinese woman who owned the store had been very reluctant to let us in. It was only after a long discussion that we had persuaded her, and now the lights had blown, which caused a lot of difficulties.

The crowds were making me a bit nervous because I was afraid that we would be attracting too much attention. But I must say that I very rarely have worked in a situation where the crowds were so co-operative. There was quite a lot of noise, understandably, and children. When we would get ready to shoot we would tell several of the people to quieten the crowd down, and they would go around telling everyone to be quiet, and they would be.

Actually, the crowds of Sophiatown puzzled me during the shooting. I wondered often why we got such marvellous co-operation, because crowds usually cause a lot of difficulty and are mostly unco-operative. Perhaps it was because we were taking pictures of them and their lives and their problems. Perhaps it was because everyone likes to be in films or feels that his place is being shown on film. Or perhaps a rumour was getting around, slowly and quietly, giving the general idea of what we were doing. But we shot many days and places in Sophiatown and always got the utmost co-operation from the people.

There were a lot of cars passing, and this also gave us difficulty because we were shooting with sound, and the noise of the cars would spoil the shot. Also the car lights kept coming into the set. So we would start a scene and would have to stop very often for all these interruptions. I like shooting on location, but this kind of interruption always caused a great deal of tension.

In this situation, where we were hoping to finish and get away without being seen by the police, our anxiety was building and building. We had all been working under great pressure for many days now, and were very tense and afraid. Then suddenly the police came from nowhere in a large squad-car.

I realised that I had to go to them immediately and tell them what we were doing before they asked us, to put them off guard. For several days, while we were thinking of how we would shoot this scene, I had been holding an imaginary conversation with myself like that which I imagined the police would have with me. For these practice sessions I would make the situation worse than it might possibly be, and my questions were always difficult.

I had decided the best tactic was to speak to them in their own phraseology. So I went up to the police and said, "You must help us. These kaffirs are getting in the way. They're spoiling our shooting. They're a nuisance. I don't know what to do with them. We can't get any work done." They nodded in agreement, but didn't make much of a move to do anything.

Then I started to explain to them what we were shooting. I told them that we were doing a film about African music and that we were shooting this thing on the street. They wanted to know why I was using this particular place. It struck me as curious why they should question this, but I said that there was a party inside and we wanted to show the entrance. "It's a party with Africans and they are going to sing and dance and this is what we want to show on film."

I suddenly realised that we were using an actual shebeen, which they were probably aware of, and it was a shebeen that was paying them off to stay open, and that was why Bright, the shebeen owner, had told us we would have no trouble from the police.

They apparently felt that they had nothing to fear at this point, and started to warm up to us, taking an interest in our filming. I decided to try to cultivate their friendship because of my plan to use real police in the scene of the arrest. I didn't have enough nerve to ask them then, but I was hoping that I would see them more often, until I got to know them well and I could try to use them in the film.

They didn't ask many more questions, but watched us filming, seeming very interested, and then they finally left. They seemed to be completely satisfied that we were all right but I was still very relieved at their departure.

Shortly after they left and we could work freely, the lights blew again. Apparently the lines were not big enough for the current we were drawing. The Chinese woman would not let us in again. I suppose the crowds and the police had put her off. We did our best to persuade her, but it was no use. We had to leave.

My nerves were frayed. Ernie was in a fury, not that I blame him, because it had taken two hours of preparation or more, plus carrying all the equipment over to the spot, and after shooting for less than an hour we had to pack up and leave, which was another long hard job. We drove off, and after turning around the corner we met the same policemen who had dropped in on us. I deliberately stopped to talk to them. They were very friendly and wanted to know what was happening. I told them that we had had very bad luck tonight. The crowds were very difficult and impossible, plus the lights had blown because of the fuses. By talking their language I had made friends with them.

But despite the fact that we had fooled the police, we were all worn out. Every day's shooting was becoming a tremendous physical effort as well as a mental strain. We had to carry the blimps, lights, cameras, sound-recording equipment, film, magazines to every set, and even sometimes with a set we used more than once we had to take all the equipment away, since there was no way of protecting it. With our small crew, it meant that the cameraman, soundman and myself had to do all this work in addition to our normal functions.

In the morning we would fill up the cars, drive to the sets, unload the equipment and set up for the shooting, shoot, break down the equipment, load the cars up, go back to the apartment and unload, then carry all the stuff up the elevator into the flat. There were only seven of us altogether, although at the flat I sometimes had some of the African "flat-boys" to help us.

We were up at 6.30 am, returning at six or seven pm, after which we would screen the previous day's rushes, unload the cameras and make our reports. I insisted on one day off, but often we found that we used this entire day to pack the film for shipment. Many nights we didn't even have dinner until 11 pm or even midnight. Our evening meal was our only pleasure and relaxation.

TECHNICAL PROBLEM

By now it was the middle of September, 1958, and it was quite clear that we would never finish the film before the end of the month, when all our visas were due to run out. After a bit of a debate, the crew decided to get their visa extensions done in Johannesburg. They all went to the Department of Immigration and Fred got his visa extended but for some reason Ernie and Milek did not. It seemed inexplicable that they would allow one member of the crew an extension and not the others, since we could not finish the film without all the people. Anyway, knowing South Africa we didn't argue, but instead went through to Pretoria. Every scene that we were shooting was being shot under more and more tension, particularly now that the visas were not granted. The hotel scene and the garage scene were shot under these conditions.

With the beginning of the rains, one night while we were screening the rushes we noticed that the film from one of the cameras was "breathing". What this means is that the image was pulsating on the screen so that it appeared to be going in and out, very much like the same movement of breathing. We watched this for the next few days of shooting and found that all the cameras were doing it, particularly the old one. But they did not seem to breathe when they were running with the synchronised motor rather than on the battery.

However, it seemed to be getting worse and worse, and when we used the cameras on battery, which of course was quite necessary for documentary "wild" shooting (i.e. without synchronised sound) when we were not on the set where we could get electricity but out on the streets. Therefore we found that we had to shoot everything after this with a "blimped" camera, which was quite heavy, and we also needed an electricity supply line. A blimp is a cover for the camera that cuts out the noise the camera makes. We suspected at this point that it might possibly be the film, since both cameras were doing the same thing, and it was doubtful that the same fault could occur in both cameras at the same time. We also discovered from talking to other people that Jamie Uys was having similar trouble. We made more tests with colour film and we found the same thing to be wrong. It was pretty desperate because we were absolutely out of time now and we needed to be able to run the cameras on battery for a lot of street scenes that we had left to do. Ernie suggested that he take both cameras to Germany himself, and they could be sent back in one week. This would be much quicker than sending them. I knew that Ernie was anxious to get home, and I was afraid to let him go because then I would be left with only one camera, and if Milek could not get his visa we would never finish. Therefore I was against his going, but on the other hand there was not much choice, so I finally agreed, with great reluctance. So Ernie suggested that we try to shoot all the sound sequences before he left the country, which was at the end of that week. It was quite a lot of shooting, and I did not know how we would manage it, but everybody put in an extra burst of energy to

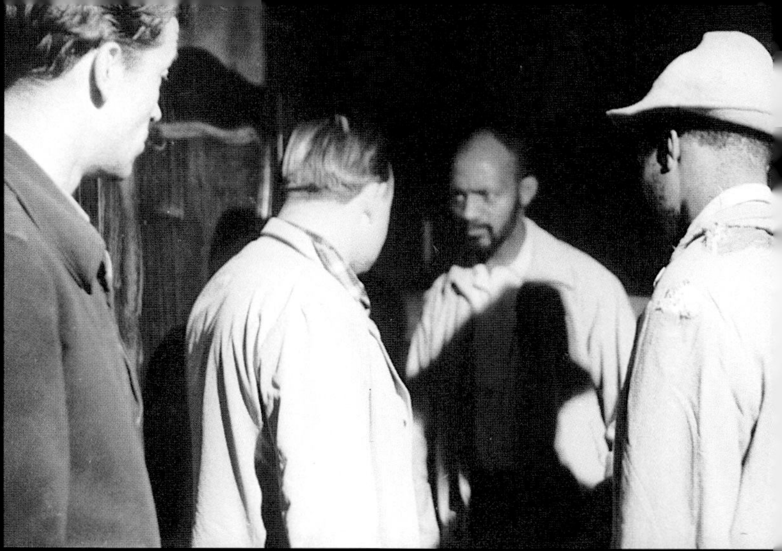

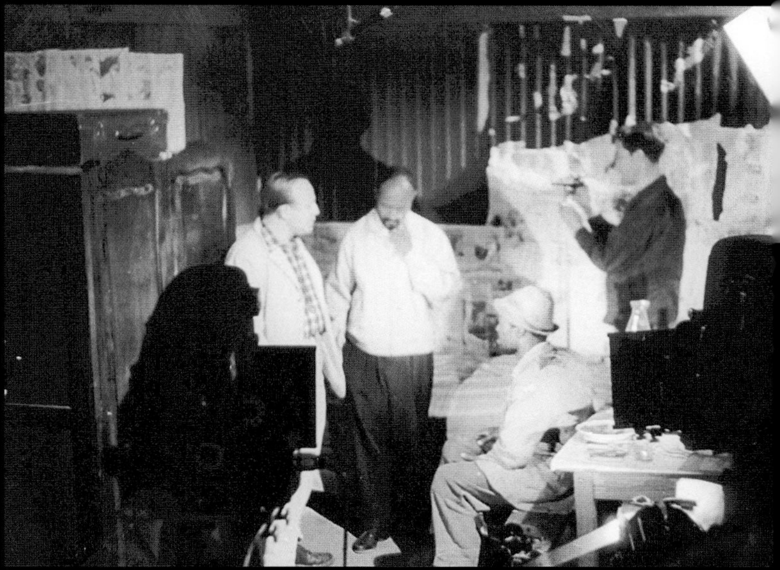

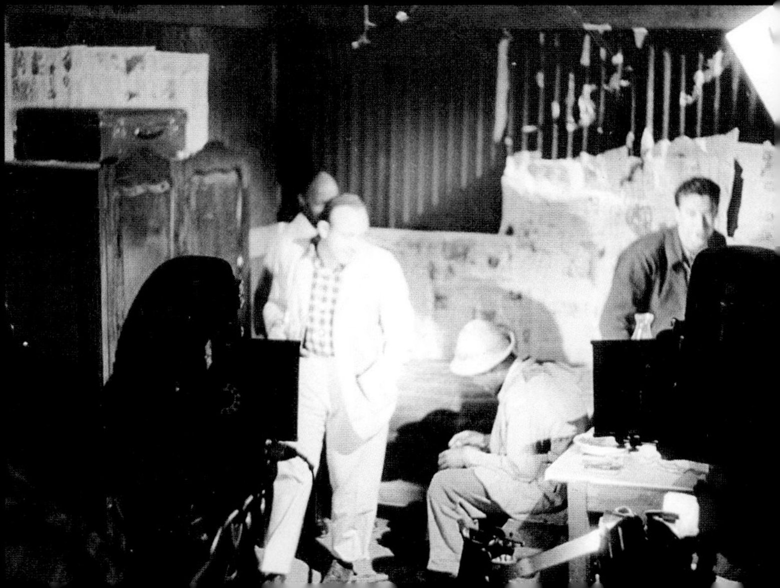

finish. It was a last-minute surge in the final dash to the end. What it finally meant was that we had to shoot two entire sequences on the last day before Ernie left, both of which were more than a full day's work. We actually accomplished this, and I think that it was partly due to the fact that by this time we were working extraordinarily well and efficiently as a team. We had learned almost a special technique of filming. We were doing everything by short cut. Of course this did not lend itself to the most impressive kind of film, because everything was done with the minimum number of angles and movements and was sometimes pretty thinly covered.

But my point of view at this time was that we had to get the film completed as simply as possible, and that the overall effect of it would be strong enough to carry the idea and only those who harp on the finer points would be concerned; and the film, I felt, would have an impact on its audience. This in itself, I would say, is an artistic decision. It is not the slickness or the polish of a film that makes it artistic or not. The film can be very rough and artistically right for its subject matter. However, audiences have been trained for a certain kind of end result, and when this is lacking they sometimes feel the film is inferior. This is something that one has to have the strength to ignore.

ROAD-GANG AND ARREST SCENES

In shooting these two scenes, because there was additional work to be done besides the actual shooting, we arrived at the location of the road-gang early in the morning, set up the cameras and shot the road-gang sequence, which consisted of several small scenes, which meant new camera set-ups for each scene and long delays because of the road-making equipment that was working all around us, causing us to stop and start. We had to lay out long cable lines. We had to get permission from the city officials to shoot this scene. We called up the city department and told them that we were making a travelogue and wanted to shoot the road-gang because we were doing a sequence of African music, and the road-gang were chanting as they worked. During this road-gang scene we used the actual foreman on the work, who was quite an amiable Boer, but the superintendent was one or our own actors.

While the equipment was being set up for the next scene with the road-gang, I rushed out to Sophiatown with Morris to look for an African policeman, since I still hoped that we would find the real McCoy. During this time Ernie and Fred were setting up for the next scene with the road-gang. I then rushed back to the road-gang location, and during the shooting, since it was done with only one camera, Milek went to take care of the uniforms of the policemen for that night's scene. I called the Greek who was to act one of the policemen and Piet Beyleveld to meet Milek at the uniform place, to try them on. The road-gang sequence was difficult because of the road-making machinery, very often we had to ask them to stop for a few minutes so that we could shoot a take. We worked at breakneck speed and were finished before noon, packed up, and while Ernie and Fred took the equipment back to the flat, Milek and I took care of other things that had to be done for the night's shooting. We gathered together at my flat, and Fred and Ernie went ahead and set up the scene and I came along with the actors, about seven or eight of them.

Finding the police for this scene had been the most difficult job of casting because I needed a rather brutal Boer type, but at the same time he had to be somebody that I could trust. It was again the same problem, people who looked the part were not to be trusted. Then suddenly Morris found a Greek at a party, South African-born, who he said would be very good. I met him and spoke to him. He did not look exactly right. His features were a bit too fine for the type, but his Afrikaner accent was pretty good and he also spoke Afrikaans, which was pretty important for this scene. He was very anxious to play the part. I am not sure if I know why, whether it was political or if he just wanted to act. Then from our circle of friends who were helping us find actors we got to a man who was an Afrikaner and yet sympathetic to the Africans, who seemed to look the part.

He gave us the name of another man who we went to see that same morning, who was the perfect Boer type, heavy features, thick nose, etc. He came from a long line of an anti-racist family and so he was in complete sympathy with the film. At the last minute, the second man — the first Afrikaner, who looked the part — backed out. He claimed a personal tragedy. The trouble may have been police trouble since he claimed he was having difficulty with the authorities. So in his place, because of the tragedy, we took the Greek.

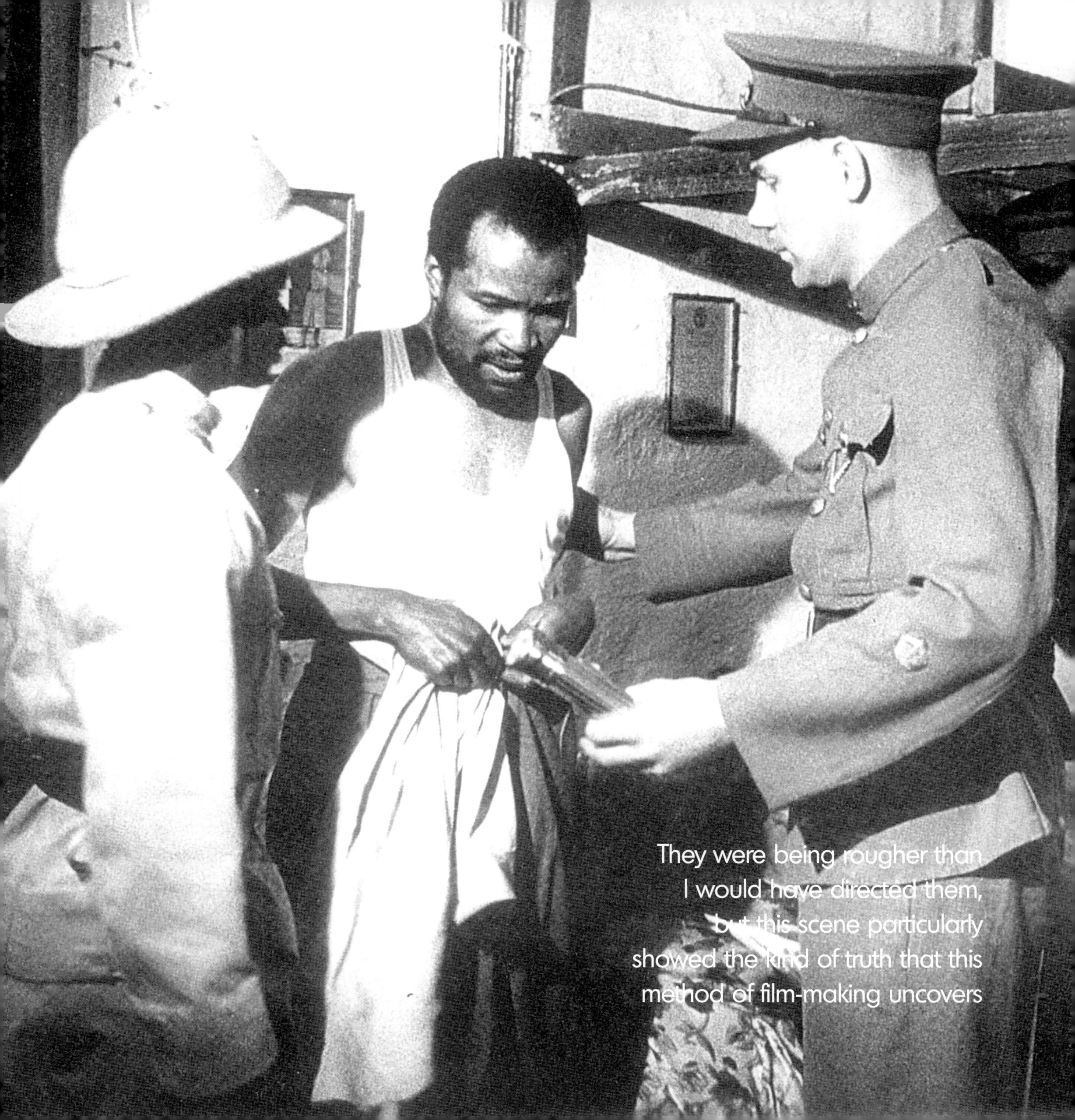

They were being rougher than
I would have directed them,
but this scene particularly
showed the kind of truth that this
method of film-making uncovers

We got their uniforms from a theatrical supply company and I hoped that they didn't report to the police the fact that we were using police uniforms. I was still tempted to use the real police but it seemed to be almost impossible at this point. Carl Lerner, our film editor in New York, told me later, when I came home to edit the film, that when I told him that I was thinking of using the real police, he thought I had gone mad. But it wasn't as bad as it sounded, and I am sure that with enough time and if we could have afforded the expense of re-shooting the scene, I could have gotten friendly enough with the police to have them give me the action I wanted. Actually, in any case, I still planned to use real policeman for the African police. Usually they go together, one or two white policemen with an African. I thought that it might be safe with an African, and I sent Morris out to look for a candidate but he was unable to find someone. Therefore, when Zacharia suggested that he had a friend for the part I agreed to take a look at him. I found that he wasn't really the right type. He was much too gentle-looking, but I did not particularly plan to feature him prominently in the scene, so I decided to use him in any case.

We shot the scene in the servants' quarters of Myrtle Berman's house, with the two African women who worked for her watching in delight. The arrest in the servants' quarters was very efficient, and the acting was excellent. I account for this by the fact that we had the advantage of using real people rather than actors. Actors from outside of this milieu would never have been able to do this scene without a great deal of work, and as a matter of fact the scene wouldn't have been good because it was something I had never seen myself and my directing was not sufficient for the scene. But the Afrikaner and the Greek were able to themselves interpret the action, and they told me that my idea of it was much too mild and that the police were much rougher. They had to break into the house quickly so that the Africans who were there illegally couldn't jump out the window, which was extraordinary when you think of a man having to jump out of a window at night for the crime of living together with his own wife. Actually, I told them to bang on the door and they said no, they must break in immediately in order to get him before he can get away. They were being rougher than I would have directed them, but this scene particularly showed the kind of truth that this method of film-making uncovers. I wanted what I showed in the film to be things that really happened to most Africans, and Vinah, who acted this scene, said that this situation had happened to her several times, and that her husband had been arrested often, and that the raids were always going on in the African servants' quarters in the area where she worked.

A rather funny incident happened during the shooting which we didn't find out until several days later: when our actor policemen were pounding on the door and I was rather fearful that the neighbours might investigate the noise and discover our work, the Africans living in the servants' quarters in the neighbouring houses heard the banging, and thinking that it was a police raid, those who were there illegally jumped out of bed and over fences and ran away into the night.

These raids were a common occurrence in Johannesburg, and we read in the newspapers that the police were arresting babies who were also illegal tenants. This shows the absurdity of the laws of South Africa. I often pondered on this and wondered why this was so, why the situation was even worse than it had to be, and I realised that once you defend a premise which is basically wrong you are then forced by the circumstance to more and more absurd action. Once you have taken the philosophy of a super race you end up by sending people to concentration camps and experimenting on human life. Once you start the policy of white supremacy there is no limit to the lengths you have to go to maintain this.

SEXUAL JEALOUSY AS BASIS OF RACIAL HATRED

Being in South Africa with my previous experience of life in America could not help but make me think a great deal about race hatred. What are the causes of this obviously irrational attitude and behaviour? There are many theories and a lot has been written and spoken about this subject, but I tend to believe that there is not one single cause but a combination of causes that creates this attitude. I think there are the economic causes. I think there are the sociological causes, and as corollary to this the historical, and there are also the psychological causes and effects, and sexual jealousy is part of this last group of causes. You will find in the mythology of any culture that has racial or group discrimination and hatreds that they imagine the members of other groups, in this case Africans, black men and women, as having special sexual attributes — that African women are more passionate and that African men are more virile, and the fact that this is forbidden fruit makes it so much more tantalising. It was common knowledge that white women in South Africa were worse racists than the men. I often suspected that this was partly due to this very cause — sexual jealousy. The women had much more to be jealous about, not only because African women were very attractive, but because it was the white men who were the most frequent offenders of the so-called Immorality Act. It was the white men who were essentially attracted to African women, and white women sensed this threat to their security and stability. And since the social punishment for such a transgression on a white woman's part would be far more enormous than for a man, sexual activity between an African man and a white woman was rare. In fact I never heard of a case where a white woman and an African man were brought to court under the Immorality Act. But once the separation of the groups has begun, and once there is a stigma placed on one group, then free rein is given to the imagination and hatred, and if whites somehow feel that Africans have greater sexual powers, it is natural that there be a subconscious jealousy by the opposite race. Such is the basis for the fury, idiotic and irrational, of whites with this mentality when they see Africans with white women. If what they suspect subconsciously were true, then they might lose their women. Of course I don't think the case can be made that this is the sole basis for racism. I think that it grows out of the other causes, but it adds to it and complicates the matter and gives it a more extreme and violent twist. It accounts for the violence of the lynchings in the American South where so often they took the form of castration, and why whites are always so quick to jump to the conclusion that Negroes or Africans wish to rape their women.

Shortly after we first arrived, there was a scandal in the newspaper about the secretary of Prime Minister Strijdom. He was a staunch Nationalist, but he was arrested under the Immorality Act for having sexual relations with an African. There was quite an uproar about the situation and from those of us who were against this whole system, a gleeful reaction. The newspaper report was quite amusing, but it was a bit pathetic as well. The man pleaded his case, and said repeatedly that he had always been an upright citizen and came from a good family, and that this would ruin him. The whole situation would have been ludicrous were it not so

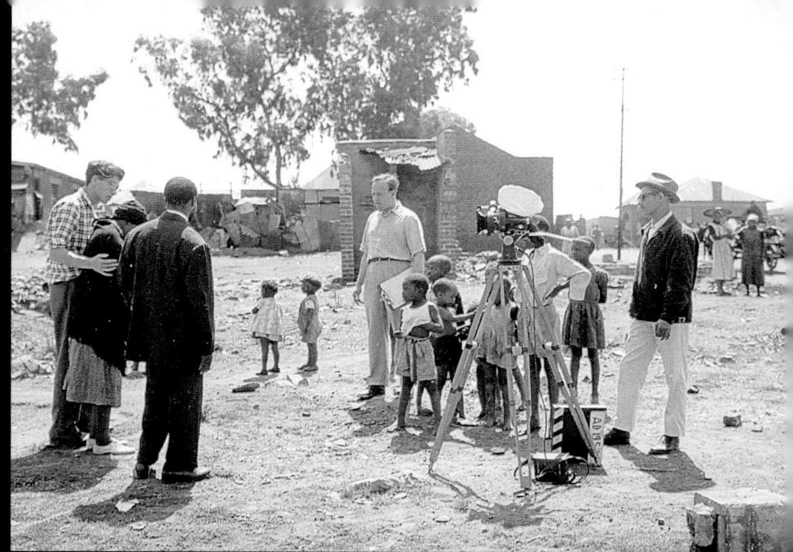

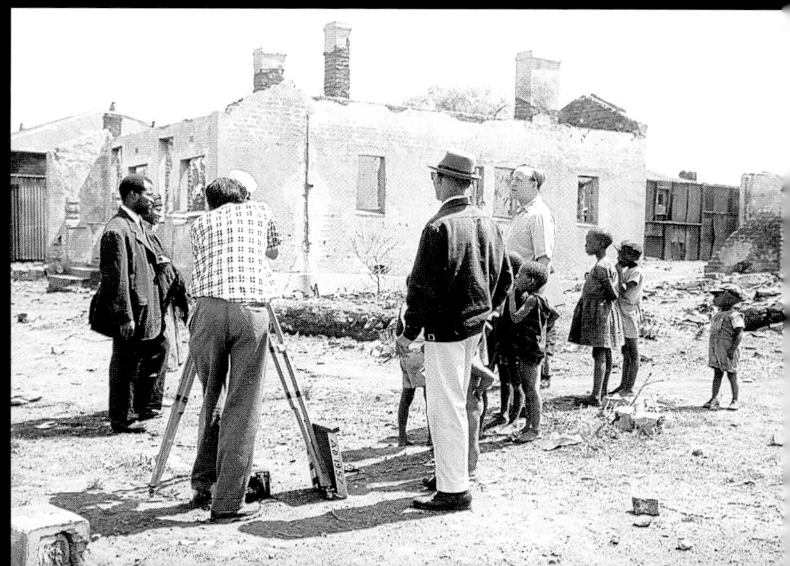

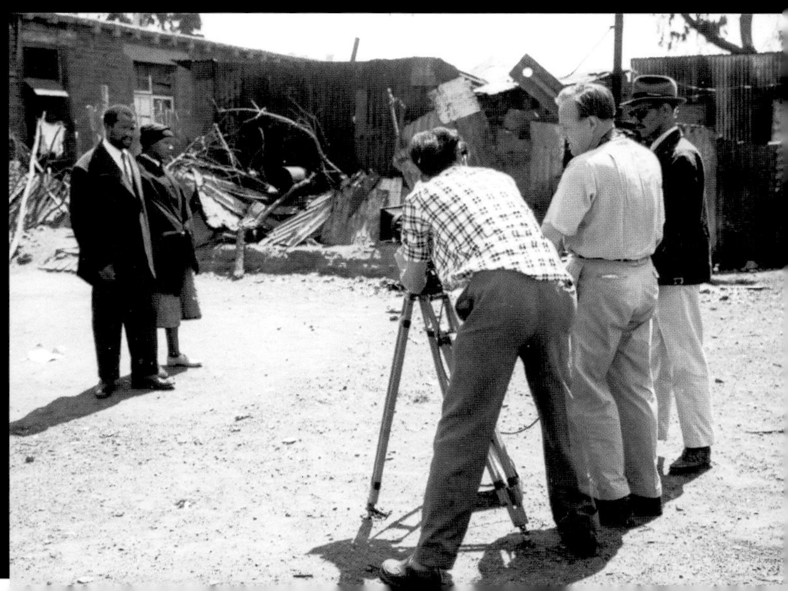

tragic. As a matter of fact, in these cases, the members of different races were tried in different courts, so you can have a situation where the African, usually a woman, would be given a sentence of three years in jail and the man would be allowed to go free. Of course there have also been cases where the men have gone to jail as well. Hendrik Verwoerd, the Minister of Native Affairs, was anxious to prevent this from happening. I was told by the Africans that if every Afrikaner guilty of this offence were put in jail, then there would be no one to run the army or the police force, and half of the manpower would be incarcerated. I have been told by African women that it is nearly impossible to walk down the streets of any city without being accosted frequently by white men. It was notorious that Afrikaner policemen quite frequently raped African girls during the raids, and this is one of the very strong reasons why African women don't want to carry passes because they can be arrested on almost any pretext and are open to such abuse. When I wrote the script I knew that I wanted Zacharia arrested at the end of the film, and finally, after long thought, I decided that he should be arrested for sleeping over with his wife, since this is so common in South Africa and so symbolic of the absurdity of the whole system of apartheid and the pass laws.

ON LOCATION: JOHANNESBURG RAILWAY STATION

After finishing the scene of the arrest of Zacharia, Ernie promptly left the next day. We still had quite a few exteriors to do, the marching sequence at the railroad and others. We had already planned to shoot this scene with Ernie helping, with no success. We could not get people to co-operate and they would always look into the camera, so I decided to go down with a pocket full of shillings and try to get a group to march through and co-operate with us. At first I got very little response. People would hardly stop. Perhaps they were suspicious or just in a hurry. Suddenly one or two gathered around, and I gave them a shilling and asked them to stand aside. Then more came. Suddenly it seemed that the group grew to enormous proportions, until I was completely surrounded by a mob of shouting Africans. I wasn't particularly concerned because they were all quite amiable, smiling and laughing and shouting, but George Malebye, our driver, and Milek and Morris, looking from the other side, became quite afraid. They said it looked quite ugly and I wasn't really aware of the situation, but suddenly I realised that there were too many surrounding me and I felt a bit uncomfortable and decided to extricate myself. Actually a man had been stabbed to death in the railway station a few days before with no provocation, so there is always apt to be some ugly character in such a crowd.

As I was trying to get away from the group, without having any difficulty, nobody was particularly bothering me, they were just gathering around, reaching their hands out for money, an African suddenly ran over and pushed aside the crowd and got me away. He was a member of the African National Congress, and one of the accused at the Treason Trial.

He had quite a wonderful face. I don't remember his name but I wanted to see him again sometime. We talked for a few minutes. He apparently knew something about the film and said that what I had done was dangerous and I mustn't do that again. Of course I was not completely unaware of the danger but never was I terribly concerned, I was so absorbed in what I was doing. Another thing is that the crowd gathered so suddenly that I had hardly had time to realise what was happening. I had been working so much with Africans, in such close relationships with them, that I had very little fear. I carried the attitude that all Africans were my friends since I was theirs, which of course was not true considering the fact that many of these people did not even know who I was — although I had the feeling that an enormous number of Africans did know who our crew were since we had been shooting almost every day for two months in Sophiatown.

I am sure that the word had spread, particularly from the kind of treatment we got whenever we filmed Africans. I also attribute this somewhat to the congeniality of the African. I think that he is very often able to be very co-operative and friendly, given no reason to be otherwise. It is what convinces me that if Africans were approached in the proper way, they in time could co-operate very well in a multiracial society. The only problem is that this will never be done until it is too late, and the Africans have become so bitter that they burst out with acts of savage cruelty.

We had other scenes to shoot that day, and we had had enough of the railway station, so we decided to come back on Sunday and try to get a group when there would be less people.

This shooting became agonisingly slow. We couldn't get anything on Sunday, and we were chased away this second time by the police, who told us that we had to get permission. We went back and got permission from the railway police, from the sergeant at the desk, and the following day we came back to shoot. We shot a few scenes, and then Milek decided to go up on the roof to get a better angle. While Milek was shooting on the roof, I suddenly noticed three or four of what seemed to me rather delinquent-looking adolescent Boers in sports-jackets running across the road from the railway administration building into the railway station. Their action conveyed to me a feeling of anger and authority, and I had the impression that they might be the police going after Milek. However, I was not sure.

Suddenly they came out on the roof running toward Milek, and their action seemed so violent that I became suddenly quite frightened, and ran towards them to tell them that we had permission from the police to shoot there. Before I was able to get close enough to do this, these ducktailed policemen rushed across the roof with such force that I thought they were going to throw Milek off. They yelled to him from a distance, "What are you doing"? Milek replied "Filming." Their reply was, "The hell with your blankety-blank film — we are going to throw you off the roof" — at which point Milek turned to them very calmly and said, "Take it easy." He said, in that unique Polish accent, "Take it easy, I am not used to being spoken to like that," and that stopped them. It worked, the same old trick worked. The Afrikaner is quite overawed by the foreigner, and they felt that Milek knew what he was talking about and had some position to back it up.

At the same time I yelled up to them that we have permission to shoot here and they asked us where our permission was. "Do you have it in writing?" they asked. At the same time, a uniformed policeman came over to me and asked to see my permission in writing. I yelled up to them that I didn't have permission in writing, but that the sergeant had given me the permission and I would go and see him. While they stood there guarding Milek, I went with the policeman to the desk. Unfortunately, there was a different officer at this stage, who said that I must go to the railway manager. When I then came back to tell Milek to come down off

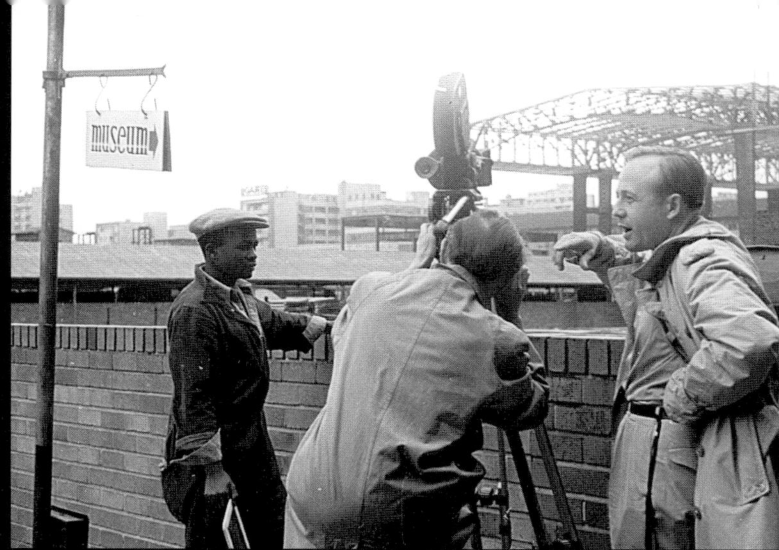

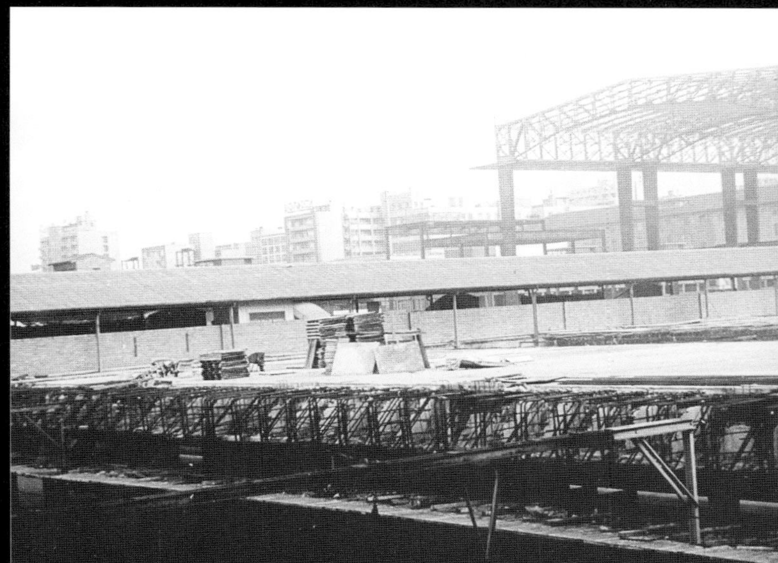

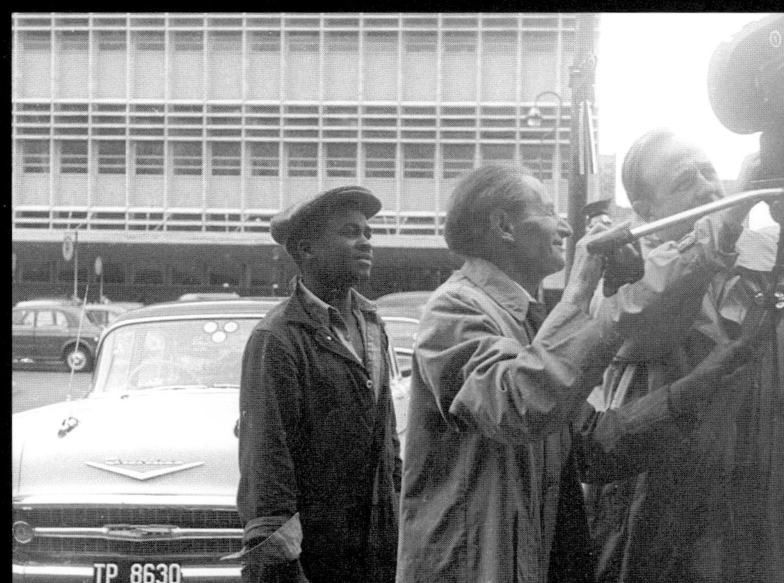

the roof, the ducktailed policemen had gone away. Milek by this time had switched magazines — we had several magazines with us so that in case the police came we could switch magazines and give them unexposed material, keeping the exposed one for ourselves — and I told the policemen that we would come back and talk to the railway manager later in the day. Milek was laughing and saying that the fools never demanded to take the film, so that we had everything we needed. George the driver and Morris and Milek were just standing around, so I said, "We should get the hell out of here fast." We loaded the car quickly, jumped in and drove off. Another narrow escape.

FEAR OF CONFISCATION OF FILM

There was a constant danger that we would be discovered and the film would be confiscated. The longer we worked, the worse this fear became, because more money and effort was being put into it. At the beginning, if this happened, the loss would not have been too great and perhaps we could have started again somewhere else. As it got towards the middle of the filming, it became worse and worse. During the day I rarely thought about it except when something happened or when we had a particular security problem, but it was at night that it bothered me the most.

After I had left the crew and was alone, getting undressed in the dark, quietly so as not to wake Ellie, I suddenly began to think, My God, what if they catch us now? Thousands of dollars will be lost, plus all of the effort. I would become intensely worked up and it seemed that my nervous system was at a key pitch. This happened to me nearly every night until after about a week I suddenly realised that I must stop. I must never think about this again, and as soon as it starts to come into my mind I must immediately stop thinking about it for the sake of the film and myself, otherwise I will work myself into such a state that I shall never be able to complete the film.

So I was able to succeed from then on in making myself forget about it. However, although I suppressed it, I am sure it was with me, because by the time the film was finished and I was back in New York I was under such emotional tension that it began to show in me in many ways and I later told my friends and family that I was terribly nervous on my arrival back home.

Practically every scene I was shooting was being rushed. I was shooting everything with the minimum number of angles and takes. Often when I had finished a scene I felt very uneasy with it. I felt a sense of pain that the scene would not be right. Very often Milek would complain about the scene, or Ernie, that it was not properly shot. My answer would be, "Let's finish the film and get it in the can before the police get us, we haven't got time to be perfect. If we have time left over we'll do it again" — knowing pretty much that we would never have time left over the way things were going.

I did manage to re-shoot one or two scenes. I should have done this with more of them that were not satisfactory, but the situation and time didn't permit it. On the few occasions that we did it the results were amazing. I found that certain scenes which we first could not seem to get proper results for, when I was able to do them over again they came out beautifully, without any effort and very quickly. From this I drew the conclusion that with non-professionals they need time to absorb the ideas into their conscious and subconscious which makes ad-libbing much easier the second time around. It was tragic that I was not able to rehearse the film with these actors for a month as originally planned.

FINAL SCENE: SHOOTING AT MISSION

We continued to shoot our interior scenes at the mission. Morris, who had never worked in films before, was turning out to be a perfect production manager, and was building the sets between the shooting of each scene. The dialogue was difficult and slowing us down. We had now come to Marumu's scene, in which he struggles with Vinah. We found the work with Marumu very difficult. I picked him originally because I felt that there was something mad about his look. He was proving to be an odd character, very likeable in some ways. He was very loyal to the idea of the film, and wanted very much to do his best in every way. But we found that he had

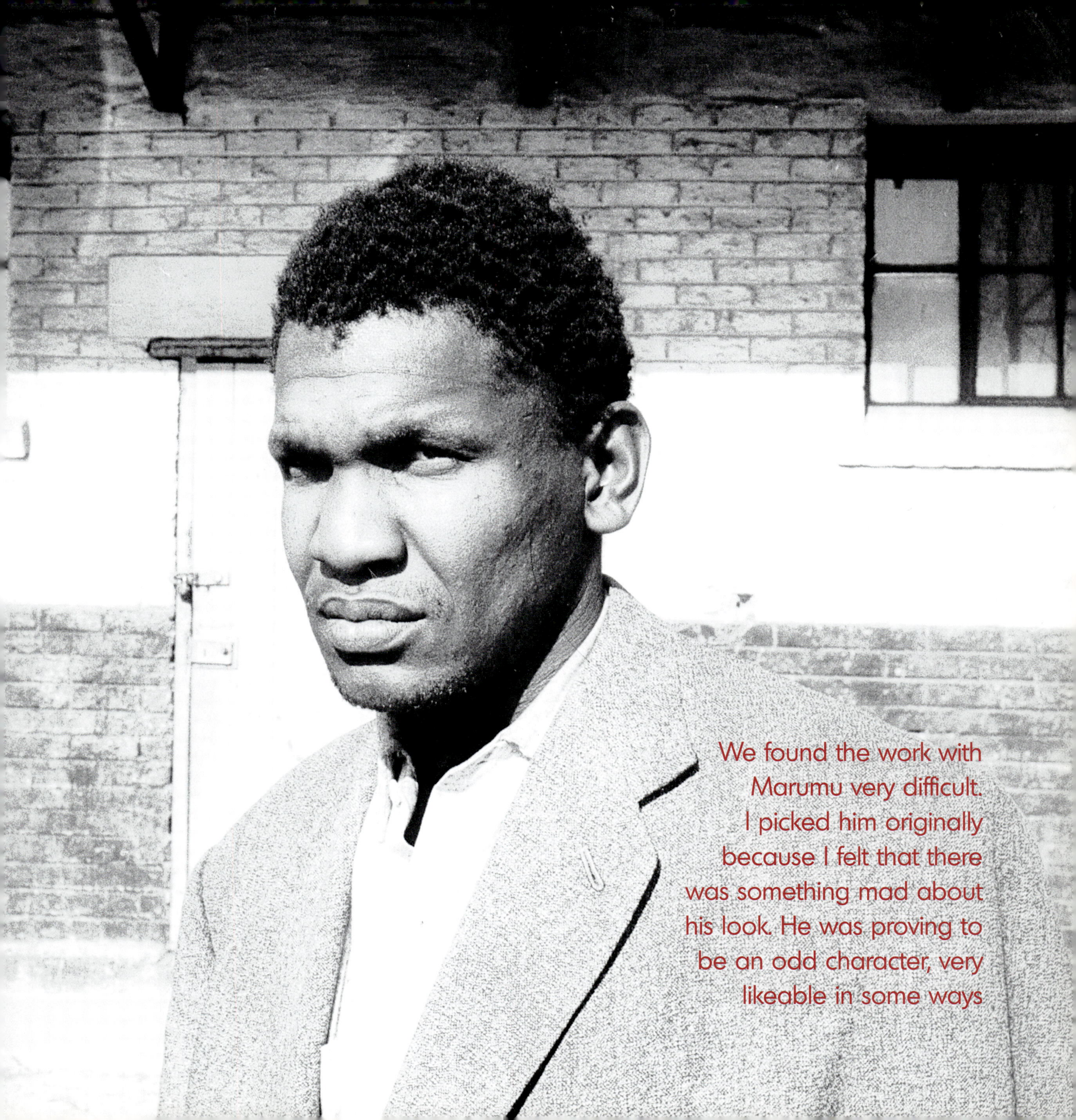

We found the work with Marumu very difficult. I picked him originally because I felt that there was something mad about his look. He was proving to be an odd character, very likeable in some ways

great difficulty in keeping appointments. We'd tell him to come to the set one day and he wouldn't show up. It wasn't because of any irresponsibility on his part. He was quite responsible in his own way, except he would come another day. Instead of showing up on Tuesday, he would show up on Monday, or on Thursday. He had no intention of not coming and he wanted to come according to his agreement, it was just that he got the days confused.

Another time we sent the car to pick him up and he wasn't there on its arrival. He showed up a couple of hours later, having walked all the way by himself. He seemed to be a bit mad, but very sweet. There was something gentle and child-like in his voice. And then one day I discovered that he had a soul. It was a day after the shooting, and we were driving home with Marumu in the car when we suddenly came upon two African girls fighting. It was quite a terrible scene since they were going at it fiercely. Nobody was doing a thing to stop them. There were some Whites there and they just seemed to enjoy the scene. The Africans stood by apathetically, they seemed afraid to become involved. After a few seconds Marumu said to me, "Please let me out of the car, I must stop them." He went over calmly and forced them apart. It was quite difficult and he put himself in jeopardy. But all of us were petrified with inactivity, and Marumu, this man, half-mad, was the only one who raised a finger to stop it. Somehow it seemed a bit symbolic of the world that we live in. Actually I had quite a bit of difficulty with Marumu in getting him to enact the scene in which he kills Vinah. For some reason he didn't seem to be able to bring forth the fierceness in his acting, perhaps because he was too afraid of his own violence. In the scene in which he is supposed to strangle Vinah to death he kept saying, "Please be quiet," in a very, very soft voice. We couldn't get this man, who apparently seemed to be full of tensions and violence, to enact the scene properly. We had to re-shoot and re-shoot.

I had decided that one of the members of Zacharia's family, his sister Josephine, would be mute. When we went to shoot this scene I found that we were having difficulty in getting the proper sound. We tried many rehearsals to get this and I finally decided to give it up until I could go to an institution for deaf mutes so that she could hear exactly how they sounded. We found one outside Johannesburg and went there with Josephine, making tape-recordings and talking to the children. When we returned to Johannesburg to the set I was amazed, and so was everyone else, at how well she was able to capture it now that she had heard it. At first I had thought that she would not be able to do it properly.

In the last scene of the film, the script has it that Zacharia goes berserk with rage on finding that his wife had been murdered by Marumu the tsotsi. When I wrote the script I had the feeling that this might be a scene much too difficult for a non-professional actor to portray. However, I felt it had to be done to give the film its proper meaning, and I decided not to tailor the script to the talents of the actors, but that the script should portray as completely as possible what I was trying to say about South Africa, and take the risk that the non-professional actors could manage. We had finally come to the shooting of this last scene and I took a great deal of preparation talking to Zacharia for quite a long time, one or two hours of preparation with him discussing the meaning of this scene, what I was driving at and how to arrive at it. After this we started to shoot immediately.

Zacharia started out with this realisation of Vinah's death and soon afterwards went into a berserk rage. Suddenly, we were transfixed. He seemed to lose complete control of himself in his acting. The entire crew was incredulous. It was hard for us to believe that his acting would have been so marvellous and that he was able to lose himself in the part so completely. However, I was afraid because of the poor camera angle that we would have to re-shoot the scene, but I felt that it would be very difficult to recapture that mood again, if not impossible. But we did come back again to re-shoot the scene. Originally I had Zacharia fall to the floor and pound on the floor in an absolute rage. The problem was that from this point the angle was very poor. Therefore, I changed it the second time. Instead of having him fall to the floor, he sat down at the table and suddenly started to beat the table with his hand desperately.

LAST SHOOT

By this time we had practically completed the filming and there only remained a long shot of Shantytown to do. This was a restricted area, and no whites were allowed in without a pass. We had been driving through this area to pick up our cast, but most of the time we sent George Malebye to do this, so there wasn't too much risk, and now we had reached the point where we actually had to take some shots of Shantytown. Our plan was to use the station-wagon if we could rig the camera up in the back and just open the door and shoot out of the back without taking the cameras out where they could be seen. It was something like those old U-boat films where they had an ocean liner fixed up with heavy guns and the sides would fall away at the approach of the submarine.

We drove to Shantytown and picked a fairly secluded spot on the road and drove back and forth until we had found the place that we thought would be the best angle and the least suspicious, and we also searched the area for police cars so that we would not be stopped during the shooting. We finally stopped and placed the car perpendicular to the road and took several shots directly into Shantytown. The angle was not good and the location was not ideal either for the picture we wanted, but at least we had it covered.

So then we decided to look for a more ideal spot, taking the magazine out and hiding it so that we would have it in case we were stopped. The best angle we could find was right next to the police station in the township. We had everything we wanted by this time, so we decided to be brazen. We stopped the car right next to the police station, and in order to distract their attention from us I told Morris to go over and ask them for directions. "Ask them how to get to Pretoria or something ridiculous." I knew Morris was a good talker and would keep their attention for quite a while. Fortunately, there was only an African policeman outside, which made it easier. Morris engaged the policeman in conversation for quite a long time, giving us plenty of time to shoot the scene. We drove away down a side road and had to turn around and come back. Suddenly two policeman came towards us, and I did not want them to come too near the car because they could then see the camera, so I sent Morris out to meet them in advance to ask them for further directions. He did this, which enabled us to back the car and get a considerable distance away from them before Morris ran back and got in the car, and we drove off.

We now had finished all the shooting necessary, and all that remained was the final preparations for going home. Actually there was quite a lot to do. The car had to be sold, and some of the equipment. We had to pack a lot of things to ship back to New York: quite a few details remained to be sorted out.

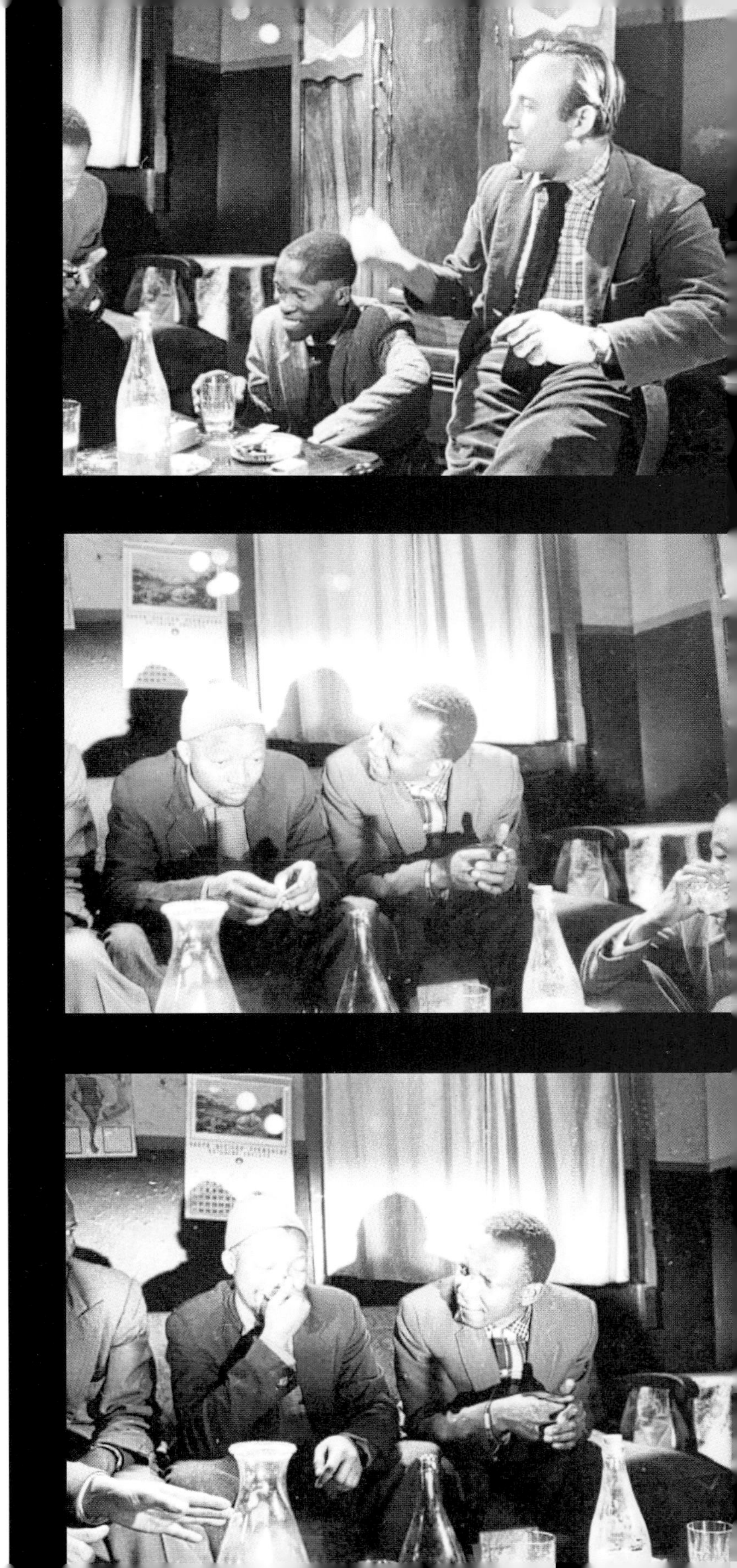

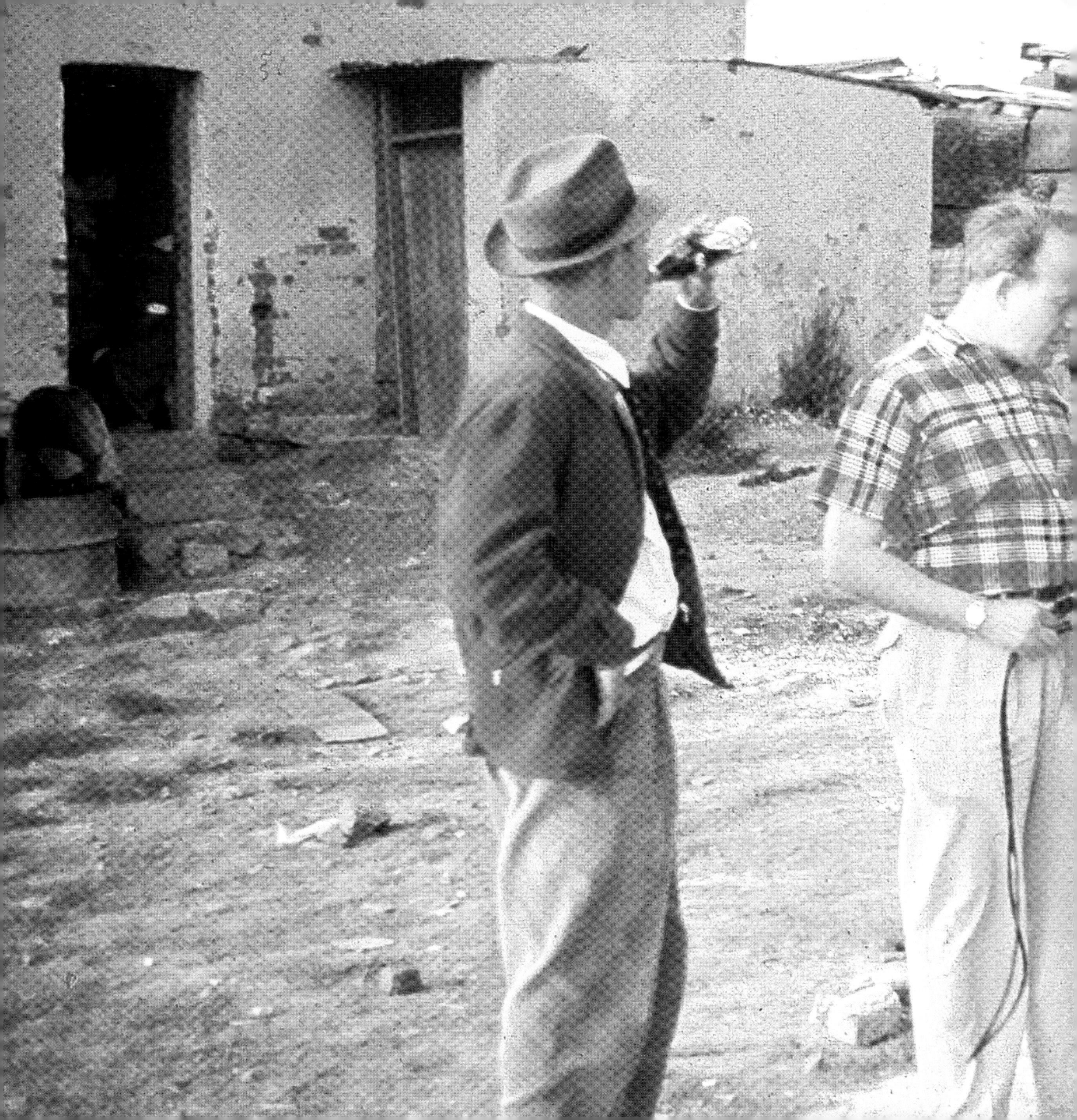

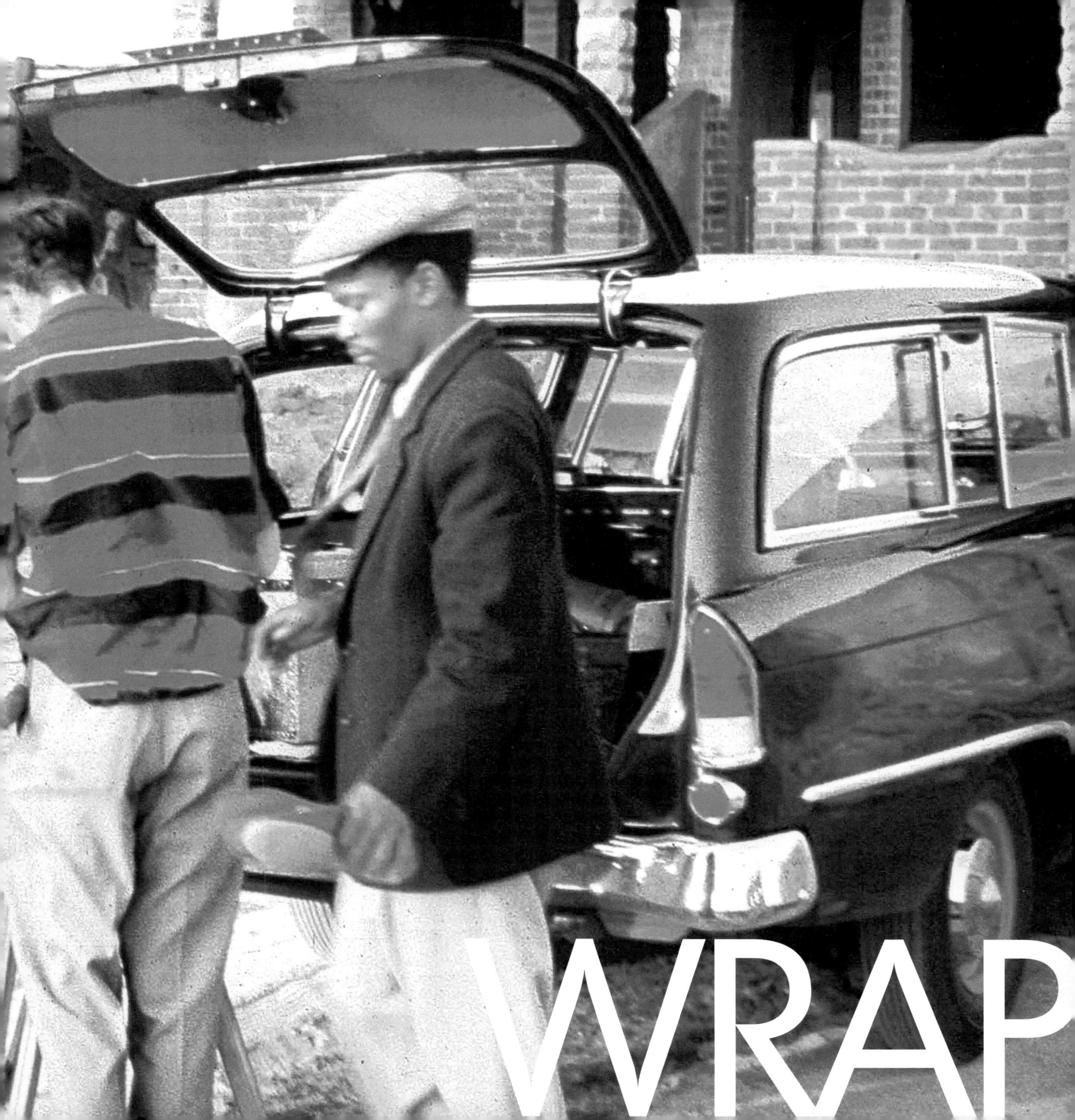

WRAP

LIBERALS OF NO HELP

I had a bit of a financial problem. This was a film that certainly would not make much money, if it even covered its costs. It was a film that was essentially made to show a very important social issue of our times. I needed more financing at this point to complete the film and I hoped that some of the whites in South Africa who had money and who were also against apartheid would be able to help. I was unable to go to them before the shooting was completed since if the film was to be done in secrecy, I had to tell as few people as possible. I asked a few of my friends if there were any South Africans like this who could help as I would like to raise at least one quarter of the budget in South Africa. I felt that somehow that was only just.

I was given a list of five or ten people supposed to be liberals or progressives. I then found out again what the African meant by liberals and I found out also again the kind of fundamental basis of liberal thinking. There were people who were supposed to be sympathetic to the Africans and were supposed to be strongly against apartheid, yet at the same time, I got no sympathy or support from them. These were all very wealthy people and one of them could have donated a quarter of the budget without the slightest sacrifice. Naturally, I cannot condemn them for not having supported this film since they were entitled to support the things they thought were important, but it was their attitude. I sensed a fear. I had the feeling that the basic reason for their lack of support was that they were afraid to become involved, for one thing, and secondly, that they were not that deeply committed or convinced about the African cause; and this was the essential argument of the Africans, that the liberals said these things and expressed these ideas, but when it came to the showdown they always backed out. The conviction is just not that deep, and also it is essentially against their own financial interests, the interest of the upper middle class.

These people were all very comfortable, they lived in wonderful houses, were cultured, respectable and presentable people, much to be admired, and in addition they knew they were on the right side, the side of civilization, the side of rationalism, the side of good thinking. The only problem with them was that they were not willing to do anything about it. They rather disgusted me. I could see how this kind of people could let down their friends among the Africans, to whom at first they might have seemed to be great people and much on the side of humanity. The mealy-mouthed liberals. Of course, liberalism means something different in every place. A liberal in South Africa would be quite conservative in Europe or America. But I am afraid that liberalism has come to mean no plan, no programme, no action, just a belief in good thinking and nice behaviour which would be all very well in a well-ordered world. However, we happen to be living in a kind of half-controlled madhouse in which a good proportion of the inmates are ready to hack the other ones to pieces, and I am afraid that this live and let-live won't do, that we have to make a determined effort to prevent this so called civilization from annihilating itself.

WRAP PARTY

Of course, we had to have a party to celebrate the end of the film. All those who were connected with the film in any way were invited, and a few others thrown in for good measure. We invited friends, and then we thought of asking some real reactionaries just to give them a little bit of a jolt. We thought it might be good for them. We decided to have the party at Myrtle's place and asked her opinion. She was amused by the idea, but felt it was dangerous because somebody who was a real extremist might call the police.

We were finally all gathered together after considerable difficulties because we were warned by one of the people who had been in the film that there was a certain house in Sandhurst that was giving mixed parties, and the police were determined to raid the next time this happened. We assumed from the conversation that it was Myrtle that they were talking about. A man told me this when I gave him the invitations, and I immediately told Myrtle, to get her opinion of it. She was not sure what was to be done. Somehow or other we did not believe it. We felt that it was an excuse on that individual's part not to come to the party. After discussing it with Myrtle's husband, Monty, their decision was to have the party. I felt a little nervous about it and almost thought that I should not do it. However, it was at their house and they said to go ahead. This stilled my fears. I thought it was very brave of them, they were admittedly taking a risk. The Africans did not have too much to lose because unless they were caught with whisky in their hands they could not be charged. Myrtle and Monty were taking the greatest risk. I had finished the film and did not have too much to lose, but I did not feel like being bothered at this stage with any trouble.

Once we decided to do it, I didn't give it much thought. This was typical of the way people like Monty and Myrtle behaved, those who had the courage to be against the racism of South Africa, that they really had been in the movement for a long time and had a great deal of courage and didn't give a damn whether the police would come, and went right on openly carrying on their work. They were all known by this time, for they could not work in secret. I was truly inspired by these people and I met a half a dozen of them. I must say that it renewed my faith in human beings to know such people.

The party went along beautifully, I don't quite know why. It was probably because all the tension was off me. Of course the others hadn't this problem, and everybody seemed to be having a marvellous time. I suppose it was partly the group that was there. Africans always add a great deal of music and dancing to any party, and gaiety. Walter Klapper and Walter Heinzl seemed to be enjoying themselves immensely. They were Austrian film-makers who were also filming in Southern Africa at the time. Walter kept coming over to me all evening and saying "My god, what a marvellous party. I've never been to such a party since I've been in South Africa. It's wonderful to feel free for once." He had never been to a mixed party in South Africa. He had associated with the wrong people and had been afraid to do such a thing on his own. Well, it was just another one of those evenings in South Africa where time seems to float by effortlessly. There were no little cliques getting together in separate groups talking to themselves, nor people dancing isolated from everyone else. It seemed to be as if everybody was mingling with everyone else, a great feeling of camaraderie.

The only unfortunate act that took place was Morris, who was becoming more and more obnoxious the drunker he became. He tried to provoke Bloke, against whom he had a grudge. He then started to annoy one of the girls there, and finally, when she got fed up with him, he sat down and went into a tirade against the world, saying that she wouldn't dance with him because he was coloured, which was completely untrue, because everybody at the party was enjoying themselves and nobody was behaving in such a way. But Morris was always feeling sorry for himself. He went on and on until finally Andre Stup, a journalist with Associated Press, said "You bore me." I hadn't said anything to Morris, but this was exactly the way I felt myself.

Finally, he started to try and provoke me as well, and the reason was that he had a grudge against me for certain things that had happened in the last few weeks. Morris behaved quite badly at times, however, I liked him. I'd feel as if I understood him, and ridiculous as his behaviour might become, I always had a sense of knowing what was bothering him, and I must say that for practically nine-tenths of the film, Morris outdid himself for us, for the film and for me. He worked very hard and did an excellent job, something that I do not think that many people would have imagined Morris capable of. At the end, he started behaving quite badly, and I really must say that he did things that were absolutely inexcusable. It was only a year or two later that I finally understood what happened to Morris and why he was so good most of the time and went to pieces at the end. I was describing him to someone, and he said, "Yes, of course, he did that because the film was finishing and you were leaving", and I suddenly realised that for Morris this was one of the few times in his life when he really felt a part of something. The idea of the film being completed and all of us going sort of shattered him. He was always a very heavy drinker, but during the film I had told him that he must not drink because we needed him, and that we could not lose time. He was really very good about this. It was only in the last few weeks that suddenly he would not show up when he was needed, and if he showed up he was often drunk.

When we started to shoot, Morris had called me up and said, "I need a job." Well, I knew how unreliable he was. He was drinking, talking uncontrollable nonsense, but I did not want to turn him down completely, so I thought I would just try him out for a few odd jobs. I told him strongly that he had to behave himself, and he came along with us. From the first few days he was such a big help and so good that suddenly he became the production manager. I started him out on an ordinary wage by South African standards, but within a few weeks I had quadrupled his salary. As the production went along, it became obvious to all of us that Morris was grafting on the side, since in his position as production manager he had to deal with people on prices and payments. I knew this and it made me quite angry, and at the same time I tried to stop it without accusing him.

At one point I wanted to throw him out during the production, but the other members of the crew restrained me, since they felt we had to put up with it. We needed him, and we just had to keep stronger control over the money. The last week of the shooting he was drunk quite a lot, and one day he did not show up at all. Because of his thievery and this last action I was extremely annoyed with him for having betrayed us, in a sense, and yet I could always forgive him no matter what he did.

Here was a man with obviously enormous potential who was completely destroyed by the society of which he was part. Morris was still in his twenties, and I could see that in another ten years he would be a wreck, possibly ending up in jail, but with all the things that he had done wrong in the past few weeks, I felt I could not let him get away with it completely. I tried to talk to him patiently, partly in my own interest but partly in the hope that it might have some small effect on him, although I knew essentially it wouldn't do much good. I told him that he had done a wonderful job for us but that he had spoiled everything by his crazy behaviour. I told him that I was planning to give him a bonus at the end of the film, but because of the way that he had let us down so badly, I would still give him the bonus but it would be less than I had originally planned to give him.

He admitted that he had been wrong, and thanked me for what I was offering him, but apparently during the night of the party the resentment that he had felt for me for what I had said to him came out strongly, and at the party he started accusing and mistreating me. Of course he was acting so foolishly that no one paid too much attention to him. The essential thing about Morris's character was that he had no real loyalty. He did have some regarding the film, it seems, but he was not able to sustain it and to me it seemed to be quite obvious that while Morris was a man who was incapable of loyalty, he was a human being for whom even his own father had no loyalty, for his father deserted him.

POST-PARTUM BLUES

After the party, Milek and I decided to see a little of Southern Africa in the short time that remained. We decided to take a trip to Swaziland, which was supposed to be quite beautiful. We also had to sell the car, equipment, left-over film and a lot of other things. Fortunately, Jamie Uys bought most of our equipment that I needed to sell. The only problem was that the money I received I was not able to take out of South Africa immediately, although the bank told me I would be able to since I had brought more than this into the country, but this is always the way such regulations work. You are told one thing, but when it comes to actually executing it you find out that there are other regulations that you were not told about. The Currency Control Board would not allow the exchange, and I should have got Uys to get an import licence. It was finally settled properly, but only after a great deal of effort.

We had a wonderful trip through Swaziland and when we got back to Johannesburg there were only a few days left before Ellie and I and Michael were to fly back to New York. Before we left, Myrtle gave a party for us. Most of the people there we had not met before, but they were all quite wonderful. Many of them had seen *On the Bowery* and thought it was a good film. Somehow or other we seemed to fit in with these people. They wanted us to stay in South Africa and not to leave. Actually for us it had become a place that was part of us and we became part of the place. It was odd. One would think that we would have been glad to get out of South Africa, but actually I did not really want to leave.

I would have liked to have seen much more of that beautiful country, and we had made a good circle of friends who seemed to be real people. The Bermans gave us a wonderful Basuto blanket before we left. There were still a lot of last-minute details to be taken care of, and Milek stayed behind to finish these off. Hazel, Vinah and Zacharia came with us to the airport with Milek and Walter Heinzl. Sadly, we waved goodbye to them all. I still remember them waving frantically from the platform. I don't think that I have ever felt quite so sad to leave a place. We got on board with our baggage, with our new cradle, to wing our way to London, then New York, with baby Michael.

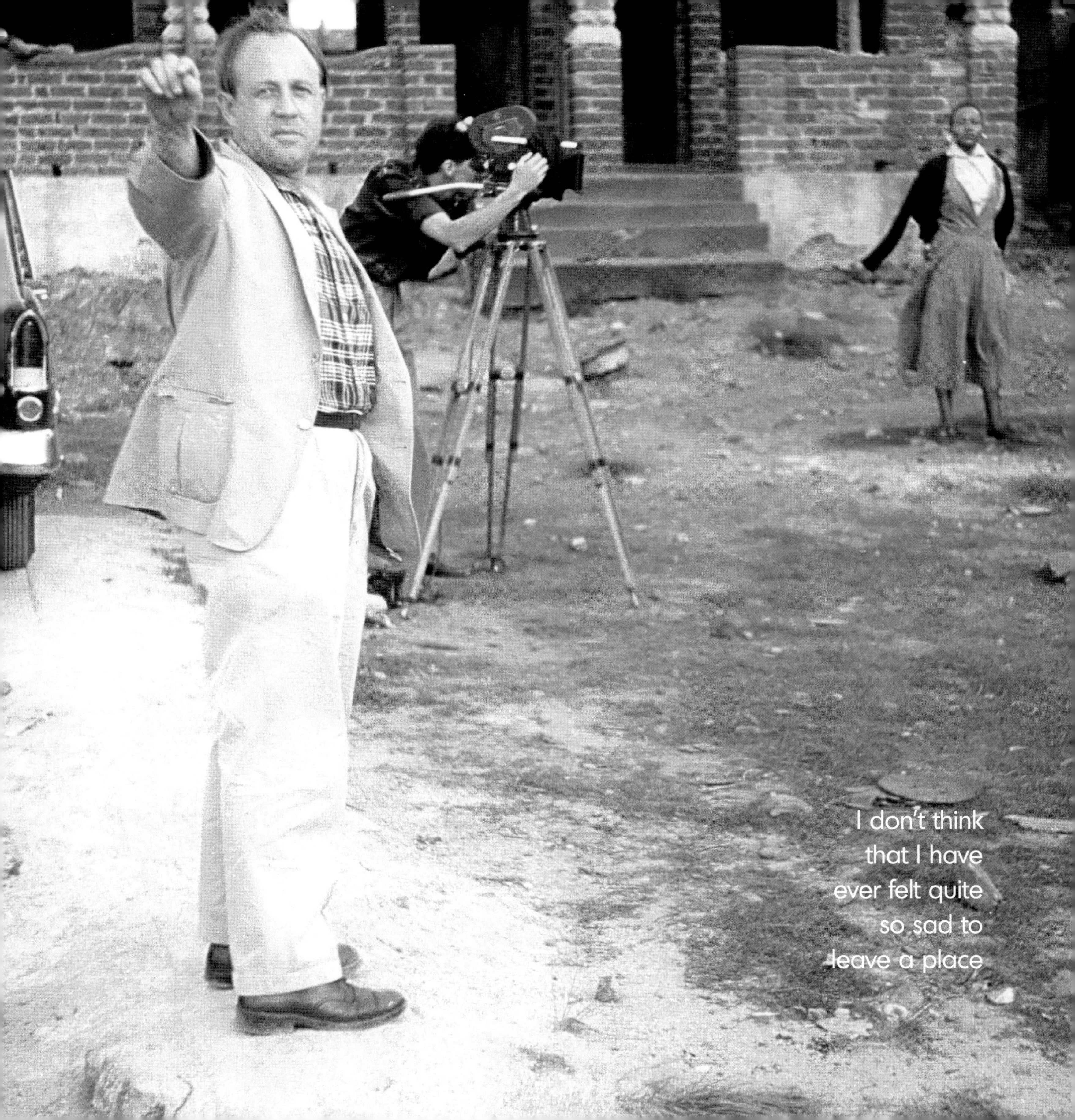

I don't think
that I have
ever felt quite
so sad to
leave a place

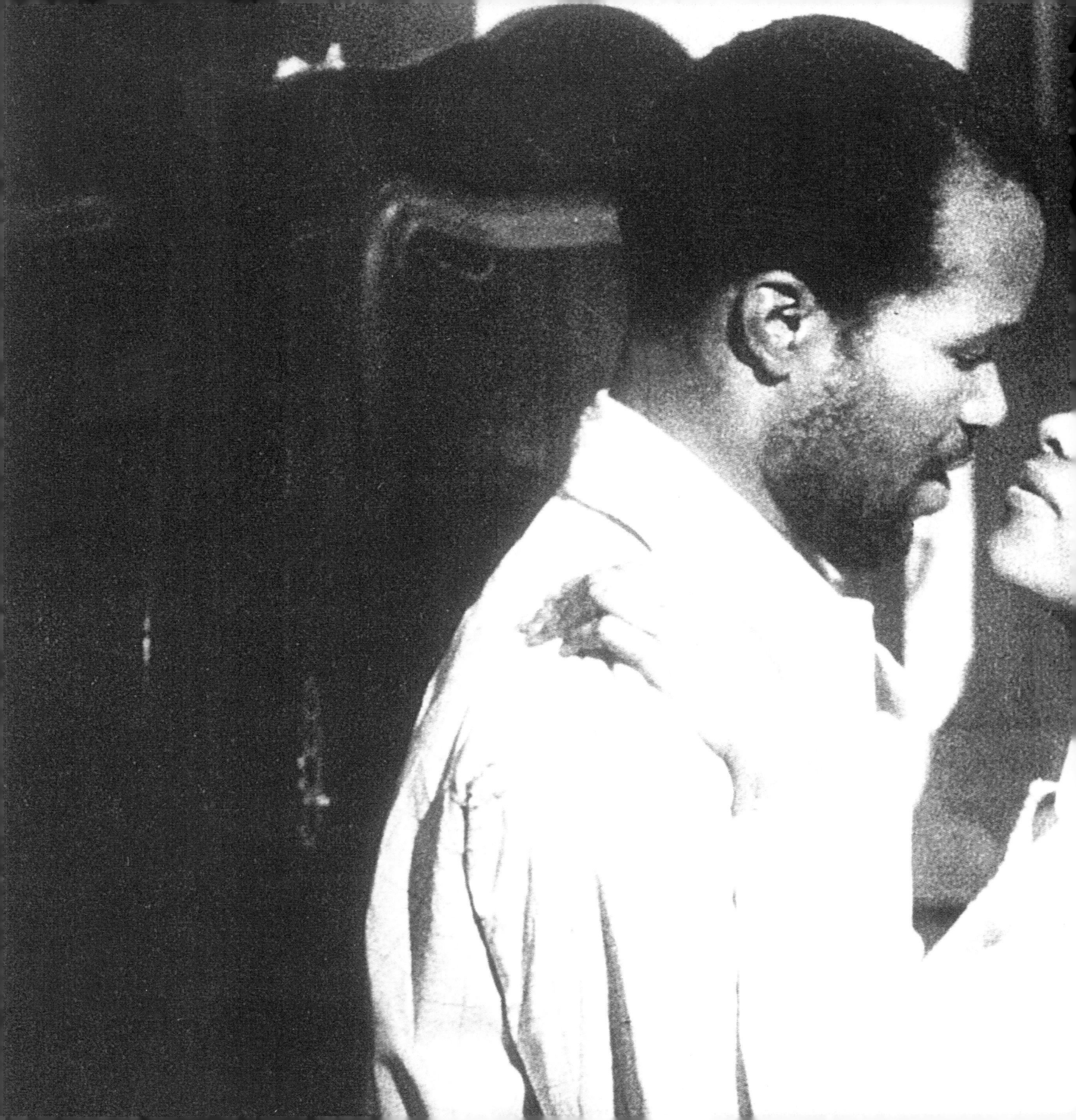

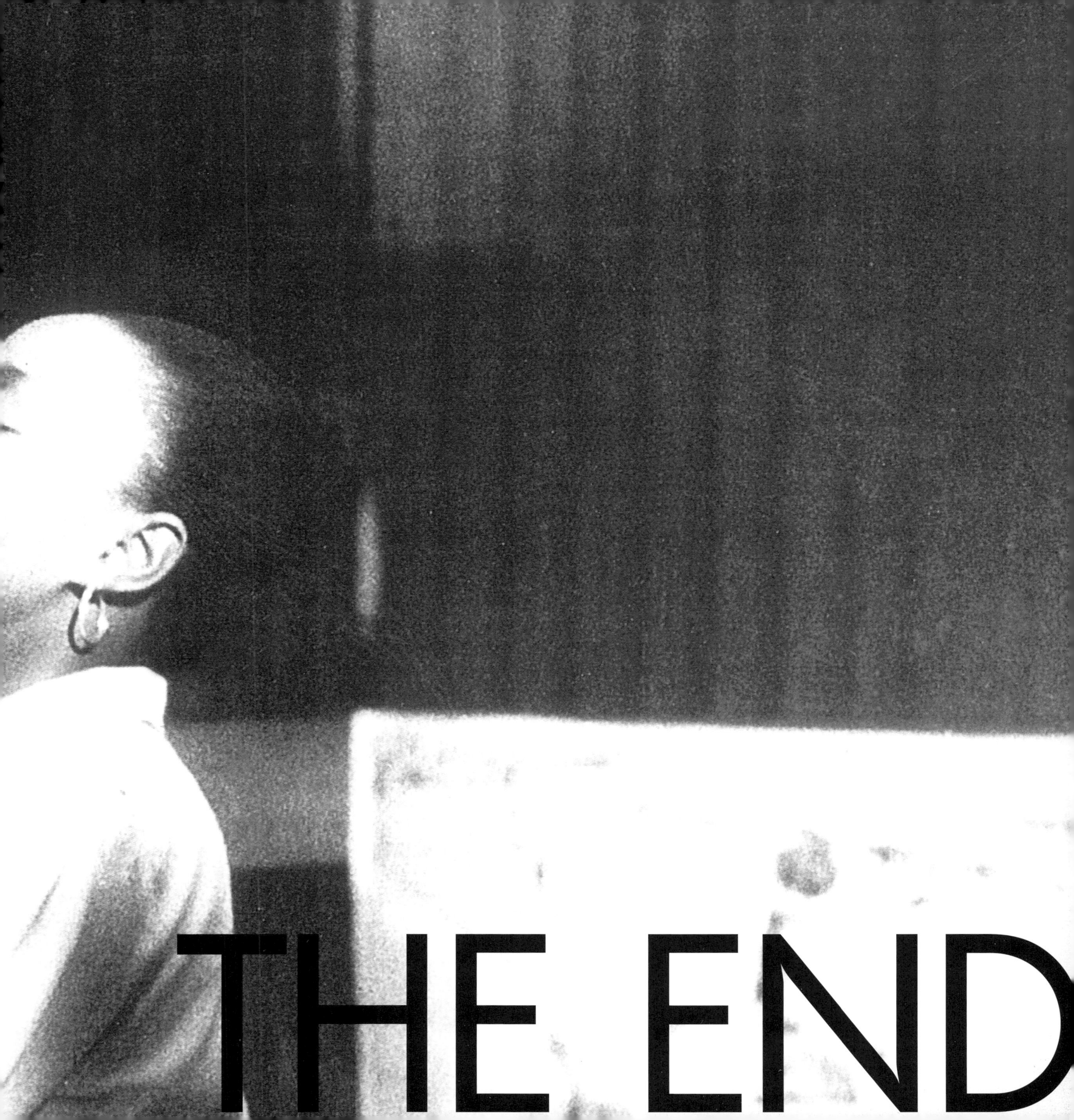
THE END

LIONEL ROGOSIN

I remember many of our African friends, Bloke, Miriam Makeba and Zacharia at the airport waving us farewell. It was a sad moment for me, SA had come to seem like home which I was leaving, never to return. We flew back to New York with a brief stop over in London. On arrival I immediately began to work on the editing with Carl Lerner. Editing the film went relatively smoothly in his able hands.

I had shot a few of the scenes in African languages and needed translations for the subtitles. The UN recommended Eduardo Mondlane. He was from Mozambique but he spoke a dialect closely related to Zulu and it was simple for him to do the translation. He was on the Trusteeship Council of the UN and dedicated to the liberation of Africa and Mozambique. Many years before he had escaped from Mozambique and enrolled in an American college and married an American student. He therefore seemed to have a strong American orientation, which when I left New York for the Venice Film Festival, I chided him about. It was ironic because he had a dramatic future and I was very surprised when a few years later I learned that he had become the leader of Frelimo, the National Liberation Movement of Mozambique.

Later, when I lived in Israel for three years he tried to find me but I had gone to New York for a short visit. I was disappointed, particularly since at our last meeting we had a confrontation about his political moderation. He had now changed drastically to guerrilla warfare against the Portuguese. His sharp turnaround was one of the great surprises of my life and it ended tragically. We finally did meet a year or two later, this time in New York. He seemed quite anxious to see me and he told me he was in the US buying guns for the revolution. This was no joke and I was quite frightened for him and thought that he shouldn't be telling me this. Talking like that could expose him but I assumed that he knew what he was doing, but I shouldn't have assumed that. It was in 1969 that I heard over the radio that Eduardo Mondlane had been assassinated by a package bomb at his home in Lourenzo Marques. It was an intense shock. Despite some minor differences I was extremely fond of him. It was said that it was the South African intelligence service that sent him the bomb.

After completing *Come Back, Africa* I applied again to enter it in the Venice Film Festival. I was surprised to be turned down, but at the same time I was invited to be a judge at the documentary festival which was held in the spring. *Come Back, Africa* was accepted out of competition and they invited Miriam Makeba to be a special guest. I then set about bringing Miriam out of South Africa – no easy task. I contacted Myrtle Berman and asked her to arrange to get Miriam out. In those days it was difficult to get Africans out of South Africa, but all such obstacles had their price in the corrupt bureaucracy of South Africa. After their original reluctance they demanded $500 as a bond for Miriam and other guarantees and fees to be paid to the Pretoria officials. After that they granted her an exit permit and we planned to attend the festival together in August.

Later in Venice I met Flavio Paulon who I knew from the previous showing of *On The Bowery* in 1956, who told me that *Come Back, Africa* was unacceptable because it was an American entry and there were too many large budget American entries, and it was an embarrassment for the festival to accept *Come Back, Africa* with its tiny budget. The US has the most powerful film industry in the world and the largest military establishment, national interests have a large influence over the decisions of festivals and juries.

The documentary festival that spring was a great pleasure. There I met Joris Ivans who became my great friend for many years. I found him sincere and compassionate. He was a communist with strong convictions and years later I showed his films on Vietnam at the Bleecker Street Cinema. I found the other judges Rene Guyonnet, Philip De Sanctos and Thorold Dickenson astute and perceptive. I think it was an excellent jury.

After the Documentary Festival, Ellie, Michael and I went to Aix en Provence in France where we had rented a flat for the summer. In the meantime I was in touch with Miriam who was planning to go to London and meet her husband, Shunna Pillay, and then come to Aix. In London, Harry Belafonte attended a screening of *Come Back, Africa* and I was told that he was very impressed and excited about it, and told Miriam he was anxious to promote the film and help her develop her career. When I heard that I was a bit apprehensive because I had a hunch that Belafonte wouldn't have the best intentions for *Come Back, Africa*. After a short visit in London, Shunna and Miriam came down to Aix and Miriam and I drove to Venice.

At Venice Miriam was an unexpected sensation. The Italians,

because of their natural curiosity seemed enthralled by her, partly, I finally realised because they had never seen an Afro. Everywhere we went she was stared at. It was all very jovial and Miriam was not offended. All this prompted me to say to Miriam, whatever you do always keep your Afro, because I wanted her to keep her authenticity and to be proud of her Africaness. Hair straightening is a demoralising and artificial imitation of white culture. Years later my Uncle Harry pointed out to me that it was Miriam's example that began the Afro fashion. At Venice Miriam was decidedly a hit and so was *Come Back, Africa*. Although shown outside of the festival it created a sensation. I was unaware of that until the next day when some acquaintances laughingly showed me the newspaper which said that showing *Come Back, Africa* out of competition was the biggest "gaffe" of the festival, and it was voted the Italian critics award as the best film of the festival. Venice was my lucky spot. There was then a large press conference and it was thrilling for me to achieve such acclaim, however despite such critical success, it was never shown in the cinema in Italy.

From Venice we went to Paris and the publicity from Venice preceded us and I was able to make a good engagement with Madame De Caris of the Pagode Cinema. In London I made a distribution agreement with Charles Cooper of Contemporary Films for a small advance, then back to New York for the big push.

Miriam came over from London and contacted Belafonte who expressed great interest in her. He impressed upon me the difficulties and expense there would be in launching her career. I had a contract with Miriam but I told Belafonte that I didn't want to be Miriam's manager and that I would be happy to turn her over to him on the basis of a reasonable compensation for my previous efforts and costs. That seemed acceptable to him, naturally Miriam would have to agree but she seemed willing. In her eyes Belafonte was an icon. He organised a reception for her at the Village Vanguard which was a fabulous occasion, everybody important in the music world was there including reporters from *Look*, the *New York Times* etc. During the festivities Max Gordon and I spoke. He indicated that there would be trouble ahead and said, "You know this is a cut throat business and you better get in there and cut throats." I wasn't attracted by this.

After this Belafonte saw that Miriam would be a sensation and decide to move in. He made me a very inadequate offer of $3 000 which I refused, I wasn't looking for an enormous fee. I was more

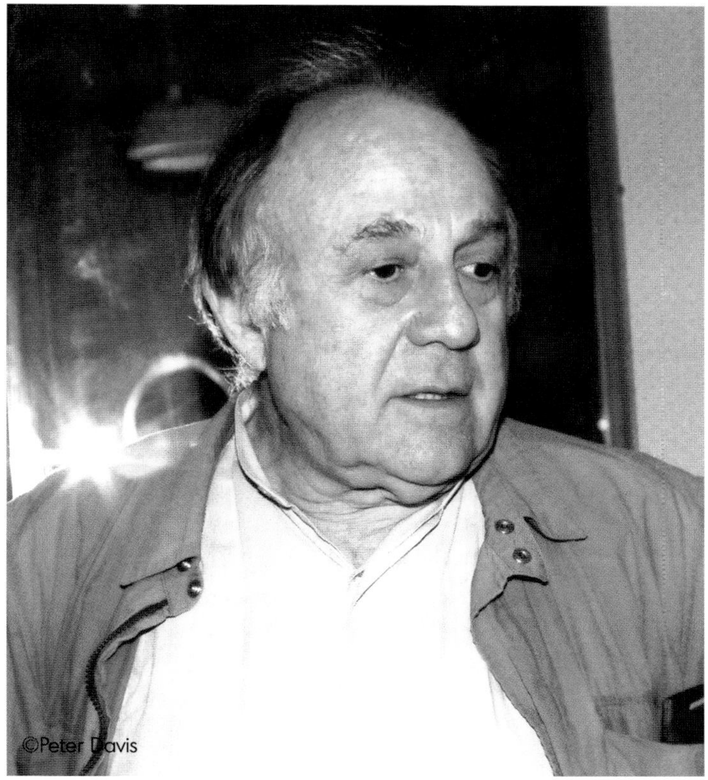
©Peter Davis

interested in collaborating with Belafonte and Miriam regarding *Come Back, Africa* but his offer was ludicrous considering the great effort that I had gone to on Miriam's behalf. However, I suspected that Miriam wanted to cut loose from me for an understandable reason. She was afraid her relationship with *Come Back, Africa* would jeopardise her mother's situation in South Africa. In that case I was sympathetic and would have released her.

Soon after I refused Belafonte's offer, Miriam came to my office and demanded a copy of our agreement. She was in a state of fury which I think Belafonte had stimulated, which in Miriam's case as a victim of apartheid was easy. What disturbed me was that our friendship went out of the window, although I had done nothing to harm her. I gave her a copy and felt that our relationship was over.

Belafonte then called a meeting and I brought my lawyer, Joe Holska, who I could see was overwhelmed by Belafonte who had his entire staff there. I felt that I was in a lion's den. I learned a lot of lessons that day, particularly how you can be sold out by your own lawyer. Belafonte immediately attacked me and started ranting about mercenary agents. I couldn't understand his anger considering that I had expressed willingness to cooperate. I got the impression that Belafonte had a power complex and there were overtones of racism in his remarks. It was becoming one of the ghastly experiences of my life, particularly since I considered Miriam a friend. I must say it pained me quite deeply. Without any further discussion Belafonte cruelly dismissed me and said that Miriam would break her contract with me. I felt completely defeated because I had decided that for ideological reasons I didn't want to attack Miriam. I was naively devoted to the anti-apartheid cause and I couldn't conceive a conflict with Miriam. It is not like me not to fight back but I had reasons for withdrawing. In retrospect I think my decision was a mistake because what I did against Miriam wouldn't have made any difference to the situation in South Africa. I had a very simple weapon against her and Belafonte which would have been very effective. Since I had a contract with her I could have slapped her with an injunction which could have tied her up for months, and both her and her champion Belafonte would have had to negotiate. I probably should be proud of the fact that I acted with high motives but I have to admit that I'm defeated by own idealism. More than ten years later she acknowledged on television that I had brought her to the US.

After the completion of *Come Back, Africa* I began thinking about starting my own cinema, because with films like *On The Bowery*, and *Come Back, Africa* it was difficult to obtain a New York opening. Since it was crucial to open all films in New York there was always a large backlog of films before you. In addition, since there was a shortage of first-run cinemas, their charges were exorbitant, $3 000 or $4 000 per week plus a guarantee of $5 000 per week for advertising. Unless the film was a great success you were sure to lose money. In between my films I would open other American and European independent films and also fill in with a repertoire of classic films. At about this time I met Lew Gittler a publicity agent who proposed to handle the promotion of *Come Back, Africa*. He was also interested in my idea of starting a cinema and while I was in Venice he started to scout around New York looking for a theatre.

Eventually Lew found the Renata Theater which could be converted into a cinema by building a projection booth. I was excited about owing my own cinema and I named it the the Bleecker Street Cinema. By March of 1960 the cinema was ready to go and we opened *Come Back, Africa* the week of the Sharpeville Massacre. Friends of mine said I was always ahead of the time. In this regard I have been fairly consistent, but it is a high risk and low reward.

Over the years we had a great variety of exciting programmes; a few American independent films and a repertoire of classics, Bunuel, Bergman, De Sica, Rossellini, etc; the American underground cinema — Jonas and Adolphus Mekas, Kenneth Anger, Shirley Clarke, and Ed Emschwiller; and radical political documentaries – Joris Ivan's films on Vietnam, *17 Parallel* and *People And Their Guns*, Felix Green's *China*, *Inside North Vietnam*, and *Cuba Va!* and Edgar Snow's *1/4 of Humanity;* and occasionally a first-run European art film.

The first year was difficult until we built up a clientele and could cut our advertising. We never had large yearly grosses but we created a sensation for the serious cineaste. We became known internationally as the best cinema in New York. We had one disadvantage, which was a flaw in my planning – location! Bleecker Street in Greenwich Village was out of the way during week days and during the weekend although the streets were mobbed, they were mostly kids who were thronging the nightclubs and gay bars, they weren't film people. However, over the years we made a powerful contribution to the art of the cinema. Our audience wasn't local, they were from all over the city.

During the editing of *Come Back, Africa* I received a cable from Bloke Modisanee stating that he was in Dar es Salaam and asking me to send him an air ticket to London, and to help with the formalities of British immigration. I was pleased and relieved to hear that he had escaped from South Africa. This was part of the plan that we had formulated when he was assisting me in Johannesburg. It was his idea to take the train to Bechuanaland and cross the border which was loosely gaurded and ultimately to reach Dar es Salaam where he could obtain permission to enter Great Britain. I promptly sent him a ticket and contacted my friend Reverend Michael Scott of the Africa Bureau to assist him, which he did with surprising alacrity and within a few days Bloke was in London.

He ended up living in Hampstead where I visited him frequently. He made steady progress in pursuing his vocation as a writer with occasional theatrical and film roles. One of his first projects was his autobiography, *Blame Me On History* published by

Andre Deutsche. It was a minor international success. Oscar Loewenstein, the theatrical and film producer, commissioned him for Genet's *The Blacks* and other plays. Over the years he obtained many roles but it was a very thin existence. I wasn't fully aware of his difficulties because he continued to maintain various projects. Eventually he went to West Germany to commence research on a book about an African uprising against Germany in Tanganyika in the nineteenth century. There he met a young German woman and after a stormy relationship they married and had a son. Before that, one summer, we took a vacation together and went to Paris where we visited Anatole Dauman of Argos Films, who suggested that we take a trip to Morocco, which we did. It was on this trip that I realised he was at a low ebb.

Finally he departed for Germany where he commenced his marriage. After his son was born the struggle became too much for him, he left his wife and later I was informed by Lionel Ngakane that he had died alone in Germany. Another tragedy of apartheid, so many of the black exiles had died prematurely.

ELINOR ROGOSIN

In the fall of 1957, six months after we had first landed in Cape Town, we returned to Johannesburg. On our arrival, the lobby of the Carlton Hotel started quivering as we stood in shocked silence. No one else was alarmed. "No earthquake," we were told, "only the settling of the mines." It was something that happened from time to time, but I never got accustomed to feeling as though the earth were rumbling beneath me with a giant stomach ache.

We settled on a furnished flat in a building owned and operated by Mrs Latoff, a large, gruff, Russian émigré woman who had taken to her bed when her lover fled to Australia. Propped up against a set of pillows as if on a throne, this bizarre queen directed the running of her enterprise without moving from her bed. She sat like a heap of protoplasm, giving orders to a number of so-called "boys", really African men, who cleaned and looked after the apartments. I was flabbergasted when we first met, and unaccustomed to paying rent in a bedroom, I was stiff and formal in our dealings.

And since I never saw Mrs Latoff leave her bed during the entire year we lived in that building, I was convinced that she had lost her legs in some terrible accident. That is, until a physiotherapist who visited me after my son was born told me the story of how and why Mrs Latoff had given up normal life. But that would be almost a year later from the time I first met this unusual, but kind woman, who had predicted that my baby would be a boy.

I began to organise our small flat and to become acquainted with my new neighborhood. High on my list after routine chores, was to find a dance school. It was my way of making contacts and friends, and in the Berea section of Johannesburg where we were living I found a studio and began studying Spanish dance. There was a possibility of my teaching a modern dance class, but when I became pregnant my doctor thought it was unwise, and I substituted classes in natural childbirth.

On one particular Sunday afternoon that proved to be providential, Lionel and I attended a performance given by the Union of South African Artists, an organisation devoted to breaking the colour barrier through the medium of entertainment. It was at that performance that we met both Miriam Makeba and Shunna Pillay, who were stars of the show, and also John Bolon, a garrulous fellow in love with showbusiness, who offered his services in any way that he could help. Shunna, a thin and handsome man with a Sinatra-like aura, was a popular singer who sang ballads and even a Yiddish song; though the prevailing African rhythms of "kwela" could be heard everywhere else.

While we were getting acquainted with life in Johannesburg, Lionel started preparations for making the film that became *Come Back, Africa*. Most of Lionel's energy now became focused on obtaining the necessary permits to bring film equipment and a crew into South Africa. This was a difficult process as it involved dissembling and obtaining false contracts, but Lionel had a type of blind faith in his own ideas, and rather enjoyed the upcoming prospect of outwitting the South African officials. None of the officials or anyone he met in the course of this aggravating and demanding quest knew the truth.

Through a business contact of his father, Lionel was able to obtain a letter of sorts stating that his intention was to film a "travelogue". In all the official interviews and visa applications he was able to keep secret his true purpose of revealing the evil of apartheid. In reality, it was a dangerous course to follow, though as American citizens we were not liable for arrest and incarceration; we would have just be thrown out of the country if the truth were uncovered.

On the surface, all seemed fair since this project had the aura of an idealistic cause that would bring world attention to the plight of the Africans living under the system of apartheid. It was a question of means justifying the end, which I understood, although dissembling did not come easily to me. It left me with a slightly disloyal opinion.

Though Lionel was sincere in his desire to make this film, I thought that in the process of fooling the cagey Afrikaner officials who demanded proof of his project, that he was echoing, on some deep level, the battles he had had with his egomaniacal and extraordinarily successful father. And yet, wanting to be helpful, I accompanied him on some of the visits to government offices. It was an added advantage that at 24 I still had an innocent looking face and would sit and nod or smile while Lionel answered the questions of the officials who were not entirely convinced at first. Perhaps when they understood that he intended to have the film developed in Johannesburg, they relented and provided the necessary papers. When not accompanying Lionel on one of these stressful visits I continued on as secretary but still had difficulty remaining mute during his dictations.

I understood from listening to hours of Lionel's monologues that he thought of making films as a way to communicate social and political injustices to the world. Movies, for him, were a forum for preaching a message of understanding and compassion rather than a vehicle to entertain. And yet, I have always thought that there has to be a structure or a story to lead audiences on a voyage into the life and worlds of the people up there on the big screen. These themes have to be absorbed into a plot line, no matter what the importance of the philosophical underpinnings were.

Lionel's idea was to base the story of this film on the real life predicaments of an African in Johannesburg, and film it with real people instead of actors. Contacts were made and a script put together with the help of Bloke Modisane, Can Themba and Lewis Nkosi.

While waiting for the bureaucratic red tape to clear, we went on a weekend excursion to Zululand where we visited with Dr Barker at his mission. I was amazed to find some of the girls wearing beaded skirts, as I thought beads as clothing had long since vanished. I felt as though I was looking at a page from childhood geography books, and I am positive if I were to travel along the same roads today, all would be changed. But I treasure the photographs I have, because at that moment in the land called Zululand, time had stopped for a moments rest.

The day was getting late on our drive back to Johannesburg, and impatient Easter weekend travellers whizzed passed us towards the Durban beaches. It was hard to stay focused as we drove in the darkness against the oncoming stream of blinding lights. Behind us lay a world were women were stylish in beads and bare breasts and men went as a rite of passage to work in the gold mines. Ahead, lay our apartment in Johannesburg. Suddenly, a car veered out of control and sent us spinning and twisting into a ditch.

The police arrived. It only took a minute for them to appraise the situation. The guilty driver was intoxicated and an Afrikaner, like themselves. We were Americans. "Was the boy driving?" one of the policemen barked as he pointed to George, a frightened, huddled, black form sitting in the back seat. "I was," Lionel replied, "and fortunately I swerved or there would have been a head-on collision, and a worse mess."

"Can you take us to a hospital?" I asked in a voice shaking with fright. I was in the fourth month of my first pregnancy and concerned. Some shattered glass from the windshield had cut my legs, but otherwise I did not think I had been injured. "Lady, we're not the American police," they snarled in the harsh, percussive brogue of Afrikaans-inflected English.

Their reply did nothing to stop my chattering teeth and my body's uncontrollable trembling. Fortunately, a car stopped and the kind driver gave me something from a first aid kit to counteract the shock of the accident. We were finally taken to a local garage where I was able to check and see if there was any bleeding, a sign of a miscarriage. Happily, I was fine. And we were able to return to Johannesburg that night.

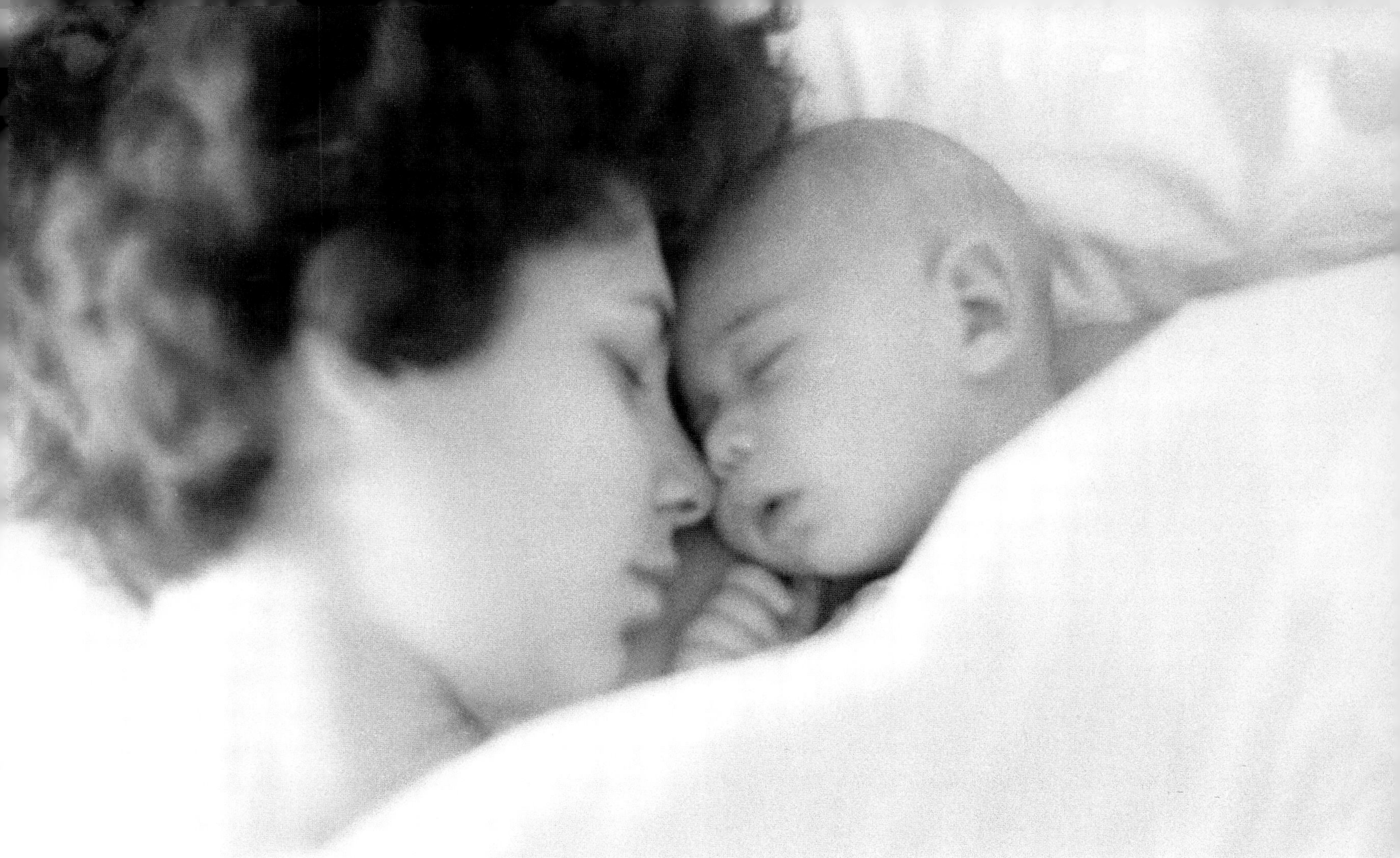

The next day, Lionel went off to Sophiatown, the freehold township where Bloke lived. Still shaken and feeling lonely, I decided to join them. However, there was no way I could get there other than walking. I set out. Along the way, a car stopped and asked if I needed a lift. Even when I told them I was on my way to Sophiatown they had me get in the car and dropped me off at the outskirts of the township. I am sure that I had an angel sitting on my shoulder for this was a most extraordinary gesture in South Africa where the hostility between the races was a constant surging of complicated games; but then, knowing I was an American, these strangers must have thought, "Well what can you expect?' But as I walked into Bloke's one-room, shanty house, Lionel, Bloke, Can, and other friends were even more astonished.

When Ernie, the soundman, Walter a cameraman, and Milek, the other cameraman, arrived, our landlady arranged an apartment for the three men. I hired a young girl, Beauty by name, who helped me prepare the breakfasts and the picnic-style lunches for the crew while they were shooting on the grounds of an Anglican Church. Dinner was often in a small restaurant in a house next to the building. We would then return to the flat and run off the days rushes. To a certain extent we became a tiny, self-contained commune dedicated to this secret project.

Lionel and Bloke checked out the long bus lines, looking for faces they wanted. Eventually, both Zacharia and Vinah, the two main characters in the film, were hired, though neither one had any acting experience. Miriam Makeba, the only professional in the cast, came on board for a scene set in a shebeen or illegal saloon. Bloke, Can and Lewis also appeared in that same scene. I was script girl or continuity, which meant that I would jot down the details of clothing as well as the location and who was in each numbered scene and a brief reference to what they were doing. I also took some production stills. As the days went by I learned that preparations for a few minutes scene would take an interminable amount of time, and I would wander over to the nursery school adjacent to the building on the grounds of an Anglican Church and take photographs.

The story of South Africa at that time revolved around the life of young men who left rural areas for a stint in the gold mines that surrounded the city of Johannesburg. The plot of *Come Back, Africa* followed the destruction of a family that resulted from this pattern of leaving the rural areas and coming to the mines of Johannesburg or "Jo'burg". A short sequence was filmed in the gold mines around Johannesburg, but I did not go along for this section, as I had gone down into a copper mine in what was then the Belgian Congo. Though I had at first been terrified as the cage slowly descended more than 16 500 feet under the ground, I had overcome my fear to become fascinated by the activity under the earth. However, I did not envision repeating the experience.

I was pregnant during most of the filming, and other than the odd contrast of my natural birth, breathing classes and the daily duties as a script girl on a subversive film, there were no problems. Though there was one rather uncomfortable evening when I spent the night with a group of Sisters attached to the Mission. The Sisters were welcoming and gentle, but I felt as though I were some kind of sinner as by that time I was noticeably pregnant. Of course, this was entirely my own imagination at work, but it made me feel uneasy as I sat with the silent Sisters over breakfast trying not to be amused by the sound of a table of Sisters crunching their way through cold toast.

The film was developed in Johannesburg and that was never a problem. Either no one ran the developed film or they did not understand what was being filmed. Then, Ernie and I would go down to the airlines and ship out the boxes of processed film to New York. He would carry in the film, and I would fill out the paperwork. For some odd reason, no one asked any questions.

It was Ernie cooking his farewell pasta dinner that not only splattered the kitchen walls with an abstract of spaghetti sauce, but sent me into labour. My son was born at noon the next day, September 17, 1958 in the Florence Nightingale Hospital. Fortunately it was the custom to keep new mothers for a week. Nightly cups of "Ovaltine" to build up your strength and daily lessons gave me time to learn how to handle a newborn. Back at the flat, I was a shaky, first time mother, clinging to my copy of Dr Spock's *Baby Book* as a guide. Michael was a colicky, fretful baby and George, who took us to our doctor's appointments, comforted me by telling me that such babies were very smart. Of course, I believed him.

Beauty helped me with the washing and ironing. English baby clothes were elegant but needed ironing. I kept myself going in the nights with doses of peanut butter and coffee. A local filmmaker, Jamie Uys, who later had a huge international success with one of his films, bought most of the technical equipment. He would come at night to pick up something or other, and was told: "No problem, Ellie is up!"

There must have been some gossip about our activity for just as the film was wrapped, a government official appeared at our apartment. Since we already had our plane tickets, there were no problems. All the same, on our return to New York in the winter of 1958, a man from the State Department visited our home.

We had left South Africa and returned to New York in November 1958 with our six-week-old son and the film *Come Back, Africa*. Carl Lerner edited the film in New York. I knew Mr Lerner from his involvement with *On the Bowery*, but once we were back in New York I became less involved with the film. Lionel did have a number of showings at a screening room for a variety of influential people, including Mrs Eleanor Roosevelt. He then arranged to show *Come Back, Africa* at the Venice Film in the summer of 1959. It was the venue where Lionel had won an award for his first film, *On the Bowery*, and I believe he expected that a showing at the festival would help arrange a distribution deal.

Lionel had also arranged for Miriam Mekeba to come to the Venice Film Festival. Michael and I remained in a small, rented flat in Aix en Provence while Lionel took the film to Venice as I was pregnant with Daniel, my second son. My feeling is that children who are born come into the world when some unknowable reason forces their souls into being. This idea of a sort of mystical attachment to pregnancy is rooted in my own hodge-podge of feelings and knowledge; but I know that when a child leaves the womb it is truly a miracle. From my own experience, I certainly knew the physical facts of the birth process, and yet when my first son was born, it was an extraordinary phenomenon, beyond all logic. I know that if you had asked me about pregnancy and birth, I would have said, yes, I know – but I really didn't know until the moment when my baby first cried and I held another human being; small, but a perfect person with his own voice.

We returned from France in the fall, and were living in Greenwich Village not far from the Bleecker St. Cinema, which Lionel had leased after finishing *On the Bowery*. He not only used the theater to project his own films, but for many years it became a place to view the work of other independent filmmakers, including Robert Downey, the Mekas brothers, and the early films of the French director, Alain Resnais.

Miriam was now in New York, preparing for a debut performance at the Village Gate, a nightclub in Greenwich Village. I had only met Miriam once or twice while we were living in Johannesburg, and as I recall it was during the shooting of the shebeen scene. We had met again for a brief moment when she was on her way to the Venice Film Festival. At that time, I had loaned her a pair of popular clear plastic shoes, but that was the extent of our relationship.

All that changed on her arrival in New York. She became a daily visitor, and I had an opportunity to know her as a friend. Miriam would come over to our apartment, and spend most of the day listening to American pop singers in preparation for her debut. We would have lunch, and Miriam would talk about her life in South Africa where she had achieved celebrity status appearing with the Union of South African Artists. I remember that I was particularly fascinated by the stories she told about her mother who was a healer in the Xhosa tribe, and whom she loved.

Miriam's exotic looks, warm voice and the novelty of her Xhosa "click" song made her an instant success. When she first arrived Miriam had a natural, untheatrical presence. Her hair was cut short in an "Afro" and a dab of Vaseline was all she used to give her face a little shine, and her costume was an evening dress she had chosen in one of our whirlwind trips through the New York department stores. Later, with the advice of Harry Belafonte, she began wearing high fashion versions of traditional African dress and was soon launched on a successful career both in the United States and in Europe.

Since Lionel's theatrical contacts and expertise were limited it was certainly in Miriam's best interest to put her future in the hands of more professionally oriented people. Even though this made sense, I felt it was unfair to completely ignore Lionel's role in bringing her to the United States; but he accused me of being jealous of Miriam. It was easier to shift blame on me than to confront the situation which involved a subtle undercurrent of reverse racism.

During the spring of 1960 Lionel decided to make an anti-war film in India. *Come Back, Africa* had been released, and it was time to start a new project. He admired the work of the Indian filmmaker, Satyajit Ray, and planned on meeting him in Calcutta, though it was decided to make New Delhi our destination. Preparations were made and we left New York City in the fall of that year.

LEWIS NKOSI

My experience with Lionel was tremendously exciting, because Rogosin arrived in the country wanting to capture something of our lives. But unlike many people who arrived knowing precisely what it is they wanted to do, Lionel seemed to want to find out from us what was involved in our daily lives. And so we spent a lot of time – he seemed to be in no hurry – just drinking and talking an awful amount.

My experience of the Fifties in Johannesburg was an awful lot of talking and drinking. Of course, European alcohol was illicit, it was prohibition days for us in the Fifties. So Lionel, simply by providing us with white alcohol, was already breaking the law before he had embarked on his film-making. But this enabled us to get to know one another. And to not only tell him about ourselves, but to hear a lot about his work in New York, for example, how he had made the film *On the Bowery*.

So suddenly there was that rapport. An American artist, who seemed a committed artist, coming to us and then suddenly discovering ways of presenting our lives to anybody who really wanted to know what we thought we were like. We spent a lot of time in Sophiatown and Lionel had to dive down on the floor of the car one evening because we were being followed by a police van. He was taking all these risks which a less than conscientious film-maker would have simply bypassed. A lot of the time we were going to his flat in Hillbrow, eating, drinking, and again discussing the shape of this film.

Bloke Modisane and I had to work on the story treatment with Lionel. It seemed much easier after that. We still argued a lot. For example, I would argue with Bloke about a presentation of a certain slice of life. At that stage, I suppose, Lionel would take his choice. That's when his own short experience of life in South Africa, what he'd read about it, and what he wanted to make, would come into play.

Lionel had a very beautiful wife, Elinor, a delicate Jewish girl and I was very young, tending to be very romantic. I was absolutely in love with her. I simply just melted whenever Ellie was around. Lionel teased me one night when we were going to Sophiatown, and he kept saying to me, "The Zulus are after my wife." We were drinking and he said, "I must protect my family, my wife from the Zulu army." It just showed that we were getting to be so close as a family that we were teasing each other a lot and laughing a lot. And the experience was good.

The remarkable thing about *Come Back, Africa*, even if we have to make allowances for some of its shortcomings, is the mixture of experience and styles of film-making that went into it. I say mixture of styles, because you can see that film as a documentary and at the same time it was not entirely a documentary. This was an invented experience. An invented story.

The people who became involved as actors had no training whatsoever. People who were playing whites in the film, were mostly progressive white South Africans. But they were so aware, so familiar with the brutalising aspects of black and white life in South Africa that they were able to project this authentically. A lot of it still makes me wince, as if I were going through the same experiences. Like when I see Myrtle as the white woman trying to hire a black servant – what goes on during that experience is both so funny, so comic, and so tragic. The pathos, and all the small bitternesses that come into the film are suddenly projected in one or two shots. And that is what I value about the experience of *Come Back, Africa*.

Its always astonishing when you think about *Come Back, Africa* and you wonder why it had to take a white American from New York City to make a film like that. To come and see what was going on in our lives. That certain people do not see what is there, not because they cannot see it if they wanted to, but because they refuse to see it. So that someone coming with a certain kind of ideological equipment, not in any concrete way, but in wanting to tell the truth about certain experiences can suddenly see what has always been staring people in the face. And you wonder why they never come up with those experiences. And this is the sense of exclusion that always amazed me.

It is indicative of Lionel's approach that in the end he was able to get away with a whole lot of things because the bureaucrats could not believe that he would make a certain kind of film. That is why, when he told them he was making a travelogue film full of dancers and so on, the officials actually believed it. Because the people who controlled self-expression when it concerned black people were white artists, and what Lionel Rogosin represents is a shift from white people trying to express a vision for blacks and allowing blacks to express themselves, to be in control of their own discourse, if you wish. And it is not as easy as saying the Africans now become film-makers. But there is an alliance between progressive artists and the black people who want to say something legitimate about their own experiences.

With *Come Back, Africa*, and I don't say it because I was a part of the film, a whole lot of languages have become available for the film-maker. What you see is not only black intellectuals articulating their own experiences so far as black life in the cities is concerned, you even hear African languages being spoken in the film, as dialogue, because Lionel Rogosin wanted to create that kind of authenticity for the urban uneducated worker.

BLOKE MODISANE

Come Back, Africa is the first authentic cinematic record of the system of apartheid in South Africa.

Only the reckless daring of a man who had the conviction to film *On the Bowery* could have risked so much to make *Come Back Africa*. Lionel Rogosin dug deep to find his story, penetrated the squalor of the locations to feel the heart-beat of the Africans. He went into the shebeens, and listened as his subjects spoke, sometimes with bitterness and at times with humour, about the injustice, the misery, the poverty that marked their lives. He got drunk with them, and I remember that one evening we dragged him through a ceremony and made him an honorary Zulu, and taught him to do the Zulu war dance.

By the time he was ready to shoot his film we had conditioned him to see black, to feel black and to react black. But for Lionel Rogosin to be black meant he had to adopt all the problems that attend that colour, and it never occurred to me that morning when he showed up at the office where I worked that I was to be enmeshed in a gigantic fraud, in a colossal challenge that was to lose me my job and earn me a friend for life.

I was a working journalist on *Drum* magazine when I met Lionel Rogosin. He walked up to my desk and said, "My name is Rogosin, a mutual friend asked me to look you up." He told me about his project, and I listened courteously. I had met too many people who wanted to make films, dishonest people who had taken African artists for a joy ride at very little cost. Exploitation of black talent by white opportunists is an old story. So I listened to his story and did not believe a word he said.

He was having trouble with the government over visas for his crew, two cameramen and a sound engineer, and for some reason that was all I needed to believe him. Anybody in trouble with the South African government was my fiend. Lionel Rogosin had to submit to the authorities details of the kind of film he was doing. After Ed G Murrow's film *African Conflict*, American film makers were suspect.

Thus began the great merry-go-round. At one time he was making a travelogue, but the government wanted to see his commission – the actual contract. Lionel had to live that lie through and produce a contract, a vague, noncommittal commission from an airline company that did not want to be involved. That was thrown out. Then he decided to film an African musical. He took this story to Pretoria, South Africa's executive capital, and wove a near-plausible tale of presenting the music of Africa to the world, to show that Africans were basically a happy people. To support his story he went round the locations shooting scenes of pennywhistle troupes, gumboot dancers, singing troupes, mine dancers, and shot hundreds of feet of film which he was preparing to screen for the Department of the Interior if ever challenged to do so. The police followed him through the townships, playing it cloak-and-dagger, and reporting all his moves. It came to be quite a game playing up to them.

After three months of this fooling and travelling the 72 miles to Pretoria every other day the visas were finally granted. But by this time Lionel Rogosin had fed the white newspapers with a story that he was impressed with Deneys Reitz's book *Commando* and that he wanted to make a film of it. *Commando* is a loaded account of the Afrikaner war against the English – the Boer War. The newspapers were enthusiastic about the project, and the government's attitude began to change.

For a while the police seemed to be off our backs, and Lionel Rogosin and I set up casting for the film. He did not want professional actors, but he wanted faces, and for two months we looked at faces in the bus queues, in the streets, at the cinemas. We went everywhere looking for a face in the crowd. I began to develop a feel for faces, to set them apart, but compared to Lionel Rogosin, I was in the kindergarten league.

I could not keep up with Lionel Rogosin, being up in the morning and looking at every face that came out the "Native's Entrance" of Johannesburg's Park Station. He bought space in a newspaper and we spent a whole afternoon looking at faces and interviewing probables, but Lionel was not satisfied. He went back to the bus queues and the ironic part of it all was that as Lionel picked a face, the person would be terrified and just run – always a man who did not have a Pass, that document of oppression which put 1 250 000 African males in jail every year. Others suspected he was a Bethal farmer, those notorious traffickers in human lives who lure Africans to jobs with fantastic salaries, the trick labour contracts which are concluded in a rush, then the horror of being shanghaied to a farm and working under slave conditions for anything up to one-and-sixpence a day. As a rule Africans don't talk to strange white men, especially those who are seemingly polite. Being in his company marked me as a traitor.

Then, one morning he rushed up to me with the exciting news that he had found the face he was looking for, but in actual fact he had found more than a face or an actor. He had found Zacharia Mgabi, himself a country man who had been forced to come to Johannesburg because the land couldn't support his needs. It was a miracle find. Zacharia didn't have to act the part – he just had to be himself, the simple rural African: inarticulate, halting in speech, coarse, very little education, but a tremendous man with a quiet dignity and integrity. And since no dialogue was written into the script he had to improvise all his lines. The words were his own, and so were the grammar and the usage.

The terrifying scene at the end when he finds his screen wife, Vinah, murdered by the villain Marumu, was even more agonising to watch. The script called for him to break down mentally, and in a rage of hysteria to smash up the crockery. The crack-up of the character and the man were so closely linked that we were all terrified at being present at the destruction of a man. It was a nightmare that we could not stop or turn our faces from, and by the time Lionel shouted, "Cut!" we were sick. The scene had come too close to the real thing and it was printed after only two takes.

When Lionel shot his exteriors, the cameras were loaded on to cars and were covered with blankets with the cameramen crouching behind them. The cars would drive away with Lionel and his white crew looking like tourists out to see how the other half, or rather, how the other three-quarters lived. As soon as the police were gone, off would come the blankets, and shooting resumed. When he was doing the safe scenes, like the itinerant musicians or a wedding, the cameras would be mounted on an open van, and sometimes we had the police come round to watch. And always at this point Lionel couldn't resist the temptation of getting the police to help.

Tongue in cheek, he would walk up to them and ask if it was safe for him to shoot in the locations. Was his equipment safe? Was there any danger of being knifed or robbed? At which point the police would advise him to be careful, and in the end he would have the police controlling the crowds that are always drawn by the making of a film. With the police keeping the crowd away from the camera, Lionel would have a whole day of uninterrupted work. And just before sundown he would be advised to stop working because the "Natives" would be drunk and troublesome. It never failed, and Lewis Nkosi and I would die laughing.

I suppose I should not admit to such a thing in print – a question of honour and all that – but it hadn't occurred to me that I was capable of many unsophisticated lies. A quality of sorts that Lionel and I shared with such generous helpings. People were always asking about the film; they wanted to know what it was all about, and we told them. It was a different story every time, until I couldn't remember which friend I had told which lie. It was stimulating to find a co-conspirator in Lionel Rogosin.

The story of the film was top secret – not even the actors were told: this more as a protection to them rather than a case of trust. If the actors didn't know, then perhaps it would be easier for them in the event of reprisal tactics by the police. Zacharia was blissfully ignorant and religiously dogmatic; he never asked questions, just did what was asked of him. The others were sophisticated enough to know and realise the time for ignorance.

After all the tensions and the back-breaking speed of shooting as much as could be done, Lionel and his wife, Eli, got extensions on their visas. And with this endorsement of goodwill in his favour,

Lionel became daring. He wanted to shoot the mine sequences, to go down a real mine and shoot the sequences of the training of new recruits, of the men going down the mines, in another world of tunnels and men with flashlights on their foreheads, the actual drilling for gold. And that, for me at any rate, was a high point in the film. The black of the skin of the miners seemed to flow into the black of the tunnels, and the flashlights on the helmets seemed to move without bodies. Moving one behind the other, and photographed in long shots, gave the impression of a long snake winding in the dark. The Africans scratched at the bowels of the earth for the gold that is the symbol of South Africa's white prosperity and the fundamental of the greed that oppressed them.

Lionel Rogosin wormed his way into the confidence of a minor official with a glowing account of making a film of South African gold mining, of showing the high technological standard of mining, its efficiency in transforming, by training, rural savages into proficient miners. And so the mine sequences were photographed – a rare privilege to be awarded to a foreign film maker.

The big interior scene, the one featuring Johannesburg's black intellectuals in a shebeen, was tricky and in a way the most dangerous. Lionel wanted it to be authentic – the atmosphere of a shebeen, real liquor, real-life intellectual drunks, a real-life shebeen queen and a genuine look-out for the police. Liquor laws in South Africa then were emphatic: Africans are forbidden to drink by law. This does not, of course, mean the Africans didn't drink – in fact 80 per cent of all liquors distilled in South Africa found their way into the townships. The Africans drank undercover.

Lionel supplied the liquor – illegally of course – and where and whenever there are free drinks going you'll find Can Themba, Morris Hugh, Lewis Nkosi, Bloke Modisane and other brethren of the Bacchus community that a mutual friend, Nimrod Mkele, derives as: displaced intellectuals in search of morality. With all immodesty I wish to add that that scene was the most authentic, for at the end when the shebeen queen throws us out, the wobbling and the leaning on each other was the real thing. And the reason that the scene came to an end at all was due to the under-sight of Lionel Rogosin who had under-catered.

If the police had surprised that sequence there would have been no *Come Back, Africa*; Lionel would have been jailed for supplying liquor to Natives, and the Natives would have been convicted of being in possession of liquor. But we were lucky: we had a good look-out and the scene was shot in the most improbable place ever – in the classroom of a mission school on mission grounds.

Lionel Rogosin's final problem was to find processing laboratories that would develop his films without a special copy being rushed to the security police. The only one technically equipped to do the job was at Irene, a suburb of Pretoria, and the studio was known to have a big contract with the state Information Department. So only the safe reels were sent there for development and then rushed to New York for processing, but the dynamite was sent straight to New York.

When it was all over and the film sent to New York we had a big illegal party, where white and black drank together, danced together and got drunk together, and I think I saw Lionel Rogosin smile genuinely: not just with the mouth, but with the eyes, the face, and his whole body. He had survived it all, and the hoax, the lies, the deceptions were all justified in his bold stating of the African's case.

MILEK KNEBEL'S NOTES ON THE MAKING OF COME BACK, AFRICA

In 1957, Mr Israel Rogosin, accompanied by his son Lionel, visited Israel. His visit and his meetings with Ben Gurion, with the Minister of Commerce and Industry, with the top economists and industrialists of the State of Israel of those years were reported daily by the local press and the radio. Naturally, when Lionel Rogosin called me and asked for a meeting, I was very surprised. He was the son of the major American investor in Israeli industry at the time, a well known film-maker, a celebrity who mingled with the elite of the Israeli establishment while I was a local newsreel cameraman with few short films to my credit.

When we met, Lionel explained the reason for our meeting: he was looking for a team that would be willing to go with him for several months to South Africa. He told me that he had reviewed most of the films done in Israel (a very tiny industry in the mid-Fifties, with a small output of mostly short films) and among them had seen the few shorts photographed by me. These had impressed him more than the other films he had seen due to their simple, honest photographic style. He told me about his new project in South Africa, which he described as a musical film but shot in a completely different way than the standard way Hollywood musical films used to be shot. On the positive side his models were the films of Robert Flaherty, some of which I was familiar with, and Satyajit Ray's films, *Pather Panchali* and *Aparajito*, which I had never seen. He wanted to make his musical film the way Flaherty shot his documentaries: no actors but real people, no studio but actual locations, no large crew but a minimal and highly professional one; those were his preliminary thoughts about the production.

After several more meetings, and after he had offered me the job as cameraman, Lionel finally told me his true intention hidden behind the facade of a musical movie, namely he wanted to make a political film that would directly attack the system of apartheid and would expose its inhuman face to the world.

I was very young at the time and my sensitivities to any injustice, and in particular to racial discrimination, were sharpened by my childhood experiences during World War Two and by a lot of Marxist literature. In those days, I believed very sincerely that any morally wrong policy had to be dealt with by an active intervention. Those sensitivities and somehow simplistic attitudes dictated many of my daily activities and were a part of my never-pronounced naive wish to improve the state of world affairs via my film work. When meeting Lionel, I was amazed to realise that although ten years older than I, and coming from such a different background to mine, he nevertheless shared my feelings. Lionel found in me an enthusiastic partner for his project and a member of the crew he was forming for the making of his film. It became obvious to me how different Lionel was from the image I had had of him, considering his father's business circles.

Later on, over the years, I was to learn that the Rogosins' father-son relations were as banal as father-son relations usually are within rich Jewish families. Nevertheless they were much more complicated than my first simplistic impression. Israel Rogosin still entertained the idea that the financial fiasco of *On the Bowery* would convince Lionel to return to his senses and join his father in his successful industrial enterprise. Lionel admired his old man but, at the same time, wished to be different. More politically aware and sensitive to social problems, Lionel wanted to be an artist rather than a businessman. His artistic inclination, in his opinion, had been inherited from his sensitive German-born mother, who had chosen to live her life as the wife of a very stubborn, strong, forceful but very courageous and successful Jew. It has always been my impression that what Lionel most wanted, as long as his father was alive and even after that, was to prove to the old man and to himself that he could be as successful as his father, but in the field of political and social film-making rather than in the rayon industry.

Lionel often read and re-read during the *Come Back, Africa* days the letters of Vincent van Gogh to his brother Theo. The book was constantly at his bedside.

I doubt whether Lionel, an American and a New Yorker, ever realized that for the Dutch painter the word "success" must have had a very different significance than it had for a New Yorker!

During my meetings with Lionel in Tel-Aviv he mentioned Walter Wettler, a soundman from Switzerland. Wettler was a specialist in recording classical music with little previous experience in film-making, but in Lionel's opinion he would be the

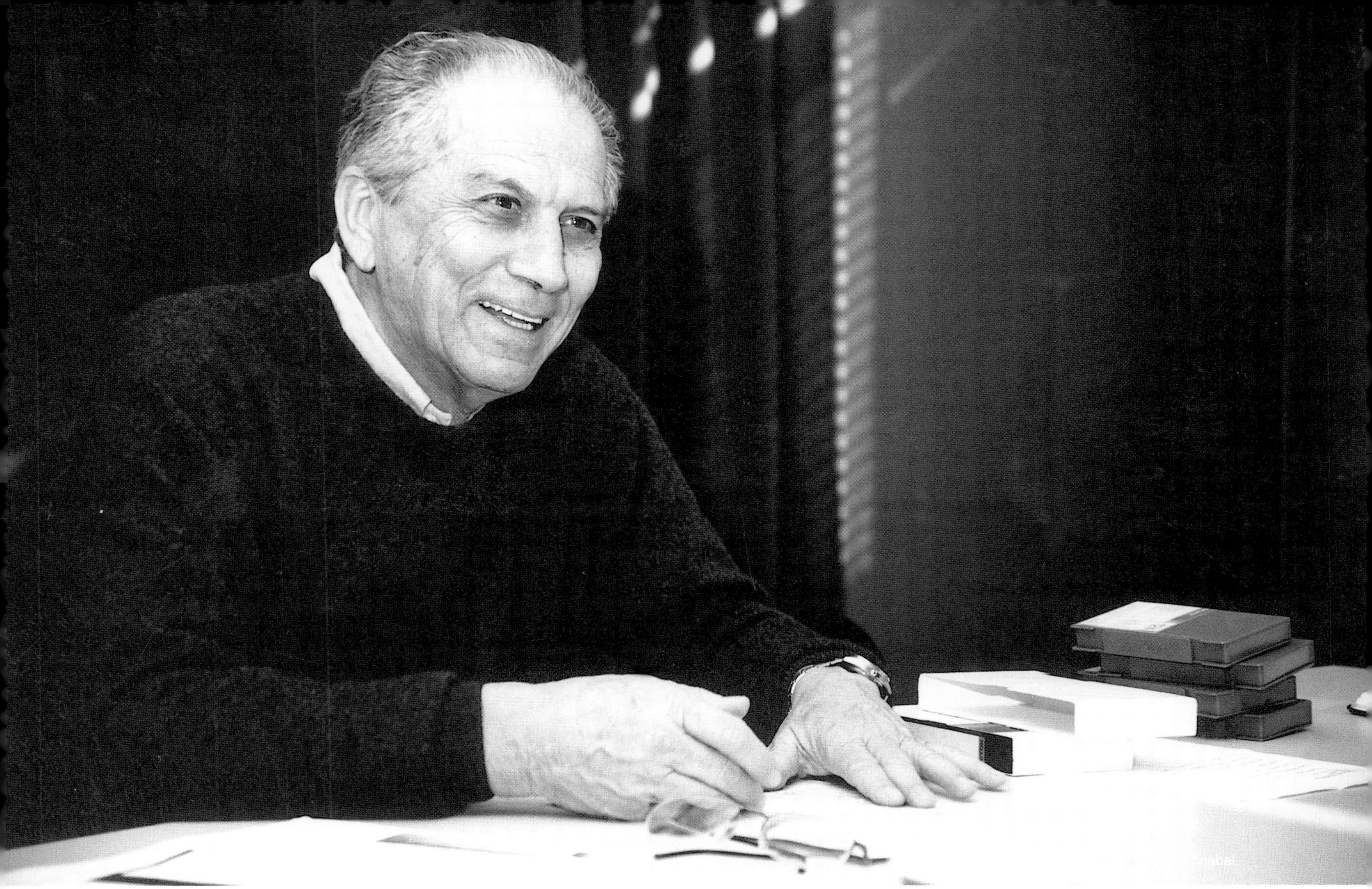

perfect man for the job. He mentioned, as another cameraman, Ernst Artaria, a Swiss cameraman strongly recommended by Wettler, but was reluctant to take his advice if he could find a suitable alternative camera person in Israel. I set up several meetings for Lionel with the majority of active Israeli cameramen at the time.

After a few meetings with some of them, Lionel decided on Artaria, relying mostly on Wettler's strong recommendation.

Lionel left for South Africa to complete the script, to cast the participants who would act in the film, and to finalise all the logistic problems. We planned to meet in Johannesburg after a couple of months.

In the meantime Lionel also needed to receive approval from the South African authorities for the project as well as work permits for the crew. Later on, I learned that a member of the South African Parliament in Pretoria, an owner of a local film laboratory in Johannesburg, who was keen to receive a client with a lot of film stock to be processed, had been very instrumental in this issue.

Upon my arrival in Johannesburg, Lionel brought me from the airport to the apartment that the members of the crew, Wettler, Artaria and I, were to share during the production months ahead. The apartment was in a large rental building located in a residential area of Johannesburg. The building was run by an old and sick

Jewish landlady who, without ever leaving her bed, dealt very efficiently with managing the place via an army of black servants – "boys" in her vocabulary; a term that applied to male and female servants alike as long as the servants were blacks. Lionel and Elinor (his wife), who was pregnant at the time, had an apartment on the same floor as ours but at the other end of the corridor. The landlady supplied us with a "boy" who would prepare our very early-morning breakfasts and a white professional cook to prepare our dinners, which were served after work in the living-room of Lionel and Elinor's apartment.

A day or two after we had settled in the apartment, Lionel called for the first production meeting. He read us the outline of the script and after the reading was completed, to my big surprise, I was the only one who asked when we would start the shooting. The others were very reserved, to say the least. Reserved, not due to the content or the form of the script, which as far as I remember were not discussed at all, but due to the production challenge that the film presented. Both Artaria and Wettler were of the opinion that in order to shoot a script like this, which called for a full feature production, the present crew, in addition to us, had to include at least another five to six professionals such as a lighting-man, a grip, a boom man, two assistants for the two cameramen, a script girl, etc. Without such a crew the project, in their professional opinion, could not take off. I was the youngest and probably the least experienced among them in feature productions. But I was far more experienced in documentary work than they both were. That is why I was convinced the job could be done provided the four of us were willing to take upon ourselves more functions than is traditionally customary. Besides, I was of the opinion that we should immediately train some local people to help us as much as possible. To make things worse, without having any previous experience with the local people, but a strong feeling for the oppressed, I was convinced their training could give excellent results. It made Artaria very upset. He was convinced we were amateurishly wasting time and money. According to his European standards, two years were usually needed to train a white assistant cameraman. To train a black assistant would probably take more time. Wettler was more flexible and was willing to try and see what would happen.

In order to prove and to convince Artaria and Wettler that things could be done even with our existing small crew, Lionel decided to change the planned schedule of shooting. The production-wise simplest scenes, he decided, would be shot first and only later on would we move to the more complicated scenes that required sync sound and lighting.

Lionel's tactical move proved to be right. Within a short time Wettler began to like the new experience of shooting a feature with a small crew. Without enlarging the crew, slowly and smoothly we moved to do the more complicated scenes. Wettler, besides being a perfect soundman who could hide his microphones in all kinds of unimaginable places and always succeeded to produce an amazingly clearly recorded sound, also filled a variety of functions. He was a driver and, on many occasions, acted as production manager and a planner of our daily work but, above all, as our continuity person (script girl). Wettler, because of the nature of his work as a soundman, was normally positioned during the shoot further off from the scene than Lionel, Artaria or I. In spite of it, in cases when a reshoot of a scene or some additional shots for a long-ago completed scene were required, he remembered and knew, better than any one of us, the fine details of the set and of the *mise-en-scene*. From the recorded sound and his carefully kept notes, Wettler could recreate the visual look of a scene weeks after it had been shot. His creative professionalism and systematic way of thinking, even under some very pressing moments, were a blessing for the production.

Artaria's difficulties with our unorthodox way of working lasted almost to the last day of shooting. He was convinced that nothing presentable would ever come out of the film, but in spite of his consistent scepticism he worked very conscientiously and hard. It was his aim and a professional ambition to keep our "amateur", in his terminology, attitude as much as possible in check.

From the first day of shooting till the last, Ernie, as we used to call him, was in full control of the lab in order to ensure the even standard of developing our negatives during the production. On the indoor or night shootings, which required lighting, he always had with him a container with a fresh developer and fixer taken in advance from the lab. Before shooting a scene he insisted on developing a test strip of film by himself in order to see the effects of the lighting created for a scene on the actual emulsion of the negative. He would do the processing on the spot, in the darkest corner of the set, and would never allow the scene to be shot before the test was completed and approved by him. Ernie always tried to shoot from a tripod even under the most unfavourable circumstances for that kind of shooting, and never used a hand held camera. For him a hand held shot was painfully improper for a feature film.

The living-room of our apartment was turned into a 35 mm mute screening room for the rushes that were supplied to us by the local lab every evening. They were screened after dinner and shipped immediately for security reasons together with the negative and sound that same night to New York City. There, in an editing room located on one of the floors of 1600 Broadway, Carl Lerner, the film editor, and his black assistant, Hue, were working on synchronising the visual footage with the sound, logging it and assembling the shots to the first rough cut of the film. Carl would communicate with us via telegrams. Often in these telegrams he would request a re-shooting of certain shots or ask us to shoot additional shots in order to enhance and enrich the rough cut or to clear out some technical continuity problems of that or another sequence.

Sophiatown, an old black neighborhood just next to Johannesburg, was the place to which our two production station-wagons were heading each morning. The neighbourhood was half-ruined; people had been moved out from there to the newly constructed black townships located further from town. These new places were built according to a plan which provided the police with easy control over the area as against the narrow and irregularly created streets of Sophiatown which were all but unfit for that purpose. Here, in a rundown mission school, were the main locations for our indoors shooting. It became our studio. The actual locations were much too small for shooting, but the sets were constructed according to the layout of the actual places and even furnished and decorated with props from the true locations.

The sequence of the shebeen (speakeasy) discussion, the living-room of Zacharia and Vinah, living quarters of Zacharia at the mine compound, the indoors of the last sequence of the film and many other scenes were all shot in the classrooms of that mission school. Most of the day and night shootings were done on the streets of Sophiatown. During the daytime, and particularly at night, few whites would dare to visit this neighbourhood. The blacks had full control of everyday life over there. Our crew was always welcomed and respected in Sophiatown. All the participants in ceremonies such as weddings or street marches, square-dances or weekend street-corner music-playing youngsters, all of them loved to be filmed. Somehow the people of Sophiatown knew or felt our friendly attitude to their predicament. Possibly someone from the African National Congress dropped a word in our favour.

During the entire period of shooting that lasted several months I don't recall any incidents in which black Africans would interrupt our work or would create an uneasy situation for us, except in one case in which Lionel was in serious danger. While shooting one of the marching crowd scenes, I was shooting from the roof of the nearby buildings while Lionel was down on the street watching from the shortest possible distance, in a close-up, one may say, the faces of the passing crowd. People's faces always fascinated him. Some of the people in the crowd noticed the camera and me above on the roof, pointed this out to the others and the passing crowd started to stare directly at the camera. In order to prevent it and to distract people's attention from the camera, Lionel started to offer coins to the mass of people passing below the shooting lens provided they would not look up. Within seconds, Lionel found himself surrounded by hundreds of people demanding their share. George Malebye, our thin, tiny and street-smart local driver, succeeded somehow in pulling Lionel out from the crowd and bringing him to safety in one of our station-wagons.

Lionel had hired George for the job as driver after screening several other candidates. Most of them were much bigger and stronger fellows than George. What impressed Lionel about George was that during the interview George asked to be permitted on his days off to walk ("footing up" as he called these walks) to his native village in order to be cured by his native village witchdoctor of the illnesses that black people usually get from too close an association with whites. Lionel loved that story. He liked George's openness and honest talk although very often he was strongly irritated by his inefficiency and easygoing attitude about things that were of mighty importance for us and completely negligible for George. For example: the suitcase. All the actors' wardrobe of the film was packed in one large and very old suitcase that was always with us in one of the station-wagons, preferably the one where Lionel was seated. Lionel, among all his numerous worries and problems, steadily worried whether the suitcase was in a safe place. Had that suitcase or part of its contents disappeared, it would have posed a terrible problem, costume-wise, for the continuity of the film. The hat with a hole in it and the rest of Zacharia's outfit were irreplaceable. We had no double sets for any of them. Lionel insisted we all watch that suitcase very carefully and never leave it in the unguarded car. For George it was just an old suitcase filled with junk and he could not understand the fuss created around it. Problems of film continuity with respect to wardrobe were absolutely none of George's concern. Sometimes he would walk freely out of the car leaving the back door of the station-wagon wide open, relying on his feelings that no one, even in the most forbidding neighbourhoods of Johannesburg, would ever be tempted to steal such an old suitcase filled with junk.

Lionel could look at and read the faces of people like an open book. In that way he had cast all the black participants of the film who had never dreamed of being or wanted to be actors except, of course, Miriam Makeba who was a well-known singer in Johannesburg. Zacharia was picked by Lionel from a crowd of people passing by; so were Vinah, Eddy, Marumu and others. Lionel never needed to shoot an actor test. He never seemed to need advice in matters of casting. He relied totally on his own judgement. For him the right facial expression of a person and his/her body language were the most important factors. Lionel's problem was in casting the whites. Here his selection possibilities were much more limited; he had to choose among those who were known as an anti-apartheid crowd of people, and who were willing to free their time for a film that fought the right cause. To act in this film, for all of them, was a part of their political activity.

Lionel was well aware that their "acting" was far below what he wished, but he had to compromise and it was eating at his heart. In vain, naively, he hoped that the serious critics and the viewers of the film would understand this difficulty, but never, as far as I know, did he publicly ask for understanding and, one may say, he proudly refused to ask for mercy.

Lionel prepared each scene very carefully, rehearsing with the "actors" on the set, changing the dialogue, allowing the actors to improvise both the dialogue and their movements. That obviously created a problem for setting the lights, mikes and camera angles, but when everything was finally ready for shooting the scene, Lionel would mysteriously disappear from the set. We had to look for him in his various hiding-places and to ask him to come on the set. I assume Lionel had some sort of a deep-seated fear of finalising the scene on an emulsion. It seldom happened while shooting the true documentary scenes, but it repeatedly happened on more complicated scenes where dialogue and acting were involved. Neither I nor anyone else ever discussed those disappearances with Lionel. It was taboo.

It seems to me today that Lionel mostly loved the true-life action scenes and did not feel completely at home with the staged ones. That is why, in my opinion, the scene of the discussion at the shebeen with Miriam singing at the end of it saw Lionel at his best. He had gathered the right group of people. He explained the scene to them and its context within the film, and provoked a discussion. No written dialogue was prepared and handed to them. At the right moment of the discussion he brought Miriam into the scene. After everything was ready for the scene, and just before shooting, Lionel instructed us, his camera people, to load as many camera magazines as possible with film stock and to be ready to cover the scene, to the best of our abilities, whatever would happen. As far as I remember there was not one single rehearsal for that scene. We had two heavy Arriflex blimped cameras and we were changing angles and the sizes of the shooting lenses as the discussion was going on. Once the scene had been completed I shot several traditional intercuts: shots of hands lighting a cigarette, hand moving a glass, etc. for editing purposes. Lionel was laughing at me. The scene was perfect as it was, and no "cut outs" were necessary in his opinion; he was so sure about it even before seeing the rushes.

One of the more difficult scenes to shoot was the mine sequence.

The mine authorities were extremely reluctant to grant us a permit to shoot even in the compound surrounding the mine on the ground level. To go down underground to the pit was completely out of the question. It was a policy that could be overruled only by a direct order from a government office in Pretoria. I remember Elinor and Lionel were working on it for weeks, until finally they succeeded to gain, as far as I remember, a one-day-only permit to shoot in the mine itself and a two- or three-day permit to shoot in the compound around it.

Ernie could not join us in the mine itself due to a claustrophobic fear he had suffered since his early childhood in any underground places. So he had to stay in the compound above the ground and the effective shots of the columns of miners walking toward the mine at early morning darkness before the sunrise, when only the lights of their miner headgear were visible, are to his credit.

Zacharia, once dressed in a miner outfit, looked completely like one of the hundreds of black miners lining up for the elevators. He refused to be taken down the pit by the elevators labeled "Blacks Only". Zacharia was scared to death that once down there, in the lower floor of the pit, he would either lose us or we might lose touch with him, and he would be regarded by the white bosses of the floor as one of the black "mine-boys" and be treated as such. Among many other things, he might be unable to leave the mine compound for several months or years; he would be imprisoned there until the contract of the present batch of miners expired. I never saw Zacharia so fearful as on that day. For his safety he insisted on going down together with us in an elevator with a sign "For Whites Only", but it was impossible. Lionel offered to go with him in the elevator for blacks, but in the system of strict apartheid held by the mine authorities that was impossible as well.

I don't recall how the problem was resolved, because I went down first to prepare the shooting on the mine floor. I just remember that I had to wait for Lionel and Zacharia many hours alone among the miners down in the pit where the temperature was extremely high. While waiting I set the lights and shot the activities around me. To my regret I was limited by the 200 feet of film I had with me. The rest of the film stock was with Lionel and Zacharia "upstairs". When they finally succeeded in joining me, after a short while there was some sort of an alarm in the mine, and we had to leave the place as soon as possible. Most of the 200 feet exposed by me, before their arrival, was included in the final print of the film.

Of great help to Lionel, during his entire stay in South Africa, were Myrtle and Monty Berman. Both of them were activists in a variety of organisations of the anti-apartheid movement. Myrtle was active in the Union of African Artists and the majority of the white cast for the film came from her circle of friends. The Berman's house was a meeting place of many black and white local bohemians. We all attended several parties organised by them where alcoholic drinks were served almost openly to black guests in spite of the very strict law forbidding it. Often during a party we would be warned that the police were nearby and the drinks had to be moved out of sight. The wrap-up party for the film was organised in this house and naturally all the participants in the film were there. It was a great event for all of us but spoiled for me at a certain point by Lionel's decision to settle some unfinished, emotionally-loaded, personal problem with Morris. Morris was neither a black nor a white person, he was racially mixed and never had known his biological parents; people around him usually did not like him very much. He was working for us as a sort of production manager and performed his functions sometimes well and sometimes badly. Lionel did not like him very much either, but definitely never showed his feelings toward him openly. During the party Lionel had had many drinks and at a certain moment asked Morris to go outside with him to the backyard of the house. There, he started a completely unexpected and most cruel fistfight with Morris whose face began to bleed profusely. To separate the two, for me alone, was impossible, so I had to call one or two people from the party and somehow we succeeded separating them. Lionel returned to the party as if nothing had happened. Morris left. I was in a state of complete shock. Until this day I cannot understand this unexpected, cruel and unjust behaviour of Lionel. After all, Morris had worked with us for many months and to the best of my knowledge had never done anything that could in any way explain, let alone justify, the amount of hatred that Lionel accumulated against him. If Morris had done something particularly outrageous, I would certainly have known about it.

A day or so after the party, Artaria, Wettler, Lionel and Elinor with their newborn son, Michael (I am his godfather), left South Africa and I stayed there all by myself. I was supposed to shoot some more mute shots on the streets of Johannesburg. Besides, I was to hear from Lionel and Carl whether they needed some additional new shots to be done after they had viewed together the rough cut of the film in New York City. One such request which arrived via telegram was for a shot that would justify, at the beginning of the film, all the marching crowd scenes. The audience would thus be informed visually from where the people were coming.

With my Arri IIC camera fully loaded, always ready, together with George I scouted for a proper location for such a shot. On George's advice I climbed on a rundown, half-destroyed bridge overlooking a railway station. Through the viewfinder of the camera I checked the possible shot. The shot looked perfect but the station's platform and the two parallel railway tracks were completely deserted. Suddenly, from behind me, I heard an approaching train. I started the camera running and one train followed by another rolled in to my preset frame. The doors of the compartments were opened before the trains came to a full stop. A sea of black people disembarked in split-second from the two fully loaded trains, and filled the empty platform of the station. I knew I had the right shot.

A few days later I got a telegram from Lionel and Carl congratulating me for what they called the best shot for their purpose.

I was preparing to leave South Africa when the chief of the Special Branch of the Security Police came again to my place. From the time Lionel and the others had left this was his third or fourth visit. The first time he wanted to know why I had stayed behind when all the others had left. My reply, that I was disposing of all the equipment left after the production, seemed to satisfy him. The apartment crowded with all sorts of equipment supported visually that reply. During other visits he questioned me about our close association with the Bermans, and some black friends. Instinctively I would give him some answers – obviously already known by him – and would refer him to Lionel for details. On his last visit he wanted to know whether I was disposing of the equipment from the top of Johannesburg railway bridges. Contrary to their image, some security police agents have a sense of humour. He asked for my passport and he promised to return it to me at the airport just before my departure, for which he set the exact date and hour. On the scheduled time two security police agents took me to the El Al plane heading for Tel Aviv.

Much was written at the time about the film being shot secretly in South Africa. There is no doubt that it was good for the publicity of the film and for the feelings of all involved in its production. Today, it seems to me that the Special Branch in South Africa at that time must have known for quite a long time about the kind of film we were making. The anti-apartheid activists surrounded us most of the time and too many people were involved in the production to keep its contents secret. So the authorities must have known the political tendency of the film. We were not stopped, it seems to me, because it would have created an international scandal. We were an international crew. Whatever we did, we did legally. The Special Branch people must have known that Lionel came from an extremely rich family, and they could assume that the best lawyers from New York City would be hired in case of a need to protect our case in a court of law. So they had to choose between two inconveniences, either an immediate scandal or a later one when, and if, the film would open. As any other bureaucratic organisation would do, they must have chosen the later inconvenience.

A few weeks after my departure from Johannesburg to Tel Aviv, at Lionel's invitation, I went to New York to assist in completing the film. At that time Carl, Hugh and Lucy were working on the sound-track. The picture was already locked, except for the very ending of the film. Neither Lionel nor Carl knew how to end it. The long debates about its ending lasted for many days and led nowhere. One day Carl and Hugh locked themselves in the editing room, asked not to be interrupted by anyone, and promised by the end of the day to come up with a solution. Indeed, later that afternoon, Lionel and I watched on a small screen of the mute, but noisy-like-hell, Carl's editing moviola of the edited suggestion for the film's end. Carl and Hugh were completely exhausted, but confident of their suggestion, as they watched our reaction. The ending was simple, emotionally moving; it summed up the entire film. It was just right. All Lionel had to do was to thank them for the best possible picture-ending of the movie. The sound-track was added later on, and during the trial screenings audiences enthusiastically applauded that ending of the film.

A few years ago, people from MOMA organised a special evening for Lionel, who had donated the original negatives of *On the Bowery* and *Come Back, Africa* to the film archives of that museum. Very few people were present. It was the last time I saw Lionel. He called me later on, several times from Los Angeles, mainly during the Oslo agreements. He wanted to come to Israel. Aware that he no longer had any financial means to make a film about the Israel-Palestine conflict, he wanted to be active personally in the peace process.

In a documentary film about the Japanese film director Yasujiro Ozu, *Tokio Ga* by Wim Wenders, the veteran cameraman of most of Ozu's films, Yushun Atsuta, states that after Ozu died he had to retire because he could not work with any other director. My participation in the production of *Come Back, Africa* was at the beginning of my film career. Since then, I have worked on many different films as a cameraman and a director, but none of the film-work I have done has been as fulfilling, engaging and satisfying as the production of *Come Back, Africa*.

SHUNNA PILLAY

The last time I saw Lionel was outside *Peche*, a fish restaurant on 2nd Avenue and 52nd Street in New York City. That afternoon necessitated a few extra margaritas with lunch as Lionel was moving to Los Angeles where within its environs is Hollywood, a netherworld of which he was not fond. Lionel put his arms around me as we were about to say farewell. "There's just the two of us left, Shun," he said, with tears in his eyes. I felt his body tremble. "Just the two of us."

My first meeting with Lionel was on a 'how do you do footing' on the set of *Come Back, Africa*. It was after this when we met again in London that we became friends, and a few years later in New York, the closest of friends. The Lionel I knew was a man with an inferno in his head, consumed with compassion over the plight of the unfortunates of the world. Tears welled up in his eyes when he spoke of the injustices perpetrated on them. Then there was the philanthropic Lionel that perhaps only I was privy to other than the beneficiaries of the thousands upon thousands of dollars he gave away. This was his own expense in the end when there was none left to give. As a filmmaker, Lionel was gifted. He had an uncanny sense to ferret out some obscure injustice, which we would thrash out lunch after lunch, often getting nowhere; but sometimes the injustice would end up in film. One such film was *Wood Cutters of the Deep South*. In this instance racist Alabama in proudly *democratic* United States, George Wallace territory. Lionel had done some reading on the lumber companies there and concluded that something had to be amiss when workers who slogged morning till night cutting trees in choking, chiggers infested forests ended the year with a salary of minus $3,000. Minus! "We'll go there!," he said to Louis Brigante, his editor and right hand man , and me, his music man. If you saw the film *Easy Rider* you could understand we'd be nervous. But Lionel was fearless. To add to it, he said we'll take along his son Michael, eight or ten years old at the time.

Residents gawked as we stepped out of an un-American car, a Mercedes, and walked into a local diner for a drink. Sheriff's men sitting at the long counter in dark glasses with guns at their sides stared us down as we stepped in. Michael ran to the pinball machine and began to play. I, with nonchalant air and in my most proper schoolboy accent, ordered tea, instructing the owner at the same time on how to brew it properly.

It worked. It often works to put on airs with this sort; it did for me many times in South Africa, even with cops. Lionel was oblivious, so that works too. Louis told me later how Michael and I had made him extremely nervous. That night Lionel took us to a motel.

You could see the fleas jumping on the sheets. Louis, Michael and I marched to Lionel's room to protest. There he lay fast asleep. That's Lionel. He thought we were behaving like ninnies, but he gave in to our bidding. I never thought I'd live to witness happiness on seeing the sign of a Holiday Inn.

Lionel quickly learned the reason for the minus yearly salary. A representative of a lumber company would lure a clerk who earned $100 week, to cut down trees for $500 to $600 a week guaranteed. The lumber company would loan him the money to buy a tractor, saws etc. and the clerk could pay back $300 or $400 a week until the loan was paid off. What the clerk was not told is that a tyre alone can wear out in a week and costs a $100 to replace. The company loans him more money to replace or repair his equipment. The clerk soon pays most of his salary towards the loan, taking home less than the $100 he'd earned in his old job.

There were two labour factions, one black one white. The lumber company kept them at loggerheads. Divide and rule. Lionel did the impossible. He brought blacks and whites together in the South to stand up against the exploitive lumber companies.

Lionel often talked about the fate of his homeland. A nation drifting farther and farther from its basic principles of democracy. Its politicians in the pockets of corporations, that includes a media which keeps its citizens in ignorance. He was angry at a United States that helps right wing military juntas and despots to overthrow other democratically elected governments. At a United States that supplies weapons to kill dissenters and freedom fighters by branding them as terrorists. A United States backed by like minded ex-colonists, particularly Great Britain, in invading sovereign countries to control its natural resources

Lionel had met Nehru and had a deep respect for him. He was disappointed in today's India that shied away from all its earlier high principles. Corrupt and fascist leaning, it is not even a shadow of the nation it was after independence.

I must say too that I think Lionel will be saddened by today's South Africa which has succumbed to corporate control, enriching the few in power, while the majority still await the Promised Land.

On a lighter note, Carole, my wife and I had Lionel's son, Michael and his family for a weekend in the country this summer. We got to reminiscing about a holiday-location scouting trip that Lionel, Michael, Carole and I took in the Navajo country in New Mexico. We reminisced about Lionel and how he could make things fun. We remembered how he sat in the back seat reading to us about Kit Carson who had roamed that territory. And how he kept passing out a variety of nuts and dried fruit, insisting that we eat it for our health, giving us lectures on health foods long before it became fashionable. That's how Lionel was, always ahead of his times.

At a memorial for Lionel at a film center in New York, I echoed filmmaker Robert Downey who spoke before me, "Save a place up there for me, Lionel. I'll be seeing you."

ROBERT DOWNEY Senior

I had a film running at the Bleecker Street Cinema and Lionel was just returning from Israel, somebody else was running the theatre that he owned. He had seen my film and I was a big fan of *Come Back, Africa* and *On the Bowery* and eventually we met just as filmmakers talking about each other's films, then became friends after that and he also distributed some of my films.

I think he was drawn to the topic of South Africa because he was always sensitive to the plight of the underdog. Also, he was always trying to make films that would mean something. It wasn't just entertainment.

Lionel could be intense and obsessive about his work but he could also be very funny. He always had such a nice sense of humour about things. He was very perceptive, he loved movies and he was always trying to help other filmmakers.

He played an active role in certain film organisations. He was part of the "Cinema 16", which was one of the bodies promoting underground films back then. He always gave money to the filmmakers' co-op and he had continued doing that right up until he died. At the filmmakers' anthology, which is where the memorial was held, I ran into Michael and his brother, Danny – such a sad day. People turned out who really respected him and his commitment to change. He was a guy who always wanted to try and change things and make them better.

As far as films went he preferred things that were a little more alternative or challenging, although if there was a good Hollywood film he wouldn't mind it. He distributed two of my films and he was also supportive in other ways. About 10 years ago I needed some help on something and he helped me get a grant.

I left California in 1997 and he stayed out there but we stayed in touch. He wanted to be near family but I don't think he loved California.

The Bleecker Street Cinema was really a kind of university of film. Every week, there was another double bill you could watch of something unique, stuff from Europe and Carl Dryer and Russian movies – all kinds of great and interesting films. There was really nothing else like it.

I would never have had any exposure as a filmmaker without it and when it closed, it was horrible, because the people who ran it after Lionel had tried to imitate what he and a guy named Marshall Lewis, who was the programmer there, did but it was never the same again. But for a while, for about 10 years, it was the best movie house in New York! You could always count on a well thought out double bill. It was the greatest. It was a great honour to me when put on a double bill with one of my films, *Chafed Elbows* and a film called *Scorpio Rising*, he ran it there for about 10 months.

The fact that mainstream cinema has never acknowledged his contribution to the art is a shock to me. *On the Bowery* is a classic! It got no mainstream attention. But through the years it's become known as a classic.

AWARDS

- Italian Critics Award – Venice Film festival –1959
- First Prize Vancouver Festival – Federation of Film Societies Award – Film with the most significant advance in content, means of expression and technique (Have original telegram)
- Time Magazine Selection, Amongst Ten Best Pictures of 1960.
- Most Worthy Picture of 1960 – Selected by Chevalier De La Barre, Paris.

REVIEWS

"The helplessness and frustration that the average African must feel in the face of the social dilemmas that exist in South Africa today are put forth with raw vitality."

Bosley Crowther, *New York Times*

"Highest Recommendation! Extraordinary film, powerfully dramatic, brilliantly photographed, splendidly played against the background of explosive South Africa."

Jesse Zunser, *Cue*

"A lucid expression of a modern tragedy even if the front pages had not lifted it into an area of special significance."

Paul V Becxley, *Herald Tribune*

"Exemplifies the tragedy in South Africa which may explode into a catastrophe at any time."

Archer Winsten, *New York Post*

"It becomes the sound of the beating of the consciousness of a waking Africa."

Jonas Mekas, *Village Voice*

"If you want to see and understand South Africa, there is no better way than this picture of Johannesburg: the bitterness of the whites,the growing anger of the Negroes and the horror of the shacks and tin shelters of Sophiatown – Extraordinary timeliness."

Archer Winsten, *New York Post*

"Burning with integrity, it is the most damning indictment of apartheid and the pass system that I have ever seen. In a climax of almost unbearable anger and frustration it beats out a question which, though unspoken, must be in the mind of everyone who sees it: How long are we going to allow these appalling conditions to exist?"

Nina Hibbin, *Daily Worker* (London)

"The very spontaneity of the scenes gives his story illumination, shock, and an intense poignancy."

Hollis Alpert, *Saturday Review*

"A timely and remarkable piece of cinema journalism: a matter-of-fact, horrifying study of life in the black depths of South African society. Filmed in secret in constant danger of arrest and deportation, *Come Back, Africa* looks deep into the private nightmare and social desperation of a man and his people."

Time Magazine

To make a film denouncing apartheid, and make it actually in South Africa, calls for qualities you will not find in many men, never mind film-men. The fearlessness of a crusader and resource of a secret agent are two of them. And both are apparent in nearly every foot of this astonishing film, *Come Back, Africa*. For it was made in the Union last year, in secret and by subterfuge, under the very noses of the police and by an American director, the same who made *On the Bowery* who has added to those qualities something of a saint's compassion. Wherever human misery, degradation, cruelty and squalor led, Lionel Rogosin took his cameras. Down gold mines he went, through shanty towns, into drinking shebeens – always with a look-out on the alert or an answer to divert suspicion. For the first time, a film shows us apartheid from the inside and with sympathy untouched by patronage.

Alexander Walker, Thursday April 14, 1960, *Evening Standard*

Come Back, Africa could not come out at a more timely moment. It is an unusual film, whichever way you look at it: as a document, as a personal expression, as a piece of propaganda. And above all it is a young film. We know Rogosin already from *On the Bowery*. We know more or less, his approach: an approach which combines fact with fiction. The acting, most of the time, is improvised on the spot, the dialogues are real, and so are the faces and situations. Even if we know that some of the situations were staged and some of the dialogue imposed, they still contain all the freshness and roughness of life. The very amateurism of the cast becomes a part of the movie's truth and authenticity. And then: there are scenes which are simply great. One is the discussion among a group of African leaders concerning their situation, which becomes a discussion of human condition in general. And the scenes in the mines, the huge Eisenstein compositions of the workers walking down the shaft ways. And then there is the final scene, a death scene, where the man does nothing but pound the table with his black fist, just this simple physical action, nothing else, which I think is about the best scene of grief and anger I have ever seen in movies. Usually, and it is the same in theatre as well as in film, these emotional scenes are very embarrassing, they seldom succeed. Here it works. It works so well that the sound of this pounding fist becomes more than an expression of grief: it becomes the sound of the dark, beating consciousness of a waking Africa. Any of the new directors of the Ninth Wave – Rogosin, Cassavetes, Frank, Morris Engel, Leslie, are better film authors than the preceding generation (Ritt, Lumet, Alrich, etc.), meaning that we see in their films more personal authorship and much less of the producer. That means that cinema is maturing. On the other hand, none of them are very familiar with film theory or film history. Neither are they intellectuals. They are, rather, emotional, unpredictable men who follow their own intuitions and visions, with little respect for any accepted conventions. And we know that the best of American cinema has been created by such emotional 'ignorants', Griffith not excluded.

Lionel Rogosin is typical of the New American film makers of the Ninth Wave. No intellectual of any sort, he nevertheless seems to have an inborn immunity against the cliches of the official cinema. By sheer intuition he is navigating American cinema into fresher, unexplored grounds.

Jonas Mekas, April 6, 1960, *The Village Voice*

CINEMA

TIME
THE WEEKLY NEWSMAGAZINE

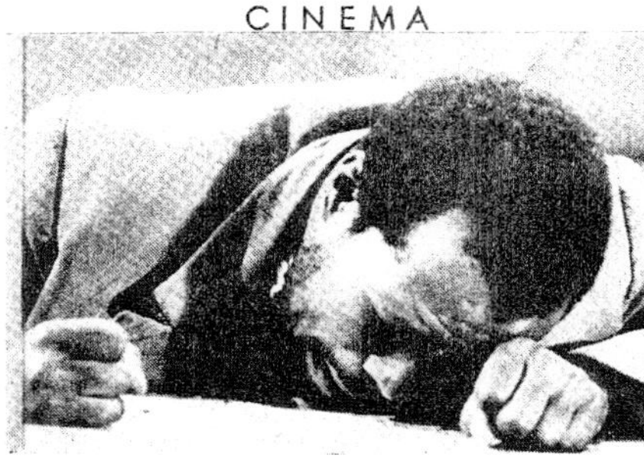

MGABI AS MGABI IN "COME BACK, AFRICA"
Like a bug in a garbage pail.

COME BACK, AFRICA

A Camera in Johannesburg

Come Back, Africa (Lionel Rogosin Films) is a timely and remarkable piece of cinema journalism: a matter-of-fact, horrifying study of life in the black depths of South African society. Filmed in secret by a 36-year-old moviemaker named Lionel (*On the Bowery*) Rogosin, who worked in constant danger of arrest and deportation, *Come Back, Africa* is necessarily crude in craftsmanship. But Rogosin's camera looks deep into the private nightmare and social desperation of a man and a people.

Lured off the land with false promises of big pay, Zachariah Mgabi (the character is named after the man who portrays him) spends several months of hard, unprofitable labor in the mines and then wangles a better job in Johannesburg: houseboy to a *baas*. But the mistress of the house soon loses patience with a "damn fool Kaffir" who can't tell mushroom soup from slops. She fires him, and Zachariah wanders thereafter, like a bug in a garbage pail, through the vast black slums of Johannesburg. He gets two jobs in succession and is fired from each for no particularly good reason. After a long layoff he allows his wife to take a temporary job as a domestic servant, and one night he stays with her in her quarters. The police break in and carry him off to jail as a trespasser. Home a few days later, Zachariah finds his wife dead—murdered by a *tsotsi* (gangster, Zulu style), who strangled her when she refused to lift her skirts for him. The End.

Dramatically, the end of the film is false, but statistically it is true; rape and murder are commonplace in South Africa's black ghettos. Indeed, Director Rogosin's reading of the facts is conservative. He is scrupulously fair to the whites, and the camera leans over backward to avoid some of the more unpleasant aspects of life in the Johannesburg slums: the open sewers and the unchecked disease. But Rogosin shows enough squalor to stun the average comfortable North American, and to prove beyond rebuttal one of his main points: that under the Nationalist oppression, black men are forced to live, as they often have to die, like dogs.

Nevertheless, Rogosin finds beauty in South Africa, too, most of it in the vital faces of the Negro population, in their sunburst smiles and roars of laughter, in the explosive imagination of their dances, and above all in the sheer demonic genius of their music. All Rogosin's candid-camera work is done with impressive skill and sensitivity. Where the director has trouble is in the acted action. Almost all his players are amateurs, and he has obviously tried to make them relax and act natural; but except in one exciting bull session among Negro intellectuals, most of them seem stilted; Rogosin thinks that they felt awkward speaking English. Zachariah Mgabi, a Zulu office worker whom Rogosin spotted one day in a railroad station, is an exception. At times he plays with a wild, shy, serious charm that is irresistible. At times his natural, gentle face suggests a black St. Peter.

. . .

Moviemaker Rogosin, the son of a wealthy textile manufacturer (Beaunit Mills), made *Come Back, Africa* (the title is a translation of an African National Congress slogan) mostly at his own expense, and the film altogether cost close to $70,000. He entered South Africa as a tourist, lived there for almost a year before he felt ready to roll his cameras. In April 1958 he applied for government permission to make "a musical travelogue." After two months of palaver with six suspicious federal bureaus, Rogosin got his permit. He dashed off his script in less than a week, then shot for three months with scarcely a day off. The police were always watching, and Rogosin could never relax security. He carefully concealed the true nature of the story from his actors; even Zachariah was not quite sure what it was all about.

Released in Europe, the film has earned good reviews and a modest amount of money. But in Manhattan, though several exhibitors liked the picture, they had no theater for it. Nothing daunted, Moviemaker Rogosin took a three-year lease on the Bleecker Street Theater in Manhattan's Greenwich Village, where *Come Back, Africa* has now been running for two weeks to small but steadily growing audiences.

16 mm FILM RENTAL: $125.00 or 50% of box office receipts, whichever is the greater. Multiple-day bookings or special screenings may be negotiated with the distributor. Available now - please list preferred play date and one alternate date with your order.

(running time: 83 min.)

AVAILABLE FROM
ROGOSIN FILMS
144 BLEECKER STREET
NEW YORK, N. Y. 10012
212-OR 4-3375

MICHAEL ROGOSIN

RETURN TO VENICE

I'll never forget the feeling of shock and sadness that I felt when I got the call that my father had died. I came down from the ladder I was working on and ran all the way home to my house. I left the next day flying from France to LA where I met my brother Daniel. We drove around desperately in the winter sun trying to sort out the grief and loss and looking for a burial place for our father. The most peaceful and beautiful place we found was an old Hollywood cemetery with high palm trees and ironically a view of the Hollywood hills and sign. Our father, the maverick rebel, would lie here in the heart of Hollywood but his soul would mingle in the ancient earth and the wild Indian soil .

Bewildered, we stumbled through the burial ceremony, the tears, the gathering, the sacred moment when the sun came out, as Dad was lowered down through the earth and we whispered our last farewells. On his desk we had found a quote from the Indian Chief Seattle; he was working on a chapter of his autobiography. We used it for the ceremony and could hear him saying how marvellous it was:

"Will you teach your children what we have taught our children? That the earth is our mother? What befalls the earth, befalls the sons of the earth. This we know: the earth does not belong to man, man belongs to the earth. All things are connected like the blood that unites us all. Man did not weave the web of life, he is merely a strand in it. Whatever he does to the web, he does to himself"

Chief Seattle, 1855

Contemplative we gathered, an odd lot huddled together; my brother and his family and I and our few close friends, the film maker Marina Goldovskaya and the waitresses and bar friends from the local lounge where he held court. There had been a big article in the LA Times, to our surprise a homage that came too late — though it brought a young film maker who came to pay his respects and then quietly disappeared.

Daniel and I then had the daunting task of going through an apartment filled with boxes that Dad had been trying to get back and had been waiting excitedly for, for months. These were all his affairs and archives that had just recently arrived. We organized things as best we could, glancing here and there through boxes. We couldn't help but read and cry and reminisce.

As I had always encouraged my father to write and we were always going over things on the phone, I knew more or less what he was up to. Even so, we were surprised to find ourselves face to face with all these memories and so many ideas, scripts, letters, theories. It was so empty all of a sudden in the flat without Dad but he was there in all these papers and boxes and the little bag full of notes and scraps of paper that he carried around.

Then by chance I stumbled across a manuscript in the *Come Back, Africa* box named Anno Domino 1957 and began to read. Here was the incredible story of the making of *Come Back, Africa*. Thus began the long journey that has become this book. Through the winter and spring I worked with John Mihirpiri and Jonas Mekas and we organised an evening in memory for dad at the Anthology Film Archives in the summer of 2001. It was a real gathering of fellow comrades and dad was coming home to New York. The cinema at the Anthology rang truly in my heart for the memorial and I remembered my childhood, running around the back alleys of the Bleecker Street Cinema, where I grew up in New York in the Seventies, watching all the film classics from a little grate under the theatre seats! I talked to Jonas about the manuscript I had found and we agreed to get it into shape.

After a few months I realized that there was an enormous amount of work and editing to be done and I remembered Peter Davis who I had met traveling around with dad at film festivals years before. Jonas agreed and Peter agreed and the work began.

One day I got a call from Peter who said that a South African publisher was interested in our story. I was a little sceptical but when I got a call from Reedwaan Vally of STE publishers I had a feeling that we had found someone good; another publisher soon called but I had made up my mind. It was to be Reedwaan. I sensed a kinship in our vision and as I checked him out everyone said that he did fine books and I believed them.

At the same time there was interest in showing dad's work in France and I discussed things with Janine Euvrard, a long time collaborator and friend of my father's. We had visions and projects and hoped to get the work out again, to be seen.

We met in Paris and decided to work with Gerard Vaugois, one of the most important independent cinema distributors in France and Janine Bertrand of the cineclubs. We met and talked and planned. There was much to be done.

It was a mess, the film materials had degraded at the Cinemateque Francaise and Dad's inventory was unclear and insufficient. Thus another quest began and it took me almost a year to get a comprehensive inventory gathered from all over the world.

We met Peter Scarlet the director of the Cinemateque at the time and he wanted to pursue a project but there were complications and materials to be checked, nothing could be done quickly.

Our group of three met in Paris at Gerards office over the next few years and each time I had another task. We realized that we couldn't bring back the films without restoring them and since the book was coming out in 2004, and a big opening in South Africa was planned, we decided to limit our efforts to *Come Back, Africa*. I discussed it with my brother Daniel, as we always do and with Reedwaan Vally as the book was coming together.

I became initiated into the world of film restoration, one of the few subjects my father didn't talk about. We were planning a big opening in Paris, but how would we get the film restored in time? I worked with Shona Barrett from the BFI who was a great help and she sent me information quickly and had things checked out, but they too could only lend a hand, but not do the restoring.

The situation in France worsened after September 2003 and in the January of 2004 things came apart. It was a bad time and arts funding and support from the old wonderful art-minded French system was drying up into an unfruitful austerity. It looked bad and I was told little could be done. Then, on this very same day, when all looked bleak and I was trying to figure out how to be ready for the opening of the book and the festivities around the tenth anniversary of democracy in South Africa, I got a call from an Italian lady asking me if an Italian group could restore *Come Back, Africa*. It was an unbelievable coincidence but the person seemed serious and we talked. It was Giulia Grassilli who was calling on behalf of an Italian foundation. I called Daniel and we talked about the possibilities, it seemed strange and wonderful and we weren't sure it would come through.

We were still holding on in Paris but the situation became too much, everyone had many other things to deal with and couldn't give the project the attention it needed. I decided to go with Giulia and we discussed the options; Giulia was a very patient, efficient and charming collaborator, but we had to wade through many steps of approval and the waters were stormy. It was up and down and very mysterious. We were waiting through the winter and spring and with only six months to go. I was worried. Giulia thought that if approved, we could get it all done, but the clock was ticking. Who were these mysterious saviors?

By the month of May it looked good and I was to finally meet my sponsors — maybe in Paris just before leaving for the States that summer. It didn't happen. I began searching for another solution, to think of another way of managing and Giulia was working full time to iron out the details; I suggested alternatives but Giulia said to wait another week. I was getting very worried .

Then the phone call came. It was done! I was to go to Bologna and meet everyone and I did. In the beginning of June I went to Bologna after discussing my options with Daniel. I met Chiara Segafredo from the Fondazione Officina Cinema Sud-Est, Gian Luca Farinelli the director of the Cineteca di Bologna and finally Giulia as well.

I had found a wonderful group of real cinema people, with real knowledge and appreciation of my father's work and on top of that they worked with one of best labs for renovating films in the world, Immagine Ritrovata. I was very impressed by Gian Luca Farinelli and the fabulous buildings and organization he has built. A truly dynamic, yet modest and sincere man. We toured the labs and met Davide Pozzi, a fine young technician with an artist's eye who would manage the restoration process.

We agreed on our plan of action and with one week to go before leaving we managed to make an agreement just in the nick of time. Then in July I was in New York with Jonas Mekas, John Mihripiri and Andrew Lambert, the new archivist at Anthology. I helped box the material up with the help of my son Elliot and my companion Pascale and the material for *CBA* was off to Italy. I had made arrangements with the BFI and Shona Barrett who'd also been following our case for over two years, and they got their material out as well from London.

Nobody took a vacation at the Bologna Cineteca in August of 2004; Gian Luca Farinelli supervising, Davide Pozzi and his team restoring, everybody was working around the clock to get the film done.

In late July when I was in Boston I got an email from Giulia — we had been invited by Marco Muller, the head of the Venice Film

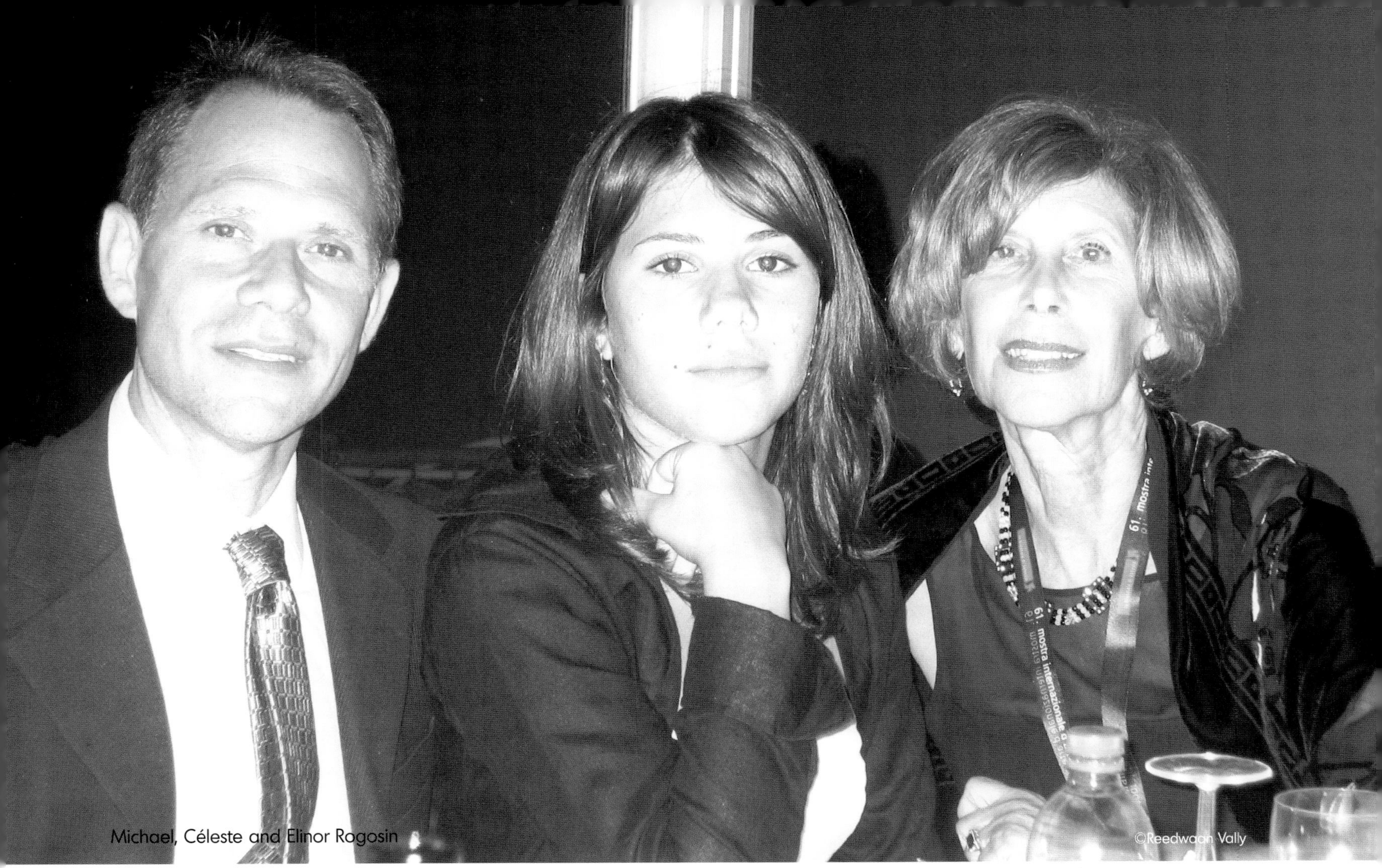

Michael, Céleste and Elinor Rogosin ©Reedwaan Vally

Festival to be a special event where my father's work had often opened and where he had won the grand prize for *On The Bowery* in 1956 in the documentary category, this was great news!

Summer went by slowly as we anxiously waited and planned our trip. Finally the great day came and I arrived with my mother Elinor and my daughter Céleste at the Lido on a fine September morning. The film was shown that Tuesday evening to the critics and on Wednesday to the general public. I found it was simply a beautiful and moving moment, the restoration showed the beauty of the images and enabled us to see the many facets of life in Sophiatown shown with tender humanity. In the many interviews and meetings that we did at the festival we were always asked how and why my father made such a film so far away from his own life. I hope this book will give the answers.

At the 1959 festival I was just nine months old and now 45 years later I felt like this was another home coming. I was born with this film and it seems that fate has carried me back again past all the obstacles of film preservation back to Italy and a return to Venice. Marco Muller gave us words of encouragement before the film started and we gave our speeches, and one could feel a bridge to another time, another sensibility and a quality of reality that we can still feel in the film came back as he opened up the Salle Volpe to us. The lights went down and I thought about what Jonas Mekas had said to me about the New American Cinema Movement of the Sixties that had been battered by the commercial system with few outlets and little money, and yet now I felt their time has come.